European Human Resource Management

Two week loan

Please return on or before the last date stamped below.
Charges are made for late return.

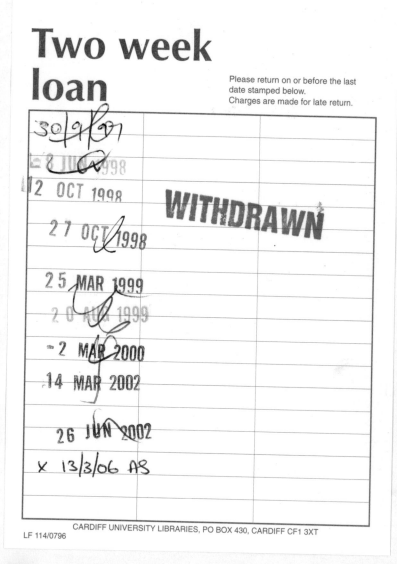

*To Alexander and Oliver who have yet to see themselves
as others see them*

European Human Resource Management

An Introduction to Comparative Theory and Practice

Edited by Timothy Clark
The Open University Business School

Copyright © Timothy Clark, 1996

First published 1996

First Published in USA 1996
2 4 6 8 10 9 7 5 3 1

Blackwell Publishers Ltd
108 Cowley Road
Oxford
OX4 1JF
UK

Blackwell Publishers Inc.
238 Main Street
Cambridge, Massachusetts 02142
USA

British Library Cataloguing in Publication Data

A CIP catalogue record for this book is available from the British Library.

Library of Congress Cataloging in Publication Data

European human resource management : an introduction to comparative
  theory and practice / edited by Timothy Clark.
    p.   cm.
  Includes bibliographical references and index.
  ISBN 0–631–19367–7 (hbk. : alk. paper). —ISBN 0–631–19368–5
(pbk. : alk. paper)
    1. Personnel management–Europe. 2. Personnel management–
Cross-cultural studies. I. Clark. Timothy. 1964–
  HF5549.2.E9E944 1996
  658.3'0094–dc20
                                    96–23267
                                          CIP

ISBN 0–631–193677 (hardback)
0–631–193685 (paperback)

Typeset in 10½ on 12½ pt Franklin Gothic by Photoprint, Torquay, Devon.
Printed in Great Britain by T. J. Press (Padstow) Ltd., Padstow, Cornwall

This book is printed on acid-free paper.

Contents

List of Figures

List of Tables

List of Contributors

Josep Baruel Professor, Departmento de Dirección de Recursos Humanos, Escola Superior d'Administració i Direcció d'Empressas (ESADE), Barcelona

Johan Berglund, Stockholm School of Economics

Timothy Clark Research Fellow in International Management, The Open University Business School, The Open University

Sebastiaan van Diepen Assistant Professor, Department of Organization and Strategy Studies, The Faculty of Economics and Business Administration, University of Limburg

Mariëlle Heijltjes Assistant Professor, Department of Organization and Strategy Studies, The Faculty of Economics and Business Administration, University of Limburg

Paul Iles, Littlewoods Professor of Human Resource Development, Liverpool Business School, Liverpool John Moores University

Alan Jenkins, Associate Professor, Département des Sciences Humaines, Ecole Supérieure de Sciences Economiques et Commerciales (ESSEC), Paris

Jan Löwstedt, Associate Professor in Organization Theory, Stockholm School of Economics

Christopher Mabey, Senior Lecturer in Human Resource Management and Head of the Centre for Human Resource and Change

Management, The Open University Business School, The Open University

Geoff Mallory, Lecturer in Strategic Management, The Open University Business School, The Open University

Steen Scheuer, Lecturer, Institute of Organization and Industrial Sociology, Copenhagen Business School

Christian Scholz, Professor of Business Administration and Management, University of Saarland, Saarbrücken

Gilles van Wijk, Associate Professor and Dean, Ecole Supérieure de Sciences Economiques et Commerciales (ESSEC), Paris

Arjen van Witteloostuijn, Full Professor of Organization and Strategy Studies, The Faculty of Economics and Business Administration, University of Limburg

Preface

The objective of this book is to provide the reader with an understanding of the nature of human resource management (HRM) in seven European countries – the UK, France, Spain, Germany, the Netherlands, Denmark and Sweden. It is intended that the reader leaves this volume not only better informed about what HRM is in each of these countries, but more aware of the diverse cultural and institutional contexts within which HRM has emerged. Such increased awareness will ensure that the reader is better able to evaluate the strength of cross-national differences.

This book evolved out of a cross-national research project called the International Organization Observatory. This is a group of researchers based at seven leading business schools in Europe: CRORA, Bocconi University, Milan; ESADE, Barcelona; ESSEC, Paris; University of Limburg, Maastricht; Open University Business School, Milton Keynes; University of Saarland, Saarbrücken; and University of Uppsala, Sweden. The common purpose of this international team is to conduct research which will help in understanding the management implications occasioned by the development of the Single European Market (SEM). If organizations throughout Europe are to be successful and operate effectively in this new, and rapidly changing, environment they will require a better understanding of, and sensitivity to, the impact of different national settings on the management task. As organizations increasingly develop their international activities in response to the creation of the SEM, they will need to distinguish between those management activities and practices which can be successfully transferred across national boundaries and those which will require modification in view of the divergence between national (that is, cultural and institutional) settings. This can be determined by initially identifying those features of managing organizations which remain constant across national boundaries and those which are divergent and then ascertaining the strength of the forces for convergence or divergence.

During the discussions which took place at the regular meetings of the research team it became apparent that the common language that we use as management teachers and researchers occasionally hides significant differences in meaning. This is important since how one seeks to operationalize a concept will depend upon the meaning attached to it. This is very apparent when we examine the concept of human resource management (HRM). In a whole host of countries there has been a change in the vocabulary of academics and practitioners with regard to the nature of the employment relationship. Previously popular terms such as 'personnel management', 'personnel administration' and 'industrial relations' have gradually been challenged or replaced by the term 'human resource management'. However, what does it mean? Although it has been the subject of considerable academic scrutiny, a detailed examination of the Anglo-American literature would show that the precise meaning of the term HRM remains unclear and is the subject of considerable controversy, it has become one of those terms that defies a single all-purpose definition and as a consequence has potentially as many meanings as people using the term. If American and British commentators are uncertain as to the meaning of HRM what does it mean to the Dutch, French or Germans?

Building on this last point, the central purpose of this book is to examine whether there is a single, shared, conception of HRM, which transcends national boundaries or a multiplicity of meanings. Is there one universal notion of HRM or many nationally specific notions that reflect a variety of cultural and institutional contexts? In other words this book seeks to answer the question: is there a similarity between notions of HRM in different countries or are there specific features of HRM which are only discernible within particular nations? As a consequence, the focus of this book is on determining the extent to which there are 'special understandings' of HRM in different nations. By examining whether HRM is uniquely understood and practised in each nation, it can be determined whether these differences are centred around a number of common elements which transcend national boundaries, or whether there are divergent understandings of HRM which cannot be integrated into a single truly 'international' or 'transnational' model. Such an approach raises the following important questions:

1. Is the term HRM being used to describe the same phenomena in each country or are notions of HRM nationally specific?
2. Does the use of the term HRM mean that a country has undergone an identical or similar sequence of transformations in its employee management practices (i.e. from personnel management to HRM) as in other countries?
3. To what extent does the diffusion of the term HRM among academics and managers world-wide represent the gradual convergence of employee management practices?

All of the chapters have been written specifically for this volume. The chapters vary considerably in their style and format reflecting both the diversity of the national HRM agendas they seek to describe and the personal stance of each author. One cannot avoid the fact that HRM is an area in which there is considerable scope for individual and idiosyncratic interpretation. Furthermore, some chapters deal with nations in which there is a well-developed and articulated debate on the nature of HRM, while others deal with nations in which the debate is currently absent or in its nascence. So some chapters seek to synthesize and convey succinctly a complex and mature debate, while others seek to nurture the beginnings of a debate. For these reasons as editor of the book I did not seek to impose a common framework on the chapters. Had that been possible I would have been guilty of communicating a particular notion of HRM when the very task of the authors was to convey the meaning as it applied to their particular nation.

I am indebted to all those who have supported the production of this book in their many and different ways. Despite the cultural and linguistic difficulties associated with cross-national collaboration I am grateful to all the contributors for the diligent and enthusiastic way in which they tackled the task with which they were faced. The process of developing the text has been significantly enriched by Greg Clark, Penny Cooper, David Grant, Savita Kumra, Christopher Mabey, Graeme Salaman, Denise Skinner and Andrew Thomson who each commented on earlier drafts of this manuscript. I would also like to express my sincere thanks to Sue Marshall for her assistance with the preparation of certain parts of the manuscript. My special thanks go to Geoff Mallory and Derek Pugh for their colleagueship but also for the many lively and stimulating discussions we have shared as a consequence of our participation in the International Organization Observatory project and which have so influenced the development of my recent thinking. Finally, I very much appreciate all the efforts of the Blackwell team, in particular I am indebted to Richard Burton and Clare Fisher for the patient and resolute way in which they have supported the development of this text.

Timothy Clark
School of Management
The Open University

1 The Cultural Relativity of Human Resource Management: Is There a Universal Model?

TIMOTHY CLARK AND GEOFF MALLORY

Introduction

During the 1980s, and continuing into the 1990s, there has been a significant change in the vocabulary of academics and practitioners in a whole host of nations with regard to the nature and management of the employment relationship. In essence the term 'personnel management' or 'personnel administration' has been increasingly challenged and replaced by the term 'human resource management' (HRM). Within the academic community, in the UK at least, this change in terminology has been reflected in the rapid increase in the number of books (currently numbering over 100 in the UK alone) and articles published on the subject, the launching of new journals specifically devoted to HRM, such as the *Human Resource Management Journal* and the *International Journal of Human Resource Management*, and the appearance of academic posts, business school departments and courses with HRM in their title. Similarly in the business community the use of the term has become more widespread, with personnel departments increasingly being relabelled human resource management departments and personnel directors being retitled human resource directors.

The purpose of this book is to examine the nature of HRM from a cross-cultural perspective. In this chapter we wish to suggest that an answer to the question 'What is HRM?' depends upon the societal setting within which it is asked. Theorists and writers from different nations will tend to come to different conclusions when seeking an answer to this question. We will suggest that differences in national cultures lead to different ways of thinking about management and organizations and thus notions of HRM may be culturally relative. It is therefore pertinent to ask: to what extent are models and notions of HRM universally valid?

In seeking to answer this question the chapter is structured as follows. We begin by suggesting that the HRM phenomenon originated in the USA and expanded in the early and mid-1980s in response to the perceived failure of US organizations to compete successfully in the domestic and international marketplace. We then go on to suggest that management theories may reflect the culture in which they are developed. Drawing on the seminal work of Hofstede (1980a, 1991) we argue that management practices and theories about management may reflect the cultural conditions in which they were initially developed and thus do not necessarily have universal validity. Very specifically they cannot simply be applied from one culture to another. In the final section we consider the nature and difficulties of making cross-national comparisons by critically examining Brewster's (1995) model of 'European' HRM. On the basis of this critique a new framework for studying HRM across nations is proposed in order to encourage and structure the way in which the reader undertakes comparisons using the material presented in this book.

The Origins of HRM

Accounts of the development or emergence of the concept of HRM tend to stress its American origins and initial diffusion to culturally proximal nations (such as the UK and Australia) prior to spreading to more culturally distant nations (such as France and Portugal) – see for example, Beardwell and Holden (1994); Beaumont (1992); Hendry (1991). Thus the development of HRM is often presented as a further example of a US management practice, following scientific management, divisionalized organizations, management by objectives, strategic planning and so forth, which has gradually become incorporated into the consciousness and activities of academics and managers worldwide.

The concept and practice of HRM that emerged in the USA in the 1980s came in part from a critique of what was wrong with American industry at a time when domestic and international competition, particularly from the Japanese, was intensifying. It therefore has specific temporal as well as geographical origins which may limit its appropriateness and transferability to other national contexts at other times. According to Beaumont (1992, p. 22) the following factors were critical to the development of HRM in the USA in the early 1980s:

- the increasingly competitive, integrated characteristics of the product-market environment;
- the 'positive lessons' of the Japanese system and the high performance of a number of exemplar organizations which accord human resource management a high priority;
- the declining levels of workforce unionization in the USA since the 1960s, particularly in the private sector;
- the relative growth of service, white-collar employment;
- the relatively limited power and status of the personnel management function in individual organizations due to its inability to demonstrate a distinctive contribution to organizational performance.

Hence, in Beaumont's view the change from personnel administration to HRM was driven primarily by fundamental environmental forces (particularly product market conditions) resulting from increased competition in the domestic and international marketplaces. Traditional ways of meeting competitive challenges were perceived as failing to stall eroding market share and halt the incursions of foreign competitors into domestic and international markets. As Hendry and Pettigrew (1990) write: 'the immediate spur, to what on the face of it looked like the values of "organization development" and the "quality of working life" movement . . . was the crisis of American management brought on by its perceived failure in the face of Japanese competition' (p. 18). In this context HRM appeared as a refreshing alternative to the dated and jaded notions of employee management associated with personnel administration. It offered something new; a novel way of improving the competitive position of US companies. According to Guest (1990), 'the apparent novelty of HRM lies in the claim that by making full use of its human resources, a firm will gain competitive advantage' (p. 378). The solution offered by HRM to the USA's competitive problems was to draw attention to the potential of a resource which was abundant in the USA – its people. The untapped, or previously ignored potential of the US worker was seen as a crucial, and by some as the main, source of competitive advantage. By fully harnessing the potential of its people the USA could gain once again its pre-eminent position in world markets.

Managers and workers alike were attracted to the solutions offered by HRM since its underlying values reinforced an ideology which has a strong appeal to many Americans. According to Guest (1990) the values underpinning HRM 'represent, in modified form, persisting themes in the American Dream' (p. 390). In particular, three central themes underpin HRM: (1) a belief in the potential for human growth; (2) a desire to improve the opportunities for people at work; and (3) a reinforcement of the importance of strong leadership. Guest (1990) argues that 'since each of these also reflects an element of the American Dream, HRM can be seen as a contemporary manifestation of that dream' (p. 391). Thus HRM was a wholly indigenous solution which sought to rebuild the USA's competitive edge by tapping into and utilizing key features of American culture. American industry would there-fore be strong again because of, rather than despite, American culture. Conceived in this way HRM can be seen as having its strongest appeal and most relevance to American managers and workers. We shall suggest in the next section that American man-agement ideas, models and theories may have less applicability and relevance in nations which do not share these underlying cultural values.

In locating its origins in the USA commentators have tended to suggest that HRM evolved from personnel administration and has now come to represent a significant and radical challenge to the way in which the employment relationship was previously man-aged. For example, Mahoney and Deckop (1986, pp. 229–34) offer one view of the nature of this shift from personnel admini-stration to HRM by identifying six specific areas in which they believe changes to have occurred:

1. **From employment planning to human resource planning**: the focus has broadened from a narrow concern with forecasting the supply and demand of labour to establishing closer link-ages between human resource strategy and organization strategy.

2. **From labour relations to workforce governance**: the traditional focus of personnel administration on the negotiation and administration of collective agreements (within a unionized organization) has broadened into a concern with the larger notion of 'workforce governance' in which employee involvement and participation in work-related decisions is being sought via several modes of workforce influence (e.g. quality circles).

3. **From morale to climate to culture**: the traditional concern of personnel administration with the job satisfaction of individual employees (the notion of workforce 'morale') developed into an interest in the notion of 'organization climate' which has more latterly been replaced by the notion of 'organization culture'.

4. **From individual to team performance**: the idea, deriving from scientific management, of selection, training, performance appraisal and compensation decisions being centred on the individual employee and the jobs they performed (supported by detailed job descriptions) has given way to the notion that performance is best achieved through effective group and team working.

5. **From behavioural effect to financial impact**: the traditional concern of personnel administration with the behavioural effects following from the reduction in employee turnover and absenteeism and improvements in the levels of job satisfaction has given way to the view that these programmes also have important financial impacts with the consequence that HRM can make a distinctive contribution to organizational performance and the 'bottom line'.

6. **From training to employee development**: the traditional focus of training on the teaching and learning of specific job-related skills has been widened into a concern with developing (both by training and non-training means) the individual's full, long-term employment potential.

Although such lists should be treated with caution in that they may tend to stereotype the past and idealize the future (see Purcell, 1993), such lists can be useful in that they draw attention to some of the possible characteristics which differentiate personnel administration/management from HRM. Mahoney and Deckop (1986) suggest that the changes noted above are 'symptomatic of a search for a unifying framework focusing on human resources in the accomplishment of organizational performance' (p. 234). Underpinning this emerging approach to the management of employees is the claim that the human resources of an organization are a precious asset, perhaps the most important asset, and that competitive advantage is derived from encouraging and channelling human potential rather than stifling it with rules and constraints. This 'soft' approach to HRM (cf. Storey, 1992) is echoed by Beaumont (1992) who, on the basis of a detailed review of the American HRM literature, writes that the emergence of HRM has meant that employees 'are now viewed as a valuable resource (rather than a cost to be minimized) which if effectively managed, rather than administered, from the strategic point of view will contribute significantly to organizational effectiveness, and thus will be a source of competitive advantage to the organization concerned' (p. 21).

In academic circles HRM's emergence is generally linked to the publication of two seminal texts – *Strategic Human Resource Management* (1984) edited by Charles Fombrun, Noel Tichy and Mary Anne Devanna at the University of Michigan, and *Human Resource Management: A General Manager's Perspective* (1985) by Michael Beer and his colleagues at the Harvard Business School. These two publications fuelled much of the interest in HRM and stimulated much of the discussion concerning the nature of HRM in the mid to late 1980s. We therefore briefly outline the main features of these two models of HRM before detailing the central themes of the American HRM literature.

The approach to HRM adopted by Fombrun and his colleagues has been termed the 'matching model' (see figure 1.1) since they assert that 'the critical management task is to align the formal structure and human resource systems so that they drive the strategic objectives of the organization' (1984, p. 37). Thus central to the 'matching model' of HRM is the notion that organizational effectiveness is dependent upon the 'tight fit', or integration, between HR strategies and organizational strategies. The basic argument is reasonably straightforward (although by no means easy to achieve in practice). It posits that competitive advantage will accrue to those organizations best able to exploit environmental opportunities and avoid or survive threats; and that the strategic management of human resources will assist organizations in this by encouraging and generating appropriate sorts of behaviours, attitudes and competencies from employees. Hence, the efforts of the HR function are directed at developing

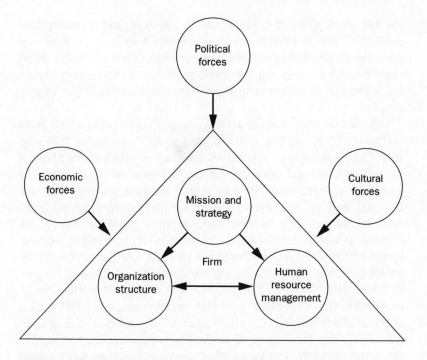

Figure 1.1 The 'matching' model of HRM
Source: Fombrun, C, J., Tichy, N. M. and Devanna, M. A. (1984), *Strategic Human Resource Management*. Copyright © 1984 John Wiley & Sons, Inc. Reprinted by permission.

coherent, planned and monitored policies on all aspects of the organization which influence or structure employee behaviour such that these generate behaviours which support the achievement of organizational strategies. As Miller (1987) puts it: 'HRM cannot be conceptualised as a stand-alone corporate issue. Strategically it must flow from and be dependent upon the organization's (market orientated) corporate strategy' (p. 348).

In this approach notions of integration are crucial. Baird and Meshoulam (1988) have sought to distinguish between two types of integration. The discussion in the previous paragraph focused on 'external integration'. This refers to the integration of HR strategies with organizational strategies so that they are consistent and mutually supporting. The second type of integration – 'internal integration' – refers to a high degree of cohesion between the various policy areas which comprise HR strategy. The elements of

the HR strategy must be internally consistent and mutually supporting. There is little point in launching a culture change programme emphasizing customer care values, for example, when
reward systems and management systems fail to reward behaviours consistent with customer care serving instead to demoralize
employees.

In their text Beer and his colleagues develop a 'map of the HRM
territory' (1985, p. 16). The Harvard 'map' (see figure 1.2) suggests that managers' actions with regard to HRM policy choices
are influenced and constrained by 'stakeholder interests' (for
example, shareholders, government, employee groups) and 'situational factors' (for example, labour market conditions, laws,
societal values and technology). In turn management policy
choices affect 'human resource outcomes' (commitment, competence, congruence, cost effectiveness – the four Cs) which in turn
affect the 'long-term consequences' (individual well-being, organizational effectiveness and societal well-being). The HRM 'map'
illustrates the circularity of HRM policy choices. HRM policy
choices affect the four Cs which have an impact on the long-term
consequences for individual well-being, organizational effectiveness and so forth. The long-term consequences themselves feed
back to affect stakeholder interests and situational factors and
policy choices.

The 'matching model' and the Harvard 'map' represent very
different approaches to the topic of HRM. The former' is located
much more centrally in the strategic management literature while
the latter relates much more closely to the human relations tradition.[1] These differences may have contributed to some of the
ambiguity, confusion and opacity which currently attaches to the
term HRM. However, despite these different approaches to HRM
various commentators have sought to identify a number of unifying themes within the American HRM literature (Beaumont, 1992;
Brewster and Bournois, 1991; Brewster and Larsen, 1992;
Claydon, 1994). While the key themes identified by each of these
writers are not identical there is general agreement and overlap
on the following areas:

● the achievement of appropriate and integrated human resource
  strategies is critical to the achievement of corporate effectiveness. This means that attempts should be made to integrate
  human resource policies with one another and with the business strategy more generally;

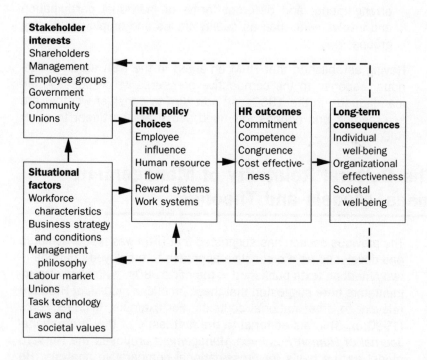

Figure 1.2 The Harvard 'map' of HRM territory
Source: Beer et al. (1985), Figure 2.2, p. 36
Reprinted with the permission of The Free Press, an imprint of Simon & Schuster Inc. from *Managing Human Assets* by Michael Beer, Bert Spector, Paul R. Lawrence, D. Quinn Mills, Richard E. Walton. Copyright © 1984 by The Free Press.

- the devolution of responsibility for HR issues to line management;
- the development of a strong corporate culture in order to support employee commitment and ensure that employees' patterns of behaviour are consistent with the values and philosophies of the senior management in the organization, with the latter being heavily shaped by the particular business plan or competitive strategy adopted. This enables senior management to reduce the risks associated with devolving responsibility by promoting employee commitment to an overarching structure of behaviour, thought and feeling;
- a focus on the individual supported by appraisals, training and development, performance-related pay, internal communications

arrangements and different forms of individual participation and involvement such as quality circles and employee briefing groups.

Having established that HRM emerged in the USA as an indigenous response to the competitive pressures which beset American industry in the 1980s we now turn to consider whether the key themes and notions identified above are pertinent to other nations.

The Cultural Relativity of Management Ideas, Models and Theories

The previous section has suggested that HRM was first articulated and developed as a distinctive approach to employee relations in two American texts published in the mid-1980s. A number of commentators have suggested that these American models of HRM are relevant to other national contexts. For example, Michael Poole (1990, p. 3) in his editorial to the first issue of the *International Journal of Human Resource Management* proposed the Harvard model as the basis for cross-national comparative analysis. He suggested that the adoption of this model as a basis for international research in HRM has a number of specific advantages (p. 3): it is the most influential model and most familiar approach so far as the international scholarly and business communities are concerned; its premises and scope are sufficiently broad for international purposes; its links to MBA programmes mean that large numbers of managers in the international business community will be familiar with its premises; and in the original Harvard studies, there are several references to international trends and patterns in human resource management. More recently, Hollingshead and Leat (1995, pp. 16–27) have also proposed the Harvard model of HRM as a framework for international comparison.

In contrast a number of writers have seriously questioned the universal appropriateness of management models and theories developed in one country. These writers suggest that the relevance and validity of a theory is limited by national boundaries (see Azumi, 1974; Hofstede, 1980b, 1983, 1993; Laurent, 1983, 1986). For example, Hofstede (1993) argues that 'management scientists, theorists and writers are human too: they grew up in a particular society in a particular period, and their ideas cannot but reflect the constraints of their environment' (p. 82). In the discussion which follows we explore the idea that the American notions of HRM outlined above are culturally bounded since they are based on certain cultural prerequisites. These ideas may therefore have little, or limited, relevance to nations which do not possess identical or similar cultural properties.

In order to explore this question from an empirical base we turn to the work of the Dutch researcher Geert Hofstede (1980a, 1991) who identified four basic dimensions to express differences between national cultures.[2] His empirical research examined the distribution of work-related attitudes among fifty-three national sales and service subsidiaries in the American multinational IBM. Statistical analysis of the data showed that the dominant values of the employees in these national subsidiaries varied on the following four primary dimensions of national culture: large versus small power distance; strong versus weak uncertainty avoidance; individualism versus collectivism; and masculinity versus femininity. Each of the nations he studied was scored high or low on these four cultural dimensions and thus given a distinctive classification.

- **Power distance** refers to the extent to which people in a particular culture accept and expect that power in institutions and organizations is and should be distributed unequally.
- **Uncertainty avoidance** indicates the extent to which people in a culture feel nervous or threatened by uncertainty and ambiguity and create institutions and rules to try and avoid uncertainty.
- In an **individualistic** culture people tend to look after their own interests and those of their immediate family (husband, wife, children). In contrast, in a **collectivist** culture there is a tighter social framework in which the person respects the group to which he or she belongs (families, tribes, clans or villages); the emphasis is on belonging and being a good member.
- In a **masculine** culture the dominant values are advancement (promotion), ambition, assertiveness, performance, the acquisition of money and material objects, and not caring for others, the quality of life or people. In a **feminine** culture values such as the quality of life, maintaining personal relationships, service, care for the weak and the environment are emphasized.

Table 1.1 clusters forty of the nations studied by Hofstede into different culture areas according to their rank scores on each of the four dimensions. The forty cultures are arranged into eight

Table 1.1 Country clusters and their cultural characteristics

1. More developed Latin (High power distance, high uncertainty avoidance, high indvidualism, medium masculinity)	2. Less developed Latin (High power distance, high uncertainty avoidance, low individualism, whole range of masculinity)
Belgium France Argentina Brazil Spain	Columbia Mexico Venezuela Chile Peru Portugal Yugoslavia

3. More developed Asian (Medium power distance, high uncertainty avoidance, medium individualism, high masculinity)	4. Less developed Asian (High power distance, low uncertainty avoidance, low individualism, medium masculinity)
Japan	Pakistan Taiwan Thailand Hong Kong India Philippines Singapore

5. Near Eastern (High power distance, high uncertainty avoidance, low individualism, medium masculinity)	6. Germanic (Lower power distance, high uncertainty avoidance, medium individualism, high masculinity)
Greece Iran Turkey	Austria Israel Germany Switzerland South Africa Italy

7. Anglo (Low power distance, low to medium uncertainty avoidance, high individualism, high masculinity)	8. Nordic (Low power distance, low to medium uncertainty avoidance, medium indivualism, low masculinity)
Australia Canada UK Ireland New Zealand USA	Denmark Finland Netherlands Norway Sweden

Source: Adapted from Hofstede (1980a), Table 7.12. p. 336

culture areas. These were identified by using the statistical technique of 'cluster analysis'. This forms each cluster by classifying together those cultures which are as alike each other as possible while being different as possible from other groups.[3] The area names were attached to each cluster after they emerged from the statistical analysis.

Three main factors appear to account for the allocation of nations to particular clusters. First, the importance of geographical proximity shows clearly since nations are generally grouped with others located in their region. The obvious mismatches are Italy in the Germanic cluster and Yugoslavia in the Latin cluster. The geographic spread of nations in the Anglo group indicates the persistent and far-reaching influence of the British Empire. In addition, the Anglo group shows that geographically distant nations can be culturally close.

Second, the nations in each cluster also tend to share a similar language. The Anglo nations speak English, those in the Nordic nations speak a variety of languages which are branches of the Germanic linguistic family. Common language groups also characterize nations in the less developed Latin and less developed Asian clusters.

Third, shared religious traditions are also an important factor underpinning the similarity of nations in each cluster. The Anglo, Germanic, Nordic and Latin clusters have a dominant Christian tradition. Japan has a distinctive national religion, namely Shinto. The less developed Asian and near Eastern clusters are less clearly characterized by a dominant religious tradition since Buddhism, Hinduism and Islam are all present in these regions.

Of particular relevance given the earlier discussion of the origins of HRM is the relative position of the USA on the four dimensions. According to table 1.1 the USA is a member of the Anglo culture cluster. Thus the cultural profile of the USA according to Hofstede's dimensions is: low power distance, low uncertainty avoidance, high individualism and high masculinity. The particular ratings on the four dimensions for the USA are as follows: on power distance it ranks 25 out of 40 nations: it is below average but is not as low as a number of other wealthy nations; on uncertainty avoidance it ranks 31 out of 40, well below average; on individualism it ranks 1 out of 40: the USA is the single most individualist country in Hofstede's study; and on masculinity it ranks 13 out of 40 and is well above average.

Hofstede (1983, 1991, 1993) argues that the way in which people see, perceive and understand management and organizations is culturally conditioned. Thus, both organizations *and* theories about organizations are culture bound. Since, in a global context, the USA has been the main producer and exporter of management and organizational theories perhaps the question should be more specifically: to what extent are American theories valid in other cultural contexts?[4] Consider the example of management by objectives (MBO) a management practice which has gained great popularity in many nations. Hofstede (1980b) discusses how well it operates in different cultures. It originated in the USA in the 1960s and was used there to spread a pragmatic results orientation throughout all levels of an organization. It has had many of its successes there, particularly in situations where results can be objectively measured rather than subjectively interpreted. It has its limitations and has received much criticism but it has proved to be one of the most popular and durable of recent management techniques. It can therefore be considered as fitting the US, and more generally, the Anglo cultural area. This is the case since MBO is based on the following cultural prerequisites:

- Subordinates are sufficiently independent to negotiate meaningfully with the superior (low power distance).
- Both are willing to take some risks – the superior is delegating power, the subordinate is accepting responsibility (low uncertainty avoidance).
- The subordinate is generally willing to 'have a go' and make his/her mark (high individualism).
- Performance and results achieved are seen as important by both (high masculinity).

This is an Anglo pattern in that it is based upon the following cultural profile: low power distance, low to medium uncertainty avoidance, high individualism and high masculinity. How would MBO work in other culture areas? For example, the Germanic area shares with the Anglo area low power distance and high masculinity. However, since the Germanic group is higher on uncertainty avoidance the tendency towards accepting risk and ambiguity does not exist to the same extent. The idea of replacing the arbitrary authority of the boss with the impersonal authority of mutually agreed objectives fits very well with the low power distance/high uncertainty avoidance of this culture cluster.

Indeed, this is the way in which MBO has developed in Germany, emphasizing the need to develop *procedures* of a more partici- pative kind. In Germany MBO has become 'management by joint goal setting'. The stress is on *team* objectives (as opposed to the individual emphasis in the Anglo culture) which fits with the lower level of individualism of this culture area.

What about the introduction of MBO in the more developed Latin group as represented by France? How would MBO work there? Since this culture group has high uncertainty avoidance – completely opposite to the Anglo group – we would expect it to encounter serious difficulties. MBO was introduced in France in the early 1960s, but after the 1968 student-led 'revolt' it became extremely popular for a time since it was seen as a new technique which would lead to the 'long overdue democratization of French organizations' (Hofstede, 1980b, p. 493). The French termed MBO 'participative management by objectives' – but according to Hofstede the title never became more than an empty slogan because the introduction of MBO was a resounding failure (see also Rojot, 1990, p. 98). The main problem was that in France a hierarchical structure protects against anxiety whereas MBO gen- erates anxiety. In a high power distance culture an attempt to substitute the personal authority of a superior by self-monitored objectives is bound to create anxiety since superiors do not dele- gate power easily and will not stop short-circuiting intermediate hierarchical levels if necessary; nor do subordinates expect them to. In a high uncertainty avoidance culture anxiety will be reduced by sticking to the old and known ways.

This discussion suggests that if a management model, theory or practice is to be successfully transferred between culture areas then these must each contain the bundle of cultural pre- requisites which exist in the first culture area and supported the initial development of the model or theory in the first instance. In other words, if nations are to adopt the management models, theories and techniques of other nations as their own, they must be culturally close rather than culturally distant from the nations where the theories or techniques originated. Referring back to the earlier discussion of the emergence of HRM in the USA, the ques- tion arises: what are the cultural prerequisites which underpin American conceptions and models of HRM and which therefore might limit their applicability to other culture areas? Based on our earlier discussion of the nature of HRM in the USA we suggest that the following cultural prerequisites underpin American conceptions of HRM:

- a willingness to delegate responsibility for HR policies and a belief that employees should be encouraged to take responsibility for their own development and performance (low power distance);
- a recognition that there are risks attached to delegating responsibility for HR issues and empowering individuals (low uncertainty avoidance);
- an emphasis on the individual resulting from: (1) a desire to nurture and release employee potential rather than stifle it; and (2) the reinforcement of the importance of strong leadership (high individualism);
- a recognition that the way in which employees are managed, such as through the development of a strong corporate culture, makes a critical difference to the overall effectiveness and performance of the organizations (high masculinity).

We would therefore expect that this notion of HRM would transfer most readily to, and be incorporated into, the management repertoire of those nations which are characterized by this combination of cultural factors (the Anglo group). As Pieper (1990) observes 'the industrialized nations of the Western world have developed characteristic approaches to HRM which do show some similarities, but are different, often contradictory, in many aspects. It seems that in practice, a single, universal HRM concept does not exist' (p. 11). Pieper (1990) goes on to suggest a number of differences between HRM in the USA and Western Europe. He identifies three main differences, which we shall discuss in turn.

1. American companies operate within a less regulated environment. Certain American employment practices are illegal in Europe, particularly those relating to the hiring and firing of employees. Strong state regulation means European organizations have a more limited menu of employee management practices from which to choose.
2. In Europe trades unionism is important and widespread. In general Europe is more heavily unionized than the USA. While trades union membership and influence varies from country to country, it is generally significant. For example, in many European nations union recognition for collective bargaining is a

legal requirement. In contrast, in the USA HRM was introduced in a context of low and declining levels of unionization.

3. A number of European nations have a strong tradition of employee involvement. In Germany, Italy and Portugal employers have to deal with workplace works' councils wherever the employees request it. In Greece, the unions can insist on the establishment of a works council where the organization has more than twenty-five employees; in the Netherlands there have to be more than thirty-five employees, fifty or more in France and Spain and a hundred in Belgium. Furthermore, employee representatives in some European nations, most notably Germany and the Netherlands, can use the legal system to delay managerial decisions in key HR areas such as recruitment and redundancy.

Using one of Hofstede's dimensions Pieper (1990) suggests that a major factor accounting for differences in HRM between nations is the degree to which they are characterized by *individualism* or *collectivism*. Management practices in highly individualistic cultures need to support individual initiative and personal achievement. Individuals accept responsibility for their own work, are achievement driven and expect evaluations of their performance. Loyalty to an organization remains only as long as individual needs are met. Anglo-American conceptions of HRM emphasize this through the shift from management–trades union relations to management–employee relations (that is, a unitarist perspective). The emphasis is on individual participation with a stress on commitment to the organization and the exercise of initiative. These are monitored and supported through such systems as individually based appraisal, training and development, merit and performance-related pay.

In highly collective cultures, it is more common for work assignments to be designed in terms of groups, with all group members sharing responsibility and rewards for successful achievement of the task. Consensus decision-making is also common, and plans tend to be formulated with a concern for the health and well-being of the employees, community and society at large. Job commitment is not an important management issue since loyalty to one's group is expected to override loyalty to one's own personal ambitions. Therefore, the frequency of particular HR policies is likely to be influenced by whether a nation is highly individualistic or highly collectivist.

In summary, the previous discussion has shown that national cultures vary across a number of important dimensions. Differences in national cultures suggest that models and theories of management and organizations, such as MBO or HRM, may have a limited applicability to countries outside of the culture cluster within which they were initially developed (that is, where the cultural prerequisites are not favourable). As a consequence, notions of HRM developed in the USA may not be applicable, or at least may have to be considerably modified to become acceptable, in nations outside of the Anglo cluster. Indeed, we noted a number of cultural factors which may account for differences between notions of HRM in Western Europe and the USA. In the next section we wish to shift the focus from a comparison between Europe and the USA to examining whether there is a single 'European' model of HRM.

Is There a Single 'European' Model of HRM?

Given that the nations of Europe do not share a common set of cultural characteristics in that they are classified to six of the eight cultural clusters in table 1.1, we turn to consider whether it is valid to talk of a 'European' notion or model of HRM. Our discussion begins by critically examining Chris Brewster's model of European HRM before establishing a comparative framework to assist the reader of this book. The reasons for focusing on Brewster's model are twofold. First, it represents the first attempt to develop a 'European' model of HRM. Second, it is illustrative of a number of problems associated with conducting cross-national comparisons, particularly those relating to the definition, use and role of culture.

Brewster's 'European' model of HRM

In a series of publications Brewster (1993, 1994, 1995) has sought to develop the notion of a 'European' model of HRM (see figure 1.3). In developing this he argues for a departure from 'an over-ready acceptance of models originating in the USA' (1995, p. 10) and the development of a 'European' model of HRM. This is necessary, he claims, because different cultural, legislative and

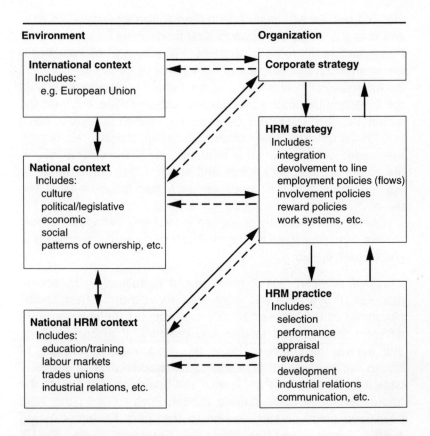

Figure 1.3 'European' (contextual) model of HRM
Source: Brewster (1995), p. 14

ownership patterns in Europe constrain organizational autonomy with the consequence that European managers have less freedom to determine and implement HR policies than their American counterparts. As a consequence, he writes that 'there is an identifiable difference between the way in which HRM is conducted in Europe and the situation in the United States of America: a difference which allows us to speak of a European form of HRM and to question the appropriateness of the American concept of HRM in this other continent' (Brewster, 1994, p. 775). He therefore proposes a model of HRM in which HR *practices* (recruitment and selection, performance appraisal, remuneration and rewards, etc.) follow from and impact upon the HR *strategy* which in turn is linked to the *corporate strategy*. The model also locates each of these factors (corporate strategy, HR strategy, HR practices) within an external environment comprising of three elements: (1) the international context (i.e. supranational organizations such as the European Union, the International Labour Office, etc.); (2) the national context (culture, legal systems, economic system, etc.); and (3) the national HRM context (education/training, labour market, trades unions, industrial relations, etc.). The dotted lines in his model are feedback loops and suggest that corporate strategy, HR strategy and HR practices can in turn influence the external environment of which they are a part.

However, as presently conceived Brewster's 'European' model suffers from four main problems. Each of these is considered in greater detail below.

Cultural diversity   Is it really useful to talk of a 'European' model of HRM when it was suggested above that different combinations of cultural characteristics may support the emergence of different management models and theories? If by Europe Brewster means the European Union this is currently a grouping of fifteen nations with diverse cultural characteristics. If we refer back to table 1.1, Belgium, France and Spain are allocated to the 'more developed Latin' culture cluster, Portugal is in the 'less developed Latin' cluster, Greece to the 'near Eastern cluster', Austria, Germany and Italy are in the 'Germanic' cluster, the UK and Ireland are in the 'Anglo' cluster and the Netherlands and Scandinavian member nations form the 'Nordic' cluster. Leeds et al. (1994), in summarizing a number of studies of cultural differences, divide Europe into seven culture clusters. As noted earlier in the chapter the different cultural characteristics of these clusters may support the development of different notions of HRM.

American versus European managerial autonomy   Brewster may overestimate the level of autonomy 'enjoyed' by American managers and organizations with respect to HR matters. It could be argued that in certain respects American organizations are more restricted than their European counterparts. Consider the example of equal opportunities legislation. This is an area of social legislation which the USA pioneered in the 1960s. The distinction between direct and indirect discrimination was first established in the American courts and subsequently incorporated into the legal statutes of many other nations. Furthermore, the contingency fee system (no win no fee) and the absence of restrictions on the level of damages awarded enables plaintiffs to seek enormous amounts in recompense for wrongdoing. For example, a Missouri court ordered Wal-Mart, the largest retailer in the USA, to pay £32 million damages to a former employee for sexual harassment (Mullin, 1995). By contrast, contingency fees are not a feature of the legal systems in most European nations thus making legal action on the part of employees prohibitively expensive. Furthermore, matters relating to equal opportunities and unfair dismissal are usually dealt with by a tribunal system in which there is a ceiling on the maximum amount of damages that can be awarded. Thus it could be argued that American organizations have less autonomy than their European counterparts with respect to equal opportunities matters.

Furthermore, as the subsequent chapters on France, Germany, the Netherlands and Sweden indicate, some of the highly centralized models of collective bargaining which have restricted managers' autonomy *vis-à-vis* employee-relations matters are gradually breaking down. Indeed, employee-relations matters in these nations are increasingly being decentralized to the firm level. Managers, as a consequence, have a greater range of options from which to choose when seeking to implement changes to employee-relations practices. Previously they were working within tight frameworks established by central negotiations between the employers' associations and employee representatives.

3 *An American or European model?* A further problem with Brewster's model is that he takes as his central notion of HRM the idea that HR strategies must integrate with, or be linked to, corporate strategies and that HR practices must be integrated with and support the HR strategy. As we stated earlier in this chapter, this is one of the themes which have dominated the American HRM literature. He may indeed be correct but at no point does Brewster develop his notion of HRM from a thorough review of the European literature. Rather he identifies the key issues and themes in the HRM literature primarily on the basis of a review of the Anglo-American literature (see Brewster and Bournois, 1991). It may therefore be the case that he has simply sought to transfer a central theme of the American HRM literature to Europe without considering the cultural boundedness of the

notion. Consequently, his model of 'European' HRM is possibly about the extent to which an American notion of HRM can be transferred to a different cultural context. Hence, his model, rather than shifting the focus from American to European notions of HRM may tend to re-emphasize and endorse the hegemony of American conceptions of HRM. As a consequence, his model is potentially culturally conditioned and inherently ethnocentric since he seeks to perpetuate the view that (depending upon the differential impact of the international context, national context and national HRM context) American notions of HRM can be found in other nations to a greater or lesser extent. Despite his claims to the contrary his model invites the question: to what extent are these American notions of HRM present in other nations?

(4) *Ethnocentrism*   The final and perhaps most critical problem with Brewster's model is that it is inherently ethnocentric. In proposing a particular model of HRM, whatever its cultural derivations, there is always the danger of cross-national comparisons becoming investigations in which scholars seek to determine whether organizations in a particular nation, or set of nations, adopt a common model of HRM. Everything is compared in terms of a common reference point (the original model) and is therefore viewed through a particular lens which tends to filter out the diversity of understandings which may exist in different nations. Researchers can therefore develop certain blindspots which result in a more unified and convergent view of the world of employee management. As a consequence they may fail to see that 'the art of managing and organizing has no homeland . . . Every culture has developed through its own history some specific and unique insight into the managing of organizations and of their human resources' (Laurent, 1986, pp. 96–7).

An approach to cross-national comparison which seeks to extend a concept developed in one nation to others without taking account of the divergent understandings in different national settings is inherently ethnocentric. In other words, it assumes that one nation's notions and models, in this case of HRM, are equally valid and relevant to those of other nations. Ethnocentrism has been defined as an 'exaggerated tendency to think the characteristics of one's own group or race are superior to those of other groups or races' (Drever, 1952, p. 86). In terms of cross-national research Adler (1984) writes 'in ethnocentric studies, one culture's "universal" theories are imposed on another culture . . .

But in comparative studies, universality exists through attempting to define patterns which emerge from all cultures studied' (p. 42). Therefore, true comparison arises from the assumption that no one nation's conception of a phenomena (such as HRM) is dominant. If commentators either explicitly, or implicitly, assume that one culture's view of something is superior to others they are conducting ethnocentric rather than comparative research. They must 'start with the assumption that there is no *a priori* dominant culture which is superior in coping with the reality of the situation. If this assumption is not made fair comparison is impossible' (Hesseling, 1973, p. 129).

In conducting ethnocentric studies researchers such as Brewster generally fail to adequately specify the nature of national culture and its relevance to the phenomena under investigation.[5] This arises since the central aim of ethnocentric research is replication. Essentially the researcher conducts a single country study in two or more nations. The main methodological goal of this research approach is standardization. As far as possible all aspects of the research design and its implementation (with the exception of language) are kept identical across cultures. However, the basic purpose of comparing phenomena, such as HRM, across nations is to contribute to an understanding of how and why employee management practices and systems are similar and different. This necessitates making comparisons between national settings which in turn requires an understanding of culture. To put it simply, it is difficult to make national comparisons without considering the distinctive features of different nations. To use an analogy, it is like comparing a squash ball with a football without considering that one is hit by a racket and the other by a person's foot. Yet where studies adopt an ethnocentric approach to cross-national research they fail to discuss explicitly the nature of national culture and more particularly how it impacts on the phenomena under investigation. These deficiencies imply that Brewster adopts a primarily 'naive comparative approach' (Cray and Mallory, 1996). This approach to cross-national comparison regards culture as the basic explanatory variable. While it looks for differences across nations and seeks to attribute these to national culture, no direct linkage is made between the observed phenomenon and the specific features of the national setting which account for the noted variability between nations. This approach is naive in the sense of being untutored or uninformed (by theory). If we fail to describe why such differences occur then the simple explanation that 'it is culture' is insufficient. Hence, while culture is the key criterion in cross-national comparative HRM research it is rarely considered explicitly and more often only defined in the vaguest terms. As a consequence culture is used as a residual rather than explanatory variable whose precise nature remains obscure and is, all too often, left to the imagination of the reader.

However, specifying culture is not a simple task. The definition of culture has been a matter of considerable controversy,[6] with the consequence that academics have failed to agree a consensual definition. As Ajiferuke and Boddewyn (1970) conclude from an examination of thirty-three comparative management studies 'culture is one of those terms that defy a single all-purpose definition, and there are almost as many meanings of culture as people using the term' (p. 161). The term has been defined in many ways. In one of the most cited studies of culture Kroeber and Kluckhorn (1952, pp. 43–56) identify no less than 164 definitions. These were classified in such categories as descriptive, historical, normative, psychological, structural and genetic.

A further problem with the term 'culture' relates to the way in which 'nation' is often substituted for 'culture'. The two terms are used interchangeably meaning that 'nation' is invariably used as a synonym for 'culture'. As a consequence, 'what are called cross-cultural differences are really only cross-national differences' (Bhagat and McQuaid, 1982, p. 654). It is a gross oversimplification to argue that the boundaries of cultures correspond to national (political) boarders. No nation is so pure that all cultural factors are shared. If culture is regarded as those deep-seated norms, beliefs and ideas which lie behind social action within different groups, these characteristics may vary within a single nation. Recognizing this Triandis et al. (1972) developed the term *subjective* culture to refer to the mind sets of different groups. They argue that any nation is a patchwork of subjective cultures. Thus, whereas two nations may share a common language, climate, political system and religion, differences in the mixture of their subjective cultures will result in distinctive belief systems, norms and values. Thus national culture reflects the unique interaction of a number of subjective cultures. Nations such as Belgium, Canada, Switzerland and the UK, in addition to the former Yugoslavia or Czechoslovakia, have, or used to have, clearly identifiable regional cultures. Nevertheless, the primary focus for comparative HRM studies remains national distinctiveness. Nationality as a representation of culture has some validity since the members of a nation share a common set of experiences and institutions which shape their belief structures and value orientations. According to Very et al. (1993) these include 'geography, climate, economy, racial mix, religious affiliations, political system, media, educational system, language and many other intangibles which result in a unique national culture that is more apparent to foreigners than to the nationals themselves' (p. 325).

An Alternative Model for Understanding 'European' HRM

We wish to incorporate national culture more explicitly into the design of cross-national comparative research projects, thereby ensuring that the relevant national attributes which account for observed differences in HRM between nations are identified. To achieve this we propose the model detailed in figure 1.4 as a possible way of structuring future analytical and empirical investigations. This encourages a move away from an ethnocentric approach to a more polycentric (that is, multi-country) approach to the study of comparative HRM. This model suggests that the nature of HRM and the type of HRM concepts and practices that will predominate in a particular nation will be the result of three factors:

1. **The international institutional context**: this refers to the impact of supranational organizations such as the European Union and International Labour Office on the character and nature of HRM in different nations.
2. **National culture**: this has already been considered in some detail and refers to the shared attitudes, values and understandings in a society which are shaped by common experiences and result in collective mental programmes.
3. **The national institutional context**: so far the importance of this factor has largely been ignored. However, Maurice (1979) and colleagues Sorge and Warner (1980) have highlighted the importance of the 'societal effect' in organizing and structuring business organizations. They highlight the importance of

examining organizations in relation to the social institutional context within which they are embedded. Thus organizations are socially constructed. Different social contexts will lead to distinctive ways of organizing. Building on this work Whitley (1990, 1991, 1992) has argued that the distinctive nature of firms in China (family business), Japan (*kaisha*) and Korea (*chaebol*) is the result of different institutional structures leading to particular kinds of firms predominating in these societies. The development of different types of firm in different national contexts suggests that there is no single way of controlling and organizing economic activities. Instead, there are a variety of successful 'recipes' which reflect the institutional context within which they developed. He argues that because major social institutions, such as legal, financial and educational systems vary between nations, different sorts of business enterprises will become dominant. He writes that 'successful ways of organizing economic activities in market societies reflect key structures and institutions of those societies, and would have developed differently in different contexts. It also suggests that managerial structures and practices need to be studied in relation to their societal contexts if we are to understand how they function effectively' (1990, p. 50).

In recognizing the importance of the argument in point (3), figure 1.4 suggests that the nature of HRM in a particular nation may be the result of a historical development within a unique institutional context. Factors such as the economic, educational, financial, legal and political systems are indicated as being of potential importance.

In contrast to the approach taken by Brewster HRM is purposely left unspecified in figure 1.4. There is no predetermined or *a priori* model or notion of HRM with all the cultural trappings that this implies. It is a black box which has to be carefully opened in each nation in order for the nature of the contents to reveal themselves. This is because, as we have sought to argue throughout this chapter, models and notions of HRM may differ depending upon the cultural and institutional setting within which they are developed. Thus, figure 1.4 is *not* a model of an Anglo-Saxon, Germanic, Scandinavian, or even European notion of HRM. It does not seek to convey a particular approach to, or model of, HRM which can then be used as a basis for comparative analysis. This

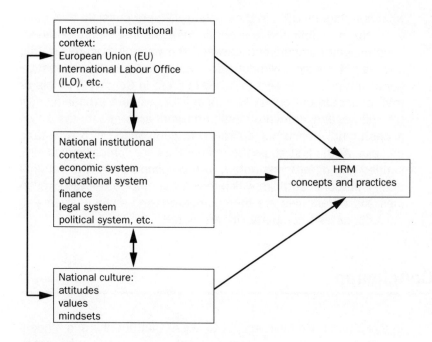

Figure 1.4 A framework for the understanding of national notions of HRM

is because we do not see the primary purpose of the comparative research task as being an attempt to answer the question: to what extent are one country's models and notions of HRM present in other nations? This is ethnocentric research. Instead we see the central question as: what do people in different nations understand as HRM? This is polycentric research.

We would encourage readers of this book to use figure 1.4 as a way of structuring their reading of the next seven chapters. These are organized according to the country clusters identified by Hofstede (see table 1.1). The book begins by examining the nature of HRM in the UK, a member of the Anglo cluster, then moves to the more developed Latin Europeans (France and Spain), then on to the Germanic cluster (Germany) and finally on to the Nordic cluster (the Netherlands, Denmark and Sweden). This will facilitate comparison between nations in the same cluster and thus enable the reader to examine the extent to which there is a common conception of HRM within a particular culture cluster. The authors of each of these chapters seek to explore what is meant by HRM in their country. Where possible they seek to locate this within the relevant cultural and institutional context. Thus making comparisons between the nations featured in this book is not possible without reference to the cultural and institutional settings. To assert that HRM differs in Country A in this or that respect from Country B is incomplete without examining how the cultural and/or institutional framework accounts for the differences found. Hence our approach to comparison is a two-stage process. At the first stage the phenomena are compared and similarities and differences noted. In the second stage the national and institutional settings which may account for observed similarities and differences are then compared, and again elements of uniqueness and comparability are noted.

Conclusion

In this chapter we have sought to argue that notions and models of HRM may vary between nations. Although a common term may be used in different nations to describe current conceptions of the nature of the employment relationship it may hide significant differences in meaning. It was pointed out that interest in the concept and practice of HRM expanded in the USA in the mid-1980s primarily in response to the perceived failure of American industry to compete effectively in traditional markets. In utilizing and reinforcing elements of the American Dream HRM offered managers a new way of conceptualizing the organization and its relationship with employees which was in harmony with key features of American culture. The new language, the new management techniques and the new conceptions of the employment relationship which HRM promoted were therefore of particular relevance to American managers and organizations.

It was argued that if this body of ideas is to be successfully transferred to other nations then the recipient nations must share a similar set of cultural prerequisites to those which underpin American conceptions and models of HRM. Using the work of Hofstede (1980a, 1991) it was noted that the USA is a member of the Anglo cluster of nations in that it is characterized by low power distance, low uncertainty avoidance, high individualism and high masculinity. The chapter suggested that we would therefore expect American notions of HRM to transfer most readily to other nations which are members of the Anglo cluster (such as the UK).

Building on the idea that different national cultures may support the development of distinctive notions of HRM, the chapter finally considered whether we could talk of a 'European' model of HRM. Brewster's 'European' model of HRM was outlined and a number of problems noted. In particular it was argued that the model is inherently ethnocentric since it seeks to determine the extent to which different nations adopt a particular model of HRM. This model is primarily based upon the key themes of the Anglo-American HRM literature. It therefore invites the question: to what extent are Anglo-American notions of HRM present in other countries? We argued that a more interesting and fundamental question is: what do people in different countries understand as HRM? This encourages a polycentric approach to cross-national research. Such an approach seeks to discover the 'special understandings' of HRM which exist in each nation and then relate these to the cultural and institutional context. Thus when reading each of the next seven chapters the reader is encouraged to ask the question: what does HRM mean in this country and what factors underpin this notion of HRM? Figure 1.4 may be a useful way of structuring this reading since it highlights the potential importance of a number of factors (the international institutional context, the national institutional context and national culture) in shaping the concept and practice of HRM in different nations.

Notes

1   See Boxall (1992) for a thorough review of this literature.
2   Hofstede's research has not gone uncriticized. Søndergaard (1993) on the basis of a review of the reviews indicates that three main criticisms have been levelled at Hofstede's original study: (1) since the data were collected between 1969 and 1973 a number of reviewers have questioned whether the results reflect the period of analysis and so are still relevant today: (2) the results are constrained by the population being limited to IBM employees; and (3) other reviewers have questioned whether a culture's values can be identified from attitude-survey questionnaires alone; multiple research methods

may be needed in order to gain a more complete picture of a culture's values.

3 The existence and general composition of these country clusters is supported by Ronen and Shenkar (1985). These authors synthesized the results of eight cross-cultural questionnaire studies published between 1966 and 1980 of work-related attitudes and values. On the basis of this analysis they identified the following culture clusters: Anglo, Arab, Far Eastern, Germanic, Latin American, Latin European, Near Eastern and Nordic. Four nations (Brazil, India, Israel, Japan) could not be classified into any one of these clusters. These were classified as 'independent' cultures.

4 In the four editions of *Writers on Organizations* which have appeared since 1964 (see Pugh and Hickson, 1993, for the complete collection) the work of sixty-two organizational theorists has been summarized. The large majority – forty-three – were American, with twelve Britons, two Frenchmen, two Germans and one Dutchman.

5 In a highly influential article Roberts (1970) noted the general failure on the part of cross-cultural management researchers to specify culture adequately. She points out that 'without some theoretical notions explaining culture and predicting its effect on other variables, we cannot make sense of cross-cultural comparisons' (p. 30).

6 Anthropologists have been attempting to define culture for over one hundred years. For example in 1877 Tylor defined culture as 'that complex whole which unites knowledge, belief, art, law, morals, customs and any capabilities and habits acquired by man as a member of society' (p. 1).

References

Adler, N. J. (1984), 'Understanding the ways of understanding: cross-cultural management methodology reviewed'. In R. N. Farmer (ed.), *Advances in International Comparative Management* (Vol. 1). Greenwich, Conn.: JAI Press, pp. 31–67.

Ajiferuke, M. and Boddewyn, J. (1970), ' "Culture" and other explanatory variables in comparative management studies', *Administrative Science Quarterly,* **15**, pp. 453–8.

Azumi, K. (1974) 'Japanese society: a sociological review'. In A. E. Tiedemann (ed.), *An Introduction to Japanese Civilisation.* New York: Columbia University Press, pp. 515–35.

Baird, L. and Meshoulam, I. (1988), 'Managing two fits of strategic human resource management', *Academy of Management Review,* **13** (1), pp. 116–28.

Beardwell, I. and Holden, L. (1994), *Human Resource Management: A Contemporary Perspective.* London: Pitman.

Beaumont, P. B. (1992), 'The US human resource management literature: a review'. In G. Salaman (ed.), *Human Resource Strategies.* London: Sage, pp. 20–37.

Beer, M., Spector, B., Laurence, P. R., Quinn Mills, D. and Walton, R. E. (1985), *Human Resources Management: A General Manager's Perspective.* New York: Free Press.

Bhagat, R. S. and McQuaid, S. J. (1982), 'Role of subjective culture in organizations: a review and directions for future research', *Journal of Applied Psychology Monograph,* **67** (5), pp. 653–85.

Boxall, P. F. (1992), 'Strategic human resource management: beginnings of a new theoretical sophistication', *Human Resource Management Journal,* **2** (3), pp. 60–79.

Brewster, C. (1993), 'Developing a "European" model of human resource management', *International Journal of Human Resource Management,* **4** (4), pp. 765–84.

Brewster, C. (1994), 'European HRM: reflection of, or challenge to, the American concept?' In P. S. Kirkbride (ed.), *Human Resource Management in Europe.* London: Routledge, pp. 56–89.

Brewster, C. (1995), 'Towards a "European" model of human resource management', *Journal of International Business Studies,* **26** (1), pp. 1–21.

Brewster, C. and Bournois, F. (1991), 'Human resource management: a European perspective', *Personnel Review,* **20** (6), pp. 4–13.

Brewster, C. and Larsen, H. H. (1992), 'Human resource management in Europe: evidence from ten nations', *International Journal of Human Resource Management,* **3** (3), pp. 409–34.

Claydon, T. (1994) 'Human resource management and the USA'. In I. Beardwell and L. Holden (1994) (eds), *Human Resource Management: A Contemporary Perspective.* London: Pitman, pp. 655–68.

Cray, D. and Mallory, G. (1996), *Managing Culture.* London: Routledge.

Drever, J. (1952), *A Dictionary of Psychology.* Harmondsworth: Penguin.

Fombrun, C. J., Tichy, N. M. and Devanna, M. A. (1984), *Strategic Human Resource Management.* New York: Wiley.

Guest, D. (1990), 'Human resource management and the American Dream', *Journal of Management Studies,* **27** (4), pp. 337–97.

Hendry, C. (1991), 'International comparisons of human resource management: putting the firm into the frame', *International Journal of Human Resource Management,* **2** (3), pp. 415–40.

Hendry, C. and Pettigrew, A. (1990), 'Human resource management: an agenda for the 1990s', *International Journal of Human Resource Management,* **1** (1), pp. 17–43.

Hesseling, P. (1973), 'Studies in cross-cultural organizations', *Columbia Journal of World Business,* **8** (December), pp. 120–34.

Hofstede, G. (1980a), *Culture's Consequences: International Differences in Work Related Values*. Beverly Hills: Sage.

Hofstede, G. (1980b), 'Motivation, leadership and organization: do American theories apply abroad?', *Organization Dynamics*, pp. 42–63. Reprinted in D. S. Pugh (1990), *Organization Theory: Selected Readings*. London: Penguin, pp. 473–99.

Hofstede, G. (1983) 'The cultural relativity of organizational practices and theories', *Journal of International Business Studies*, **13** (3), pp. 75–89.

Hofstede, G. (1984), *Culture's Consequences: International Differences in Work Related Values* (abridged version). London: Sage.

Hofstede, G. (1991), *Cultures and Organizations: Software of the Mind*. London: McGraw-Hill.

Hofstede, G. (1993), 'Cultural constraints in management theories', *Academy of Management Executive*, **7** (1), pp. 81–94.

Hollingshead, G. and Leat, M. (1995), *Human Resource Management: An International and Comparative Perspective of the Employment Relationship*. London: Pitman.

Kroeber, A. L. and Kluckhorn, C. (1952), *Culture: A Critical Review of Concepts and Definitions*. Cambridge, Mass.: Museum.

Laurent, A. (1983), 'The cross-cultural diversity of Western conceptions of management', *International Studies of Management and Organization*, **13** (1/2), pp. 75–96.

Laurent, A. (1986), 'The cross-cultural puzzle of international human resource management', *Human Resource Management*, **25** (1), pp. 91–102.

Leeds, C., Kirkbride, P. S. and Durcan, J. (1994), 'The culture context of Europe: a tentative mapping'. In P. S. Kirkbride (ed.), *Human Resource Management in Europe: Perspectives for the 1990s*. London: Routledge, pp. 11–27.

Mahoney, T. A. and Deckop, J. R. (1986), 'Evolution of concept and practice in personnel administration/human resource management', *Journal of Management*, **12** (2), 223–41.

Maurice, M. (1979), 'For a study of the "societal effect": universality and specificity in organization research'. In C. J. Lammers and D. J. Hickson (eds), *Organizations Alike and Unlike*. London: Routledge, pp. 42–60.

Maurice, M., Sorge, A. and Warner, M. (1980), 'Societal differences in organizing manufacturing units: a comparison of France, West Germany and Great Britain', *Organization Studies*, **1** (1), pp. 59–86.

Miller, P. (1987), 'Strategic industrial relations and human resource management: distinction, definition and recognition', *Journal of Management Studies*, **24** (4), pp. 347–61.

Mullin, J. (1995) 'Lewd talk costs US retail chain £32m in sex harassment case'. *The Guardian*, 30 June, p. 1.

Pieper, R. (1990), 'Introduction'. In R. Pieper (ed.), *Human Resource Management: An International Comparison*. Berlin: Walter de Gruyter, pp. 1–26.

Poole, M. (1990), 'Human resource management in an international perspective', *International Journal of Human Resource Management*, **1** (1), pp. 1–15.

Purcell, J. (1993), 'The challenge of human resource management for industrial relations research and practice', *International Journal of Human Resource Management,* **4** (3), pp. 511–27.

Pugh, D. S. and Hickson, D. J. (1993), *Great Writers on Organizations: The Omnibus Edition.* Aldershot: Dartmouth.

Roberts, K. H. (1970), 'On looking at an elephant: an evaluation of cross-cultural research related to organizations', *Psychological Bulletin,* **74** (15), pp. 327–50.

Rojot, J. (1990), 'Human resource management in France'. In R. Pieper (ed.), *Human Resource Management: An International Comparison.* Berlin: Walter de Gruyter, pp. 87–108.

Ronen, S. and Shenkar, O. (1985), 'Clustering nations on attitudinal dimensions: a review and synthesis', *Academy of Management Review,* **10** (3), pp. 435–54.

Søndergaard, M. (1994), 'Hofstede's consequences: a study of reviews, citations and replications', *Organization Studies,* **15** (3), pp. 447–56.

Triandis, H. C., Vassiliou, G., Tanaka, Y. and Shanmugam, A. (eds) (1972), *The Analysis of Subjective Culture.* New York: Wiley.

Tylor, E. B. (1877), *Primitive Culture: Researches into the Development of Mythology, Philosophy, Religion, Language, Art and Custom* (Vol. 1). New York: Henry Holt.

Very, P., Calori, R., and Lubatkin, M. (1993), 'An investigation of national and organizational cultural influences in recent European mergers', *Advances in Strategic Management,* **9**, pp. 323–46.

Whitley, R. D. (1990), 'East Asian enterprise structures and the comparative analysis of forms of business organization', *Organization Studies,* **11** (1), pp. 47–74.

Whitley, R. D. (1991), 'The societal construction of business systems in East Asia', *Organization Studies,* **12** (1), pp. 1–28.

Whitley, R. D. (1992), *European Business Systems: Firms and Markets in their National Contexts.* London: Sage.

2 Human Resource Management in the UK: a Case of Fundamental Change, Facelift or Façade?

CHRISTOPHER MABEY AND PAUL ILES

Introduction

During the 1980s the term 'human resource management' (HRM) came increasingly to be used by both practitioners and academics. In the space of a few years, HRM challenged and largely replaced terms such as 'employee relations', 'industrial relations' and 'personnel management'; in some academic institutions it even took 'organizational behaviour' into its orbit. As Beaumont (1993) points out, 'students . . . appeared to respond relatively positively . . . to courses with the former title, whereas courses concerned with industrial relations matters did not have anything like the same pulling power' (p. 1). In addition, a number of chairs in HRM were established (there had never previously been chairs in personnel management), two new journals were established in 1990 (*the Human Resource Management Journal* and the *International Journal of Human Resource Management*) and the magazine of the Institute of Personnel Management, the leading professional association in the area, subtitled itself '*the Journal for Human Resource Professionals*' as well. Many departments of personnel management and many textbooks of the subject similarly changed their titles to include human resource management rather than personnel management. A number of academic critics in particular have wondered whether this is merely a change of label (to keep up with fashion or to advance professional interests) or whether it represents a fundamental change in the way people and employee relations are now managed in the UK.

Addressing this question will help to articulate what is distinctive about the development and current status of HRM in the UK. First we trace the historical antecedents of HRM, noting a number of discernible phases over the last century that have each helped to shape its modern-day conception. We then assess the evidence for the practice of HRM in the UK in the 1990s. This inevitably throws up questions about *how* it should be defined, recognized and evaluated – both as a body of theory and as an empirical phenomenon. Views on this differ markedly – perhaps more so in the UK than elsewhere – and the divergence of these interpretations is the subject of the third section of this chapter.

Origins of HRM in the UK

It could be argued that the function of human resource management in the UK originated in the nineteenth century, and since that time has evolved in a piece meal, unplanned fashion in a climate where the state has traditionally adopted an abstentionist rather than an interventionist role in industrial relations. Five major phases in the evolution of HRM in the UK can be identified (Berridge, 1992; Torrington and Hall, 1987).

Phase 1 – the welfarist phase

Many leading Protestant (especially Quaker) industrialists in the nineteenth century saw their role (or more often, the role of the ladies of the family) as extending to care and concern for the physical and moral welfare of their employees (albeit from instrumental as well as purely altruistic reasons). Health and safety legislation led to the formal appointment of 'welfare workers' against a background of anti-union actions and the recruitment of untrained supervisors. Though the 1980s witnessed a growth of interest in employee counselling, substance abuse, stress management and employee assistance programmes, this has been primarily directed from a business-orientated perspective. Indeed, the personnel 'profession' has long struggled to shake off this 'welfare' image; one could argue that the recent move to HRM provides support for such a stance, given its business and strategic orientations. The Welfare Workers' Association was founded in 1913 as the first occupational association in this area.

Phase 2 – the industrial efficiency phase

This interest in working conditions and in their effect on labour efficiency was married in the early twentieth century to an interest in Tayloristic work study, industrial engineering and 'scientific management'. These concerns were boosted by the experience of two World Wars, which led to an interest in 'scientific' selection techniques, psychometric tests and worker morale and its effect on productivity. An interest in job design and ergonomics led to many 'people management' activities being subsumed into engineering and productivity services departments, often staffed by the same specialists (Berridge, 1992). The Institute of Welfare Workers was renamed the Institute of Labour Management in 1931, reflecting the change of emphasis.

Phase 3 – the personnel administration phase

From the 1930s, industrial relations became of growing importance to the personnel function with the rise of the trades unions, the growth of collective bargaining and rising levels of industrial conflict. As more sophisticated methods became standardized in such areas as recruitment and selection, training, job design and job evaluation, the personnel function became more bureaucratized and administrative. As personnel administration separated from its industrial engineering elements, it came more under the influence of inputs from the behavioural sciences, psychology and sociology. One example is the growing influence of the US 'human relations' school and its focus on issues of group behaviour, leadership and social systems. In 1946 the Institute of Labour Management was renamed the Institute of Personnel Management.

Phase 4 – the industrial relations (IR) phase

From the 1950s, industrial conflict, bargaining and the importance of managing employee relations were together seen as the critical contingency for personnel management. Attempts to assert greater control over working practices, productivity and the introduction of new technology led to more contractualized employment relationships. At the same time a concern with motivation and communication led to greater receptivity to research and consultancy in the behavioural sciences in such areas as selection, leadership, training, job satisfaction, motivation, job design and organization development. The personnel administrator role became more professionalized with the growth in influence of the Institute of Personnel Management, the increasingly lengthy and specialized nature of professional training, and the tendency for practitioners to identify with their professional body rather than their organization. Increasingly the state acted to legislate in such areas as employment contracts, sex and racial discrimination, health and safety, training, union recognition and industrial relations, which placed a premium on legal skills and knowledge and on skills in negotiating with the trades unions in collective bargaining. The dominant issues of management control and the challenges to it towards the end of this phase are perhaps summed up in two of John Storey's earlier works (1980 and 1983), as well as in Graeme Salaman's (1979) work and his article with Craig Littler (Littler and Salaman, 1982). For academics, personnel practitioners, line managers, trades unions and employees, the workplace seemed to be 'contested terrain' (Edwards, 1979).

Perhaps the most academically developed research area characteristic of this industrial relations era was the attempt to map the different 'patterns', 'ideal types' and 'styles' of industrial relations in British industry (e.g. Fox, 1974; Purcell and Sisson, 1983). For example, traditional conceptions of labour as a factor of production and constitutional conceptions of acceptance of trades unions and the need to institutionalize conflict and police collective agreements are distinguished from emerging 'sophisticated human relations' and 'consultative' approaches. In the consultative style, unions are recognized, with an attempt to build up 'constructive' relations via extensive discussions, the provision of information, and the use of team briefing, share options, profit sharing, joint working parties and quality or productivity circles to boost 'commitment'. This style pre-figures much of the approach that came to be seen as HRM, and is perhaps even more characteristic of those continental European approaches to HRM based on the notion of the trades unions as 'social partners'. The final style, 'sophisticated human relations', involved internal labour markets, attitude surveys, flexible reward

systems, appraisal, communication systems and internal griev-
ance, disciplinary and consultative procedures to enhance individual loyalty and commitment. These tactics, together with
the bypassing of collective bargaining and collective institutions,
are perhaps even more resonant of the HRM approach, and seem
characteristic of many UK-based US multinationals in particular.

Another approach in the mid-1980s which captures some of the
shifts from personnel management to HRM is the study by Tyson
and Fell (1986) of the personnel function. They distinguish the
'clerk of works' or reactive administrator of personnel procedures
(characteristic of the function in its 'personnel administration'
phase) from the' contracts manager' seeking to develop comprehensive systems and procedures to ensure uniformity, efficiency
and the policing of tight contracts. This role is clearly characteristic of the 'industrial relations' phase, and Torrington and
Chapman (1979) also identified the 'contracts guardian' as a key
role. However, these authors emphasized the technical, servicing
role of personnel management in developing 'payment', 'control',
'work' and 'collective consent' contracts, while others (e.g.
Thomason, 1976) sought to put personnel managers in a more
professional advisory or 'custodian' role, guarding the corporate
conscience and identity while also guarding the employer's legal
duties, the employees' rights, and the physical and cultural identity of the organization.

However, it is Tyson and Fell's (1986) discussion of a third role,
that of the 'architect' who takes a more proactive, innovative,
strategic, integrative and planning-oriented stance and focuses on
the organization's learning and capabilities that clearly presages
many of the characteristics associated with HRM. This more
proactive, innovative stance had earlier been picked up on by
Legge (1978) who gave emphasis to the dynamic roles played by
personnel managers, either as 'conformist innovators' reflecting
dominant orthodoxies and seeking acceptance through cost-
benefit analysis or as 'deviant innovators' acting more independ-
ently and entrepreneurially.

Phase 5 – the HRM phase

The evolution of personnel management in the 1980s is often
seen as showing a clear break from earlier conceptions and from

past models: a movement towards HRM is seen as being precipitated by a number of inter-related developments. These included the influence of American and Japanese employment practices, the economic and political policies pursued by the Thatcher government, the recession, changing patterns of product and labour markets, the influence of new technology, and the impact of influential management thinking, especially over 'culture and excellence' and 'human resource management' (Berridge, 1992; Beaumont, 1993; Mabey and Salaman, 1995).

The 'radical right' Thatcher government was associated with the erosion of manufacturing industry, high unemployment, the reduction in trades union power, the growth of enterprise-level bargaining and single-union agreements, the privatization of large sections of British industry and the public utilities, and the adoption of market or quasi-market disciplines in education, health and social services. In particular, it attempted to promote a more individualistic 'enterprise culture' with an emphasis on enhanced performance, results and customer orientation.

Much of the thrust of these initiatives was echoed by those management writers and consultants, typically American, who preached the virtues of 'excellence', 'total quality' and 'cultural change' (e.g. Peters and Waterman, 1982). Though often 'searching for excellence in second-hand clothes' (Iles and Johnston, 1989) with many ideas borrowed from the organization development (OD) theorists of the 1960s and 1970s and even further back from the 'human relations' school of the 1930s, their influence was immense, not so much on personnel managers as on chief executives and line managers. Many of these authors sought to explain the growing success of Japanese and other Far Eastern companies in the 1970s and 1980s in terms of their commitment to quality, corporate culture and the commitment of employees. This placed human resources at the heart of the business and made them of central concern to line managers and top management rather than merely the responsibility of personnel professionals. Such texts, both the original American ones and their British imitators (e.g. Goldsmith and Clutterbuck, 1984), not only sought to persuade and cajole but also to reassure, providing many case studies and pen-pictures of Western 'excellent companies' and Western 'transformational leaders'. The message seemed to be that a 'success formula' for creating organizational and managerial excellence had been identified and could be followed. A message moreover that placed such 'soft systems' as staffing, structure, style and leadership at the fore-front, in contrast to the 'hard systems' traditionally empha-sized in Western management thinking and business school curricula.

In the United States such rethinking led to the development of a new MBA core course at Harvard, the first for many years, enti-tled 'Human Resource Management' with accompanying texts (Beer et al., 1985). Such academic ideas were influential through business school courses (the 1980s witnessed an explosion in the number of managers undertaking MBA courses in the UK as well as courses at certificate and diploma levels), academic writ-ings, conferences, workshops and the dramatic growth in con-sultancies presenting ideas often drawn from the excellence, culture change and HRM schools of thought.

A more direct influence was felt from international business. The 1980s was very much a decade of 'inward investment' and internationalization in the UK, with a rapid growth in the number of foreign-owned and foreign-managed businesses. Many, especially the Japanese and American companies, had a tradition of paying greater attention to quality and making greater investment in employees skills by training them in relevant technologies. While American multinational companies offered many examples of an individualistic HRM approach, it was the Japanese manufacturing companies with their more collectivist, team-oriented approach to employee relations that seemed to offer the greatest challenge and inspiration to British personnel management. Practices including extensive communication, skills training, multi-func-tional team-working, changes in supervisory styles, and enhanced levels of employee participation, involvement and commitment represented an apparently radical break with British practice and managerial assumptions about employee relations. In addition, the introduction of single-union and no-strike agreements, total quality management, just-in-time, quality circles, harmonization and single-status working all emphasized this difference, and such practices appeared to be successful. Though British aca-demic research has questioned some of the received wisdom over Japanese management practices in the UK, there is no doubt that the centrality of HR in the Japanese approach (rather than the centrality of personnel management as performed by personnel specialists) has had a considerable influence on British HR thinking.

Despite this Japanese influence, the model of HRM imported into the UK in the early 1980s came from the USA. Though (unlike in the UK) the term 'HRM' is often used interchangeably with or as a replacment for the term 'PM' (personnel management), what was new about the 1980s American approach to HRM was its stress on *strategic* HRM. The two main models derived from very different traditions. The Fombrun et al. (1984) model is very self-consciously in the 'strategic management' tradition, emphasizing the 'resource' or 'hard' connotations of the term HRM, while the Beer et al. (1984) model is much more in the 'human relations' tradition, emphasizing pluralism and the existence of 'multiple stakeholders' in a way that gives more emphasis to the 'human' or 'soft' connotations of the term HRM. An implicit theory of HRM can be discerned in earlier emphases on human resources as organizational assets, human capital theory and human asset accounting. Although Morris (1974) had already exposed some of the tensions and contradictions in HRM in his distinction between 'human resources' and 'resourceful humans', it was the introduction of these two models into the UK by Hendry and Pettigrew (1986) in particular which stimulated both critical evaluation and empirical research.

Both models of HRM emerged in the USA in the early 1980s, according to Hendry and Pettigrew (1990, p. 18), as part of a sustained critique of US strategic behaviour, cultural values and HR practices and also of a normative mission led by 'academics and management gurus, with one foot in the consultancy and one foot in the academic world, putting themselves at the service of industry to bring about the turnaround' in the face of Japanese competition. However, Hendry and Pettigrew go on to argue that 'HRM arrived in the UK around 1985/1986 without this broad underlying critique . . . .. it presented itself as a more or less fully formed set of values and prescriptions' (1990, p. 19), despite the existence of a number of similar elements such as recession, restructuring, loss of competitiveness, the introduction of new technology, anti-union legislation and a new legitimacy for entrepreneuralism. In addition, the criticisms of tactical, short-term, non-strategic thinking in British industry (Tyson, 1983), a series of critical reports on British managers' education, training and development (e.g. Handy, 1987; Constable and McCormick, 1987), as well as a stream of well-publicized cases of HRM-inspired company turnarounds, laid the foundation for the acceptance of the HRM model in the UK.

The Evidence for HRM in the UK

However, receptivity is very different to realization. To what extent have these 'new' HRM approaches taken root? One feature of HRM in the UK has been the numerous surveys and the extensive case study analyses of strategic approaches to HRM. Here, we report a sample of these key findings and briefly sketch the industrial relations context within which these events are taking place.

Survey data

Guest and Hoque (1993) report that in a national sample of a little over 2000 establishments employing twenty-five or more staff only a minority employed a personnel specialist of any sort (17 per cent). North American-owned firms were significantly more likely to adopt the HR title. They found no consistent pattern to suggest that firms with the 'human resource' title actually practised a more coherent set of HRM policies. These firms are more likely to have merit pay schemes, more likely to use team briefings and quality circles and to make systematic use of the management chain for communication purposes. However, such practices do not amount to a distinctive and coherent set of HRM policies and practices. The authors conclude that 'HRM' has found a very modest existence in some head offices but at establishment level is scarcely breathing.

In 1989 the Cranfield School of Management in association with management consultants Price Waterhouse launched a Europe-wide study of HRM practices. The survey provides a unique quantitative statistical base of HRM policies and practices comprising 15,000 organization responses in eighteen countries collected during the four-year period from 1989–93. Some of the key findings to emerge so far are:

- Differences in HRM practices are usually more closely related to national factors than to organization size, sector or ownership.
- Few organizations take HR into account in the development of corporate strategy and board membership excludes more than 50 per cent of HR directors.

- There is a common trend to decentralize pay bargaining and increase pay variability.
- Training is central to HRM, yet a high proportion of organizations do not know how much they spend on training.

The survey results have led Brewster (1994) and his colleagues to propose a 'European model' of HRM, drawing attention to the lack of employer and managerial autonomy in many European countries, in contrast to the assumptions behind the US model of 'strategic HRM' (see figure 1.3 in Chapter 1 of this book). Brewster (1994, pp. 328–9) writes that

> What is happening in Europe is that there is a move towards the HRM concept but one which, within a clearly established external environment, accepts the duality of people management. Thus, objectives include both organizational requirements and a concern for people; the focus on both costs and benefits means fitting organizational policies to external cultures and constraints; union and non-union channels are utilized; the relationship with line managers at all levels is interactive rather than driven by either specialists or the line.

Wood and Peccei (1990) surveyed 171 British firms across the whole spectrum of manufacturing and service sectors to assess whether the then approaching Single European Market (SEM) was stimulating a more integrated, business-led and proactive approach to HRM. The survey, together with a more in-depth study of two industries – furniture and insurance – found widespread complacency and insularity in attitudes towards Europe and to the SEM. However, firms already operating in Europe, particularly those with specific business plans for 1992, were most likely to have business-led personnel policies 'although more often than not they are developed downstream from corporate strategy and treated as "third-order" within the strategic planning process' (Wood and Peccei, 1990, p. 86).

A good indication of how British managers' attitudes towards HRM have changed over the period 1980–90 is reported by Poole and Mansfield (1992). From a random sample of 1058 members of the British Institute of Management in 1980, and another 827 in 1990, they found broad endorsement for the adoption of HRM in many British firms. For instance, employee involvement was favoured (providing it did not challenge the managerial controlling functions) as was employee shareholding and profit sharing and there was pronounced support for training and management development. However, as the authors note, this espoused concern for the motivation and development of the human assets of the firm does not necessarily represent a transformation from personnel management to an integrated and strategic approach to HRM by the firms in question. The reality of such changes is provided – at least in part – by a survey of 600 British managers conducted over a three-year period (1992–4), who were asked to describe the involvement of key individuals in HR changes in their organizations (Skinner and Mabey, 1995). In two-thirds of the cases, the Chief Executive was personally involved in the initiation of HR strategies and the top team/directors were involved as a group in 39 per cent of cases. Possibly as an outcome of this wide board involvement, which contrasts with earlier views (for example, Purcell, 1989), a high degree of linkage between HR strategy and business strategies (61 per cent) was reported; this linkage was seen as slightly lower at the planning (53 per cent) and implementation (44 per cent) stages however. The HR director, as an individual rather than as a member of the top team, was perceived as having had a high degree of involvement in 31 per cent of cases overall. More surprisingly, in most cases the HR director does not appear to play a major part in the *implementation* of HR strategies. If the Shipton and McAuley (1993) model were to hold true, and HR directors were reactive 'business managers' rather than proactive members of the board, they could have been expected to score well in the implementation stage. However HR directors were perceived to have had a significant role in only 37 per cent of cases overall. In conflict with the findings of the Price Waterhouse/Cranfield study, that HR directors took a major role in implementation and more often in the initiation of a strategy, it seems that in most companies the HR director is not perceived as having a leading role in either activity.

Two notable studies which attempted to go beyond the inevitable superficiality of survey analysis are those by Storey (1992) and Pettigrew and Whipp (1991). (The latter is discussed more fully later in the chapter.) Storey conducted 350 interviews in fifteen core-case 'mainstream' British companies, supplemented by data from twenty-five panel organizations. His conclusions concerning the extent and depth of change to actual practice and behaviour, relying largely on non-HR sources (80 per cent of the sample) was that:

some organizations, for example, steered a major new approach to labour management in a step-by-step manner; others launched total programmes. Some of the changes were progressed in a top-down, cascade way, others were bottom-up in character. In some cases the human resource or personnel/IR specialists were intimately involved; in others the process was clearly driven from elsewhere and these specialists were either marginal or even acted in opposition. The overall lesson about managing change was that there is no set formula.

Storey, 1992, p. 120

However, Storey does note a significant tendency for the change process used by the organizations he studied to move toward the 'top-down systemic' type, where there was a greater willingness by management to operate outside the negotiating machinery, a greater degree of careful planning, and attempts to integrate different human resource initiatives rather than making changes in an opportunistic fashion.

The stance and role of the personnel function with respect to HRM varied considerably. In some cases the values, concepts and methods of HRM 'clearly provided a fillip to personnel's flagging fortunes' (Storey, 1992, p. 186) and an enhancement of credibility in the eyes of senior management. In other cases, it was the latter who were championing change initiatives, with personnel specialists cast in the role of handmaidens of change or in some cases playing no part at all in their conception or implementation. Generally speaking, the line manager's involvement in people-management roles, such as selection, direct communication, target-setting motivation, training and development, was found to be expanding, with a likely erosion of personnel's traditional contribution.

Finally, in assessing managerial approaches to industrial relations Storey found:

little evidence of any forthright move to abandon pluralism in favour of a wholehearted commitment to an individualistically based human resource programme. Instead, the general tendency was to maintain the previous machinery in a ticking-over mode while experimenting rather more enthusiastically with policies and approaches which signalled a departure toward new priorities.

Storey, 1992, p. 258

Specific HR strategies

Team working is one important element of the claimed new approach to the management of human resources (see Buchanan, 1992). For instance, Cameron et al. (1992) report that despite some resistance from supervisors and middle managers the team concept is spreading rapidly in industries other than the motor industry, such as aerospace, electronics, food processing, steel and financial services. General Electric, for instance, is reported to have 20 per cent of its 120,000 employees working within the team concept. This has also found expression in the rush by western managers to attempt the introduction of Japanese work practices into their organizations. Gleave and Oliver (1990) reported that two-thirds of *The Times* top 1000 companies were using, or planning to use, just-in-time production and 95 per cent were using, or planning to use, total quality control. This, they suggest, is due to the demonstrated capability of the major Japanese corporations to engineer a good 'fit' between their manufacturing strategy and their human resources strategy.

Also of importance are work changes which, again borrowing from the Japanese, attempt to overcome the classic disadvantage of the traditional, scientific management forms of work organization: low levels of worker motivation and commitment resulting in poor-quality work and insignificant creativity, and poor balance of the flow of work through the assembly process. The Japanese shop floor system of work organization, through quality circle programmes, aims to 'empower' workers so that, in groups, they become involved in aspects of management decision-making such as quality and problem-solving, and in management decisions relating to tools, materials-handling layout and improvements. This system seeks to make every worker a quality inspector, to be responsible for continuous change and improvement, and through 'just-in-time' production methods and improved supplier-and-user relations seeks to balance the assembly process. These methods, particularly just-in-time material flow systems, quality circles and team working, have been applied in the UK and hailed as a revolutionary break with previous practice and a crucial stage in the achievement of competitive levels of quality and efficiency. However, as Hill (1991) notes, quality circles have only succeeded in the UK when embedded in a more comprehensive culture of quality consciousness. Where this is the case results – both attitudinal and commercial – have been dramatic (Giles, 1989).

What is significant about several of the cultural change interventions reported in recent years at organizations such as British Telecom, Royal Dutch Shell, British Airways and Manchester Airport is the way multiple leverage points were used to initiate and support the changes and the way organization-wide human resource practices were deliberately modified to reinforce desired cultural changes. Apart from the fundamental presumption that culture can be changed in a deliberate and predetermined manner to implement strategic initiatives, culture change programmes based around shared values have been criticized for relying on managerial, top-down assumptions (Beer et al., 1990); for overlooking the inherent contradictions of an organization striving for a 'strong culture' on the one hand and skills flexibility and devolved responsibility on the other (Legge, 1989; Ogbonna, 1992); and for underestimating the cynicism of professional knowledge workers in the 1990s who are increasingly more resistant to corporate cultural manipulation (Hope and Hendry, 1994).

Another significant area of change, which also reflects the pursuit of flexibility but at an organizational level rather than at the level of work design, is the move among many organizations towards types of structure which achieve the twin goals of accountability of management decision making and sufficient management control over delegated decision making. This is attempted by decentralization, reduction of bureaucracy, reduction of layers of management, and thus the separation of parts of the business into discrete, accountable business units, autonomous within a structure of financial controls and corporate policy. These developments have not only occurred within the private sector. British Rail and the National Health Service have also been exposed to decentralization and division into profit-responsible divisions. These developments represent an effort to achieve an optimum relationship between the corporate centre and operating companies. Goold and Campbell (1987) in a study of seventeen multi-divisional British firms identify three types of centre–operating company relationship, each of which is empirically apparent and each of which solves some problems and raises others. A similar sort of development is the move towards formal and explicit service-level agreements between service departments and their internal customers. For example, within local authorities discrete divisions may now be required to install service agreements formally specifying what each division agrees to supply to its internal customers. For external services they are required to arrange for competitive tendering as usual. Interestingly, one result of this move is to increase the quantity of bureaucratic paperwork, with the details of each interdepartmental relationship being formally specified.

Changes have also occurred in the traditional areas of personnel: selection, assessment, payments systems and training. A study by the Institute of Personnel Management reported that nearly 20 per cent of the organizations surveyed had a formal performance management programme, three-quarters said they had performance-related pay, and a third TQM programmes (Bevan and Thompson, 1991). Yet here too, the evidence is inconclusive. While follow-up studies have confirmed the growth of performance-related pay schemes, claims about their impact on performance management appear unjustified (Guest, 1993, p. 221; Storey and Sisson, 1993, p. 136).

Changes in the industrial relations context

The past fifteen years have witnessed underlying social, economic and political changes encompassing a shift towards free-market economics in Europe and elsewhere. The period has been characterized by episodic recession and continuing high unemployment and a movement towards individualistic attitudes and values. In the UK these and other factors have had a significant impact upon IR and arguably changes in government policy towards the labour market together with the IR legislation have been the most important developments in terms of eroding trades union monopoly power (McIlroy, 1991). Such events have progressively removed state support for collective bargaining, depoliticized trades unions, restricted the opportunity for trades unions to organize and engage in industrial action, and denied unions access (via the Trades Union Conference) to government policy-making.

At a workplace level the decline in collective IR is reflected in the decline in trades union membership since 1980, together with an increase in the proportion of establishments with no union representation. Another development has been the growth of union de-recognition (or decline in recognition), together with the reluctance of both existing non-union workplaces and newly formed establishments to provide recognition in recent years. A further manifestation of the decline in collectivism concerns the coverage and structure of collective bargaining itself. Collective pay determination has declined together with an associated strong emergence of individual forms of pay determination such as individual performance-related pay. While the fracturing of collective bargaining has gained momentum, it is not yet clear whether these changes 'can be seen unambiguously as deliberate steps on the way to complete de-unionization' (McLoughlin and Gourlay, 1994, p. 15).

Insofar as industrial relations now encompasses 'new style' agreements, flexibility agreements and other new employment practices such as employee involvement, TQM, team working and empowerment, then it could be argued that the new IR is more compatible with HRM than 'traditional' IR. Moreover, there seems to be some convergence between a modified collectivist approach as evidenced by the new IR and HRM strategy which is more 'pluralist' in orientation. However, some commentators, such as Pemberton and Herriot (1994), are more cautious. They cite BT and Cadbury-Schweppes as organizations which have de-layered radically and whose remaining employees express anger concerning increased job insecurity, distrust about employers' motives and loss of pride in working for their companies. There can be little confidence that those who remain want to deliver what the organization requires, particularly within what some employees perceive as a 'culture of fear' which is undermining the effective implementation of business changes because of a focus on short-term results. They conclude that 'the willingness to improve customer care through building long-term relationships is likely to be undermined by the (employee) desire to get out the minute an alternative job opportunity arises. The exhortation to grow with the job and embrace multi-skilling is being undermined by a desire to get even; digging in and resisting overtly or covertly the organization's agenda' (Pemberton and Herriott 1994).

The surveys, case studies and IR climate reviewed above reveal a great deal of change in the way UK organizations – in all sectors – are managing their human resources. For all of them debate continues on two fronts: how empirically pervasive are these changes and what is their significance? Is there a major and qualitative change in the design of work and the structuring of work organizations? Is the design of key personnel processes signifying a comprehensive programme of strategically driven change?

Or are these undeniable developments either so piecemeal, uneven and variable in their implementation or so driven by opportunism and a traditional concern for tightened management control, that they cannot possibly be seen as indicating any major strategic transformation?

Interpretations of HRM

This brings us to the final section of this chapter in which we seek to spell out the current views concerning the 'state of play' of HRM in the UK. We consider four very different interpretations or views which might be termed pragmatic, purist, processual and polemic.

A pragmatic view

Arguing that many critics of HRM read too much into the term, Beaumont (1993) points out that HRM can be seen as simply a generic term for employee – management relations or as containing a central message: 'the need to establish a close two-way relationship between business strategy or planning and HRM strategy or planning'. That such linkages have rarely been found by research is seen as unsurprising given the iterative nature of strategic decision-making and the felt need for short-term responses: 'In short, I think rather unreasonably high standards are frequently applied in terms of whether HRM exists in many organizations at the present time' (1993, p. 5).

In the United States, much attention has been given to elaborating the links between HRM strategy and generic competitive strategy, product life cycle and organizational life cycle. And it is this approach that Beaumont (1992, 1993) has developed, especially in his work on selection strategies and quality/flexibility strategies in Caledonian Paper (Beaumont and Hunter, 1992). He argues that 'certain key changes in the environmental context of the 1980s, particularly in the product market area, triggered a number of changes in management and organizational practice that pointed in the human resource management direction', citing 'the increased priority attached by senior line managers to human

resource management issues, the retitling of personnel management departments . . . and the reduced priority attached to collective bargaining and joint consultative arrangements' (1993,
p. 1).

What research has demonstrated, according to Beaumont
(1993), is the key importance in employee–management relations of 'how an organization seeks to compete effectively in the
product market' (p. 5). While accepting that much of the relevant
literature is a confusing mixture of prescription and description
and contains naive assumptions about the processes of organizational change and strategy, Beaumont concludes that 'in summary, I personally view HRM as a useful generic term and one
which contains a key message which accords well with the practical experience of modern times' (p. 5). As he points out, 'the
very fact that a personnel director in a leading company is more
interested in talking about training . . . than changes in the level
of collective bargaining, is indicative of thinking and moves along
these lines' (p. 6).

A variety of obstacles to moves along the HRM path are discussed by Beaumont, including low-wage competitive strategies,
decentralized labour-management, pressures for short-term operating results, the need for clarification of uncertainties, and the
need for a national HR strategy. However, 'it seems difficult to
write off human resource management as simply another fad . . .
there is simply too much going on in individual organizations that
is part of the HRM approach' (p. 7). He acknowledges that 'there
are important unresolved issues and debates . . . both within and
external to individual organizations that will need to be played out
before the rhetoric and organizational reality of HRM are more
closely aligned' (p. 22). His position seems to be that it will take
time for the HRM approach to be fully implemented, and that for
this to happen several weaknesses need to be addressed: (1) the
weakness of much underlying HRM theory, lacking explicit theories of motivation and commitment, for example; (2) the
need to incorporate a more 'political' understanding of internal
decision-making processes; (3) the need to consider extra organizational influences; and (4) the unaddressed role of government
in HR practice. Despite the inherent logic of models which propose the integration of HRM with business strategy and competitive performance, there is – as yet – very little empirical evidence
of the widespread incidence of firms which have achieved this

linkage. Bassett's (1986) account of IBM's alterations to its man-power planning, performance management and communications system in relation to projected changes in its market environment and that by Arthur (1994) correlating productivity and labour turnover in American steel mills with HR systems, are isolated examples.

A purist view

Despite the limitations noted above, writers have continued to work on the development of a theory of HRM which achieves 'fit' or integration between human resources and strategic manage-ment. For example, Guest (1987) suggested that human resource management comprises a set of policies designed to foster the commitment, flexibility and quality of the workforce.

Although commendable in themselves, these policies only deliver real competitive advantage when *integration* with business strategy is achieved. This, in turn, is only realistic where human resource policies cohere with other areas of policy and with each other, where line managers accept that managing people is their responsibility, where employees feel integrated into the business, and where the firm adopts a long-term perspective on human resource planning in place of short-term expediency (Guest, 1987, p. 512; Guest, 1989, p. 42). And lastly, strategic integra-tion is more likely to be achieved where the organization suc-ceeds in creating an all-embracing HRM philosophy (Hendry et al.; Pettigrew and Sparrow, 1988). The central notion of commitment is retained, but placed in the context of the Harvard Framework (see figure 1.2 in chapter 1 of this book). Guest (1992) recog-nizes 'the failure of personnel techniques, derived largely from organization psychology, to have the expected impact on organiza-tions' (p. 128).

Guest's approach is useful because, in his words, it offers a set of testable propositions which can be used as an interpreta-tive framework to make sense of the reality of human resource management within different contexts, for example between union and non-union firms. The four policy goals of integration, commitment, flexibility and quality are at the centre of Guest's model and all must be present to guarantee delivery of the desired organizational outcomes. It is implied in the model that the organization's ability to improve its performance can be directly influenced by applying a cohesive set of HR policies. In addition, supportive leadership, a strong culture and a conscious strategy need to be in place to provide the cement to bind the HR system together and ensure that it is taken seriously in the organization (Guest, 1992, p. 128). In practice, this might involve the identification of a profile of core competencies or behaviours that are required to implement an emergent corporate strategy, and the subsequent establishment of an integrated recruitment, performance management, career planning and training and development structure designed to achieve it (Mabey and Iles, 1993; Sparrow and Bognanno, 1993).

However, the HRM approach typified by Guest's model has been criticized on a number of fronts.

1. It fails to overcome the three inherent contradictions pointed out by Legge (1989): how is it possible for a firm to pursue individualized HR policies (e.g. performance-related pay, development centres, fast tracking) at the same time as initiatives to improve teamwork (quality circles, functional flexibility)? How does an organization reconcile long-term strategies to improve quality by a steady enhancement of skills over time with simultaneous requirements to attain congruence and cost savings via functional flexibility which may imply deskilling? How can a firm achieve a 'strong' culture of shared values and corporate commitment at the same time as cultivating flexibility, creativity and adaptability (Noon, 1992, pp. 23–4)?
2. It appears to regard the link between strategy, structure and HR policies as a rational, causal relationship (Hendry and Pettigrew, 1990).
3. It seems to imply that a congruence of interests across all members of an organization is both desirable and feasible, which neglects the structural and political reality of such social institutions (Keenoy, 1990).

Furthermore, Noon (1992) has questioned the theoretical utility of Guest's model. There is, as yet, little empirical evidence to demonstrate that the model reliably explains and predicts the impact of HRM. So, on the one hand the 'theory as it stands may be just too broad for it to be tested adequately . . . or on the other hand so bounded that it is only relevant for growth industries, using high technology, with a predominantly white-collar work-force, traditionally non-unionized and espousing a strong corporate image' (Noon, 1992, pp. 25 and 27).

A processual view

Another British HRM approach which addresses many of the above weaknesses is located in a literature attempting to analyse organizational change. By exploring the implications of a variety of approaches to strategic management it emphasizes the importance of understanding the importance of context, content and process. Much of this work is associated with research under the leadership of Andrew Pettigrew at Warwick University's Centre of Corporate Strategy and Change (see Hendry and Pettigrew, 1990; Pettigrew and Whipp, 1991). It adopts a sophisticated longitudinal, historical and cross-sector methodology described in detail by Pettigrew (1988) and requiring resources beyond the reach of most research groups. This overcomes the criticisms of 'bounded' theorizing, the assumptions of rational strategy and implementation and the adoption of unitarist values levelled at the Guest model. Pettigrew and his colleagues borrow from the Harvard HRM model (Beer et al., 1984) by extending its analytical elements and down-playing its prescriptive outcomes. Empirical testing of this model leads them to be sceptical about any straightforward relationship between HRM and competitive performance. This is in part due to 'the fragility and impermanence of many HRM instruments' and the difficulties facing any firm seeking to control 'the social, political and educational forces of the competitive process' (Whipp, 1992, p. 52).

Despite all this, they see the struggle to unravel the complex forces that shape an organization's effectiveness as worthwhile.

> Our research at firm level in four sectors of the UK economy confirms the findings of the critical school of writers – that in practice the development of a HRM approach within a firm cannot be assumed. In the same way its positive contribution to competitive performance cannot be taken for granted. The dimensions which the vast majority of writers in the first minimise we see as paramount: the process by which human resources are developed such that they can contribute to the ability of the organization to accomplish strategic change and generate competitive bases.
>
> Pettigrew and Whipp, 1991, pp. 210–11

Their research examines the successful and the less effective management of strategic and organizational change in eight British companies over more than twenty years to 1989. One of the central factors seen as critical for managing change for competitive success was treating human resources as assets and as investments rather than costs. This involved: (1) *ad hoc* cumulative, supportive activities at various levels; (2) linking HRM action to business needs, with HRM as a means, not an end; (3) devolution of responsibility to line management; and (4) constructing HRM actions and institutions which reinforce one another.

Over and above these supportive mechanisms was the conditioning of those concerned both prior to and during the HRM implementation. In particular, they found this to consist of raising HRM consciousness in the organization, using situationally appropriate features to create a positive force for change and demonstrating the need for business and people change. In short, successful organizations paid as much attention to the process of human resource change and its degree of progressive acceptance outside the HRM department as they did to the substance of the policies and procedures themselves.

While such research helpfully raises the profile of internal decision pathways and the mobilizing of support for change in organizations, doubts remain about the internal consistency and possibility of human resource strategies (the tension between 'hard' and 'soft', the possibility of achieving integration, the possible conflicts between aspects of HRM and so on). Furthermore, the findings do nothing to dispel the suspicion that many of the apparent human resource strategies are more to do with increased employee control and a focus on cost control and the 'bottom line', than on initiating a new form of, and approach to, the management of staff.

A polemical view

Despite the enormous public espousal of 'soft' HRM values by senior manages, the evidence on levels of installation of such key elements of HRM as training and development, and the integration of HR practices and business strategy suggest that 'Britain still has a long way to go . . . Senior managers are either not practising what they espouse or they are installing new initiatives in an incompetent and ineffective way' (Storey and Sisson, 1993, pp. 50–1). In short, there appears to be a massive gap between rhetoric and reality.

For some writers, however, the importance of HRM is much more, and much wider, than the various practices which do or do not reflect its operationalization. While there are undoubtedly many changes occurring in organizations that impact on the structure and process of work and employment, these are argued to be less significant as indicators of a new strategic approach to human resources, and more important because of their simultaneous appeal to powerful new values and assumptions and reliance on old forms of power and control (Mabey and Salaman, 1995).

In contrast to the pragmatic, purist and processual views, we describe this as a polemical view because it represents a radical critique of HRM. HRM is conceived as a powerful and new form of managerial rhetoric, whose power lies not in its impact on performance, but in its capacity to reflect current societal values and political priorities, and to represent managerial conceptions of the organization, and of intra-organizational relationships. It is thus seen as a new form of managerial control. Not simply control through managerial practices and organization change and restructuring, but control of the ways in which organizations are thought about and understood, and the ways in which organizational dynamics and purposes, and critically, organizational members, are conducted and framed. Such an approach would argue that the preoccupations of management remain the same as ever. Namely, to achieve control, ensure and increase productivity and profitability, yet at the same time to ensure that as far as possible, employees are willing to do what is required, are compliant, co-operative and creative. This is the essential paradox of management. If HRM offers anything really new, it offers new techniques, and new language and constructions of meaning, with which management approaches this dilemma.

Furthermore, there may well be a connection between changes in work organization which require discretion on the part of workers, and an approach to management, organization, training and culture change. These seek to ensure compliance on the basis not of formal (rigid) rules, but on the basis of 'shared norms of understanding, a common grammar of interpretation . . . the internalization of the organization's "goals" or "norms" to ensure that the individual interprets the area of discretion correctly from the organization's point of view' (Townley, 1989, p. 103). As

Keenoy and Anthony (1992) remark: 'to understand the HRM phenomenon in Britain it is necessary to treat it as a cultural construction comprised of a series of metaphors which constitute a
'new reality'. HRM reflects an attempt to redefine both the meaning of work and the way individual employers relate to their
employees' (p. 234). It has also been noted that one of the key
elements of HRM thinking – the focus on market forces and relationships, and these on the value of enterprise (together with the
practices and organizational technologies which are inspired by
this focus) – is essentially coterminous with the political-
economic-social project of Thatcherism (du Gay and Salaman,
1992, p. 627).

There will perhaps come a time when the distinction between
rhetoric and reality becomes blurred and meaningless. But by
then, the rhetoric may have already become real in its consequences because HRM will have helped to re-define management,
organization and the employee. When HRM is used to impose a
conception of how managers and employees relate to each other
and to the organization (and the customer) as liberated autonomous, enterprising employees, such a conception will be difficult
to resist because of its resonance with, and dependence upon,
wider societal/political conceptions of the market and the primacy
of market forces and values, and conceptions of the individual. In
other words, the rhetoric – and language – wherein HRM is
explained and developed and justified, the activities in which it
results, are inextricably related to practices and systems which
define, develop, reward and empower the individual. In the same
way that the American excellence literature was received so readily and unquestioningly because of its cultural and economic time-
liness in the USA (Guest, 1992), it could be argued that HRM
rhetoric and practice in the UK connects not only to the challenges of recession and the increased competitive threat, but
also to the constant attempt to devise new strategies, cut costs
and improve margins.

In other words, interpreting the significance of HRM will inevitably require some understanding of the prevalent values, economic
priorities and cultural context of the country concerned. In her
assessment of the influence of English culture upon business
organizations, Monir Tayeb, an Iranian, notes that when it comes
to: 'leadership style and management-employee relationships,
one can also trace many of their features to the cultural, political
and economic characteristics of English society. Deference to

authority (culture) plus a high degree of unemployment (economy), for instance, could together explain the absence of serious trade union challenge to management's prerogatives and right to manage' (Tayeb, 1993, p. 61).

Conclusion

In the early part of this chapter we made a case for HRM in the UK owing its intellectual origins to the philanthropic human relations movement, then tracing its quest to occupy a more central place among the organization's decision-making elite. For this elevated position of HRM to be sustained and maintained, at the very least its policies and actions must be seen to add measurable value to the business. We have seen in the foregoing analysis that this is by no means self-evident. There are three issues here.

1. There is a tendency to accept the link between environmental triggers and changing business strategy and the process by which HR strategies are formulated and implemented as unproblematic. This ignores the complexities and realities of organizational politics and culture within the managerial hierarchy, to say nothing of the differing cognitive maps and personal agendas of the individuals involved.
2. Despite the self-styled 'bottom-line' orientation of the HRM paradigm, and the various models which propose a relationship between various HRM policies and different business strategies there is very little evidence to support the thesis that HRM practices have had a positive impact on organizational performance. Noted in this regard was the relative absence of case studies which reveal strong relationships between, for example, employee involvement and productivity, or between performance and performance-related pay.
3. There is Legge's (1989) concern that HRM is underpinned by an ideology which is simply designed to make unilateral management action more acceptable.

In addition to these issues, there is the wider question of whether HRM in the UK can be treated in isolation from its international context. The development of the Single European Market in particular means that the 'domestic market' for UK firms no longer stops at national borders. Wage levels, jobs, inflation rates and

interest rates are increasingly influenced by pan-European decisions and HRM is no longer able to address purely local or
national issues. In addition, European social policy, as embodied
in the Treaty of Rome and amended by the Single European Act of
1986, is having an increasing impact on a range of HRM issues
by creating principles which fall within the jurisdiction of the European Court of Justice and which domestic legislation in a whole
range of areas needs to take into account. Such issues include
the right to freedom of movement, to equal treatment, to
employee participation, and to equal pay and benefits. Even
according to the narrow yardstick of economic performance alone
it is doubtful whether the Anglo-American model of HRM, with its
focus on employee autonomy, deregulation, mobility, and enterprise-level strategies in terms of pay, recruitment and training, is
a superior pathway to competitive success compared to the HR
approaches pursued by countries like Japan and Germany.

HRM promises a great deal; its influence on recent and current
programmes of organizational restructuring has been enormous.
To a major degree HRM supplies the agenda for programmes of
organizational change: the introduction of internal markets within
the British National Health Service; the subcontracting and priva-
tizing of public utilities; the de-layering and devolving of many previously centralized businesses; the introduction of JIT, TQM,
team-working and PRP; and so on. However, our analysis of HRM
in the UK context has shown that it is characterized by a number
of basic problems, limitations and contradictions: it means a variety of different things ('open' versus 'closed', 'hard' versus 'soft')
it makes a set of recommendations which could well conflict; it
claims high moral purposes but seems to be vulnerable to short-
termism. Possibly the most important feature of HRM is not simply the changes – many of them far-reaching and pervasive –
which are taking place in organizations. Rather it is the way the
concept and language of HRM supplies a new, authoritative theory of how organizations work and how individuals must be managed, rewarded and directed. Furthermore, HRM has strong links
with associated notions of 'excellence', the role of markets and of
enterprise, all of which had a timely resonance with the prevailing
political, economic and cultural context of the late 1980s/early
1990s UK.

Whether HRM continues to have such a defining influence as
this political and international climate of the late 1990s inevitably
shifts, remains to be seen.

References

Arthur, J. B. (1994), 'Effects of human resource systems on manufacturing performance and turnover', *Academy of Management Journal,* **37** (3), pp. 670–87.

Atkinson, J. (1984), 'Manpower strategies for the flexible firm', *Personnel Management,* August.

Bassett, P. (1986), *Strike Free.* London: Macmillan.

Beaumont, P. (1992), 'The US human resource management literature: a review'. In G. Salaman (ed.), *Human Resource Strategies.* London: Sage, pp. 20–37.

Beaumont, P. B. (1993), *Human Resource Management.* London: Sage.

Beaumont, P. B. and Hunter, L. C. (1992), 'Competitive strategy, flexibility and selection: the case of Caledonian paper'. In B. Towers (ed.), *The Handbook of Human Resource Management.* Oxford: Blackwell, pp. 392–403.

Beer, M., Spector, B., Lawrence, P., Quinn Mills, L. D. and Walton, R. (1984), *Managing Human Assets.* New York: Free Press.

Beer, M., Spector B., Lawrence, P., Quinn Mills, D. and Walton, R. (1985), *Human Resources Management: A General Manager's Perspective.* New York: Free Press.

Beer, M., Eisenstat, M. and Spencer, B. (1990), 'Why change programs don't produce change', *Harvard Business Review,* November-December, pp. 158–66.

Benjamin, G. and Mabey, C. (1990), 'A case of organization transformation', *Management Education and Development,* **21**, pp. 327–34.

Berridge, J. (1992), 'Human resource management in Britain', *Employee Relations,* **14**, pp. 62–92.

Bevan, S. and Thompson, M. (1991), 'Performance management at the crossroads', *Personnel Management,* November, pp. 36–9.

Brewster, C. (1994), 'The integration of human resource management and corporate strategy'. In C. Brewster and A. Hegewisch (eds), *Policy and Practice in European Human Resource Management.* London: Routledge, pp. 22–35.

Buchanan, D. (1992), 'High performance: new boundaries of acceptability in worker control'. In G. Salaman (ed.), *Human Resource Strategies.* London: Sage, pp. 138–55.

Cameron, S., Francis, A. and Storey, J. (1992), 'Structural strategies'. In *'B884' Human Resource Strategies.* Open Business School, Milton Keynes, Open University.

Constable, J. and McCormick, R. (1987), *The Making of British Managers.* London: British Institute of Management.

Du Gay, P. and Salaman, G. (1992), 'The cult(ure), of the customer', *Journal of Management Studies,* **29**, pp. 615–33.

Edwards, R. (1979), *Contested Terrain.* London: Heinemann.

Fombrun, C., Tichy, N. and Devanna, M. (1984), *Strategic Human Resource Management.* Chichester, Sussex: John Wiley.

Fox, A. (1974), *Beyond Contract: Work, Power and Trust Relations*. London: Faber and Faber.

Giles, E. (1989), 'Is Xerox's human resource management worth copying?' Paper presented to the Annual British Academy of Management Conference, Manchester.

Gleave, S. and Oliver, N. (1990), 'Human resource management in Japanese manufacturing companies in the UK: 5 case studies', *Journal of General Management,* **166**, pp. 54–68.

Goldsmith, W. and Clutterbuck, D. (1984), *The Winning Streak*. London: Weidenfeld and Nicolson.

Goodstein, L. and Burke, W. (1991), 'Creating successful organization change', *Organization Dynamics*, Spring, pp. 5–17.

Goold, M. and Campbell, A. (1987), *Stratetgies and Styles: The Role of the Centre in Managing Diversified Organizations*. Oxford: Blackwell.

Guest, D. (1987), 'Human resource management and industrial relations', *Journal of Management Studies,* **24**, pp. 502–21.

Guest, D. (1989), 'HRM: implications for industrial relations'. In J. Storey (ed.), *New Perspectives in Human Resource Management*. London: Routledge, pp. 41–55.

Guest, D. (1992), 'Human resource management in the United Kingdom'. In B. Towers (ed.), *The Handbook of Human Resource Management*. Oxford: Blackwell, pp. 3–26.

Guest, D. (1993), 'Current perspectives on human resource management in the United Kingdom'. In A. Hegewisch and C. Brewster (eds), *European Developments in Human Resource Management*. Kogan Page: London, pp. 210–32.

Guest, D. and Hoque, K. (1993), 'The mystery of the missing personnel manager', *Personnel Management*, June, pp. 40–1.

Handy, C. (1987), *The Making of Managers: A Report on Management Education, Training and Development in the US, West Germany, France, Japan and the UK*. London: NEDO.

Hendry, C. and Pettigrew, A. (1986), 'The practice of human resource management', *Personnel Review,* **15**, pp. 3–8.

Hendry, C. and Pettigrew, A. (1990), 'Human resource management: an agenda for the 1990s', *International Journal of Human Resource Management,* **1**, pp. 17–43.

Hendry, C., Pettigrew, A. and Sparrow, P. (1989), 'Changing patterns of human resource management'. *Personnel Management*, November, pp. 37–41.

Hill, S. (1991), 'Why quality circles failed but total quality management might succeed', *British Journal of Industrial Relations,* **29** (4), pp. 541–68.

Hope, V. and Hendry, J. (1994), 'Corporate cultural change: is it relevant for organisations in the 1990s?' Paper presented to the 9th Annual Workshop for the European Institute for Advanced Studies in Management, St Gallen, Switzerland.

Iles, P. A. and Johnston, T. (1989), 'Searching for excellence in second-hand clothes', *Personnel Review,* **18** (6), pp. 26–9.

Keenoy, T. (1990), 'Human resource management: rhetoric, reality and contradiction', *International Journal of Human Resource Management,* **1,** pp. 363–84.

Keenoy, T. and Anthony, P. (1992), 'HRM: metaphor, meaning and morality'. In P. Blyton and P. Turnbull (eds), *Reassessing Human Resource Management.* Sage: London, pp. 233–55.

Lane, C. (1992), 'European business systems: Britain and Germany compared'. In R. Whitley (ed.), *European Business Systems: Firms and Markets in their National Contexts.* London: Sage, pp. 64–97.

Legge, K. (1978), *Power, Innovation and Problem Solving in Personnel Management.* Maidenhead: McGraw-Hill.

Legge, K. (1989), 'Human resource management: a critical analysis'. In J. Storey (ed.), *New Pespectives on Human Resource Management.* London: Routledge, pp. 19–40.

Littler, C. and Salaman, G. (1982), 'Bravermania and beyond: recent theories of the labour process', *Sociology,* **16**, pp. 251–69.

Mabey, C. and Iles, P. A. (1993), 'The strategic integration of assessment and development practices: succession planning and new manager development', *Human Resource Management Journal,* **3**, pp. 16–34.

Mabey, C. and Salaman, G. (1995), *Strategic Human Resource Management.* Oxford: Blackwell.

McIlroy, J. (1991), *The Permanent Revolution? Conservative Law and the Trade Unions.* Nottingham: Spokesman.

McLoughlin, I. and Gourlay, S. (1992), 'Enterprise without unions: the management of employee relations in non-union firms', *Journal of Management Studies,* **29**, 669–91.

McLoughlin, I. and Gourlay, S. (1994), *Enterprise Without Unions: Industrial Relations in the Non-union Firm.* Open University Press: Buckingham.

Morris, J. (1974), 'Developing resourceful managers'. In B. Taylor and G. Lippitt (eds), *Management Development and Training Handbook.* New York: McGraw-Hill, pp. 274–93.

Noon, M. (1992), 'HRM: a map, model or theory?'. In P. Blyton and P. Turnbull (eds), *Reassessing Human Resource Management.* London: Sage, pp. 16–32.

Ogbonna, E. (1992), 'Organization culture and human resource management: dilemmas and contradictions'. In P. Blyton and P. Turnbull (eds), *Reassessing Human Resource Management.* London: Sage, pp. 74–96.

Oliver, N., Delbridge, R., Jones, D. and Lowe, J. (1993), 'World class manufacturing: further evidence in the lean production debate'. Paper presented to Annual British Academy of Management Conference, Milton Keynes.

Pemberton, C. and Herriot, P. (1994), 'Inhumane resources', *The Observer,* 4 December.

Peters, T. and Waterman, R. (1982), *In Search of Excellence.* New York: Harper and Row.

Pettigrew, A. (1988), 'Introduction: researching strategic change'. In A. Pettigrew (ed.), *The Management of Strategic Change*. Oxford: Blackwell, pp. 1–13.

Pettigrew, A. and Whipp, R. (1991), *Managing Change for Competitive Success*. Oxford: Blackwell.

Poole, M. and Mansfield, R. (1992), 'The movement towards human resource management: evidence from a national sample'. Paper presented to the Annual British Academy of Management Conference, Bradford.

Price, C. and Murphy, E. (1987), 'Organizational development at British Telecom', *Training and Development*, July, pp. 45–8.

Purcell, J. (1989), 'How to manage decentralized bargaining', *Personnel Management*, May, pp. 27–9.

Purcell, J. and Sisson, K. (1983), 'Strategies and practice in the management of industrial relations'. In G. Bain (ed.), *Industrial Relations in Britain: Past Trends and Future Prospects*. Oxford: Blackwell.

Salaman, G. (1979), *Work Organizations: Resistance and Control*. London: Longman.

Schuler, R. S. and Jackson, S. E. (1987), 'Linking competitive strategies with human resource management practices', *Academy of Management Executive*, **1**, pp. 209–13.

Skinner, D. and Mabey, C. (1995), 'How do organizations conceive, design and implement human resource strategies?' Paper presented to the 10th Anniversary Workshop on the State of the Art of SHRM and its future, Brussels, March.

Sparrow, P. and Bognanno, M. (1993), 'Competency requirement forecasting: issues for international selection and assessment', *International Journal of Selection and Assessment*, **1**, pp. 50–8.

Storey, J. (1980), *The Challenge to Management Control*. London: Kogan Page.

Storey, J. (1983), *Managerial Prerogative and the Question of Control*. London: Routledge and Kegan Paul.

Storey, J. (1992), *Developments in the Management of Human Resources: An Analytical Review*. Oxford: Blackwell.

Storey, J. and Sisson, K. (1993), *Managing Human Resources and Industrial Relations*. Open University Press: Buckingham.

Tayeb, M. (1993), 'England: English culture and business organizations'. In D. Hickson (ed.), *Management in Western Europe*. Berlin and New York: Walter de Gruyter, pp. 47–64.

Thomason, G.F. (1976), *A Textbook of Personnel Management* (2nd edn). London: IPM.

Torrington, D. and Chapman, J. (1979), *Personnel Management* (2nd edn). London: Prentice-Hall.

Torrington, D. and Hall, L. (1987), *Personnel Management: A New Approach*. London: Prentice-Hall.

Townley, B. (1989), 'Selection and appraisal: reconstituting social relations'.

In J. Storey (ed.), *New Perspectives in Human Resource Management*. London: Routledge, pp. 92–108.

Tyson, S. (1983), 'Personnel management in its organizational context'. In K. Thurley and S. Wood (eds), *Industrial Relations and Management Strategy*. Cambridge: Cambridge University Press.

Tyson, S. and Fell, A. (1986), *Evaluating the Personnel Function*. London: Hutchinson.

Whipp, R. (1992), 'Human resource management, competition and strategy: some productive tensions'. In P. Blyton and P. Turnbull (eds), *Reassessing Human Resource Management*. London: Sage, pp. 33–55.

Wilson, D.C. (1992), *A Strategy of Change*. London: Routledge.

Wood, S. and Peccei, R. (1990), 'Preparing for 1992? Business-led versus strategic human resource management', *Human Resource Management Journal*, **1**, pp. 63–89.

3 Hesitant Innovation: the Recent Evolution of Human Resources Management in France

ALAN JENKINS AND GILLES VAN WIJK

Introduction

The recent changes in personnel/human resources management (HRM) in France have to be seen as closely related to broad historical and social processes of the management of social consensus and of industrial modernization. They have been conditioned by the 'institutional' interaction of tone-setting governmental policies, the sometimes reluctant endorsements of employers (the *patronat*), employee representation on various boards and councils, the political options of the labour unions, and ultimately, in-firm innovations. This multi-layered process becomes even more complex when it is recognized that many labour traditions, some of them dating back to the 1930s with the *Front populaire*, are still in force and that business leaders are on occasion the advocates of the government's social philosophy. Among the HR-relevant policy issues permanently on the national agenda are public education, professional training and social protection. Their consideration invariably interacts with problems posed by the emergence of a more recent emphasis on liberalism, and the difficulties inherent in the development of a more modern and dynamic French economy.

In enacting social and organizational change in France it has often been found difficult to modify the social *avantages acquis* (benefits which must not be relinquished) without awakening fierce resistance and hence threatening social consensus. If the French like to think of themselves as individualists and autonomous actors (d'Iribarne, 1989), they have displayed on many occasions a remarkable capacity to stage massive resistance against attempts to curtail their perceived rights or social benefits. Over the past few years, the social situation has repeatedly been delicate to manage: more than 11 per cent unemployment, difficult integration of youth into working life, and business more concerned with its competitiveness than with the social situation, which is usually considered to be the natural domain of the state. The most effective occasions for change have been periods of slow growth and recession which made the moves 'inevitable'. Yet these periods also exacerbated a number of the weaknesses of the employment system, in particular providing work for the young.

To provide a basis for understanding the nature of HRM the chapter is organized as follows. The first part describes the roles of the main social actors in shaping an employee relations ideology or philosophy coherent with the multiple constraints sketched above. The second part gives a flavour of the plurality of approaches and schools of thought in practice and in academic work. The French HRM literature is characterized by its variety, including original and creative academic work, 'traditional' Anglo-American influenced contributions, and 'official' pamphlets written by consultants and business opinion leaders, propagating the accepted social philosophy. Elements of descriptive evidence will emphasize the gap between these often pious statements and actual practice. The third part addresses the practical problems as they have emerged in the field, and describes how they have been solved by French companies in the past few years.

The Spread of a New Employee-Relations Ideology in France

The abundance of social actors historically intervening in the definition of employment and personnel policies in France often suggests a fairly static situation, with little variation from business to business. Important changes have nevertheless occurred since the 1980s, and they have been accompanied by the emergence of what we may call a new employment ideology. Business rather

than the state is now considered to be more responsible for overall social well-being, and the need for business to be successful is
recognized if it is to be able to fulfil its social responsibilities. The
idea of the *Etat Providence*, the all-providing state, has receded
but not yet vanished. In this new spirit wage stability and job
security have become things of the past, but welfare protection,
inherited from the *Front populaire*, and professional training
(needed more than ever for competitive efficiency) are still very
much valued. However the notion of *solidarité nationale* remains
very strong as the presidential campaign of May 1995, with its
dominant themes of *fracture sociale* and *exclusion*, revealed.

Much broader ideological changes have taken place over the
past twenty-five years, more particularly since 1981 under the
Mitterrand administration. They have accompanied three phases
in the evolution of the concrete management of employee relations, which we can refer to as (1) the 'era of doubt' (roughly from
the social crisis of 1968 to 1975); (2) the 'era of experimentation' (from 1975 to 1986); and (3) the 'era of transition' up to the
present. Across these three periods a number of inter-related
changes have taken place within the French firm :

1. The very idea of 'management' held by the *patronat* has
   evolved (Morville, 1985). Authoritarianism and a traditional
   over-reliance on bureaucracy and technical expertise have
   receded in the face of the imperative to build on worker's skills
   and promote more and more organizational flexibility.
2. Industrial relations have been modified. As the weight and traditional power of the trades unions has waned, new forms of
   direct dialogue with the workforce have (with stimulus from the
   state) become institutionalized and organs such as works
   councils (the *comités d'entreprise*) given new responsibilities
   (Gallie, 1985).
3. What was traditionally called personnel management has, as
   in other countries, become modified. Its label changed quietly
   in the 1980s, the period of workplace experimentation, and
   many commentators and practitioners proclaimed a revolution.
   The new mission of personnel/HRM was to be the strategic
   service of business objectives (sometimes defined in terms of
   a mission or *projet d'entreprise*, often in terms of an 'organizational culture') with a planned and coherent blend of recruitment, training, remuneration and other such policies. Dream
   or reality? We shall come to this issue later.

For the moment let us return to the realm of societal ideologies to see how the role of the state has been crucial in the evolution of mentalities, how business has reacted to this, and how a number of management opinion leaders have endorsed and propagated a new neo-liberal message.

The influential state

In the economic domain the state in modern France has to face up to a number of contradictory responsibilities. It must manage a sometimes fragile social consensus, prepare the ground for a modern competitive nation, and deal with pressing problems like unemployment. One of the standard ways of doing this is to intervene actively in the way employee relations are managed in the firm. The state acts both directly by way of law, and indirectly by funding advisory agencies and persuading innovative and highly visible firms to implement and propagate new practices. Since the profound reforms of the Auroux legislation in 1982,[1] this tendency towards state-guided innovation has been very marked, and this is not confined to Socialist administrations.

A significant example concerns the important legislative programme drafted under the recent Balladur government, and referred to as the *Loi quinquennale pour l'emploi*. This law defines a whole host of regulations and mechanisms to develop the 'insertion' of school-leavers and youth into working life, accelerate 'reinsertion' of the jobless, to encourage manpower development and part-time employment. Some of the provisions of the law have been hotly debated and abandoned under popular pressure, but the process is exemplary of the kind of centralized intervention to structure aspects of human resources management in the firm. The failure of the provisions intended to facilitate access to jobs for the young (via the CIP, *contrat d'insertion professionnelle*) illustrates how public opinion can suddenly show fierce resistance to bureaucrat's decisions. The promulgation of the CIP articles in effect triggered widespread unrest and at times violent responses from masses of teenagers who felt cheated at the prospect of having proportionally reduced salaries, and this after having completed increasingly demanding educational programmes. It is likely that this discontent is also fuelled by the feeling of an increasingly uncertain future. Backing out on this programme, the government generated much scepticism regarding the effectiveness of the other provisions of the law

While a variety of attempts are made to fight unemployment, and youth unemployment in particular, through long-term arrangements, temporary incentives (such as tax relief), or isolated measures (one-time early VAT reimbursement, for instance), there is also an awareness that the problems stem in substantial part from a poorly qualified labour force (Delmas, 1992). Efforts in developing a hands-on, pragmatic education, different from the over-theoretical and humanistic programmes (Cannac, 1985) have had little effect. This is partly due to the widespread attraction in France of elitist education, epitomized by the *grandes écoles* system, but also to the failure of the professional education programmes to respond to the needs of business. In order to transfer the burden and the responsibility of professional training to firms, a new tax arrangement was devised. It was determined that a firm has to spend 1.5 per cent of its revenues on employee training by offering internal programmes, by subsidizing relevant educational institutions, or by collaborating with a trade school to offer apprenticeship programmes. Though many firms devote more resources to train their employees, the obligation of committing at least 1.5 per cent of revenues has created a norm to which most small firms adhere. Investment in training has thus become 'institutionalized'.

Recent efforts aimed at improving the integration between education and working life have favoured a system in which apprentices alternate between on-the-job training and school sessions. Though these programmes have been intrinsically successful they have been difficult to popularize. Firms were not ready to take on the additional cost of developing *ad hoc* training curricula, and devoting the necessary supervision. The efforts of the central administration to give these programmes some momentum are illustrative of the spirit and the ways in which such national-level programmes are often implemented. The timing of the efforts looks right as they take advantage of enduring economic difficulties with high levels of unemployment. The usual preference for long and abstract studies gives way to more pragmatic concerns such as simply getting a job. Formal incentives include a reduction of the mandatory social coverage expenses for the firm, and financial support for the schools involved. Finally, in order to build consensus and demonstrate the effectiveness of the programme, its implementation is staged. It is unofficially co-ordinated by national and regional government representatives among reputable firms and visible educational institutions. A swift and successful implementation is ensured by giving such a programme a valid and even desirable image as an educational alternative; it is hoped to achieve a snowball effect. Communication about these developments is relayed to known experts (consultants and managers) whose endorsement is then used to promote the new measures. This process of breathing new life into the old scheme of apprenticeship by combining formal legislation and informal implementation is illustrative of the state's action in such domains.

State-led efforts are also remarkable for their continuity. Fundamental equilibria are not disturbed; socialists and conservatives have not interfered, except on rare occasions, with long-term orientations. In the 1981–3 period, job protection, social benefits and a reduction of the length of the working week were introduced or reinforced, but these changes were either reversed later or left to wither under the pressure of economic problems. Other equilibria have, significantly, never been touched, though they have often been challenged. The *patronat* has requested for many years that their obligatory contributions, currently exceeding one-third of labour expenses, be reduced. These contributions pay for 80 per cent of health expenses, hospital fees, private pension plans, public transport, aid to the poor and unemployment compensation. The resulting level of labour costs faced by firms leads to a situation in which firms prefer to invest in sophisticated equipment which replaces labour rather than to recruit expensive employees. This in turn underscores the contradiction, fought by the *patronat*, of both requesting the creation of jobs and of being modern and competitive. Indeed, the continuation of this other state-inspired industrial policy, keeping the nation competitive through 'modernization', has not been called into question either by the conservatives, or by the socialists.

Logically, firms' choices have leaned towards more and more capital intensive equipment which has also been supported by a favourable tax structure. As a result productivity has increased steadily. Reductions in working time and economic upturns have not generated more jobs. In effect, the potential for productivity increases is likely to take some time before it bottoms out (Moscovici and Hollande, 1991). Ultimately, the unemployment problem has become so acute that it has become an important political issue. This provides sufficient reason for the administration's bureaucrats to try and work out alternative solutions and significantly reduce labour costs.

As in many of the other domains, the state sets the pace. Whether for recruitment, for social benefits, for professional training, for pension plans and even for levels of income, either through legislation or by influence, the state defines and establishes relatively narrowly boundaries for the management of human resources within the firm.

The increased relative autonomy of business

The changing ideological environment has resulted in an assumption of the importance of more autonomy for business in general, and less centralized control over personnel matters in particular. This change has not occurred, however, in an even and uniform fashion. Some HRM domains have remained under state influence, while others have been decentralized with varying degrees of success. Business has not been spontaneously eager to become more involved – the efforts required to develop apprenticeship programmes are an example. Recruitment and lay-off practices suggest that the adoption of the new ideology often relinquishes social concerns to second-tier importance. There is generally no question that firms are now mostly aiming to achieve satisfactory economic performance and competitiveness. This is not only popularly accepted, but much hope is also vested in the success of French firms abroad. Except for some rare cases, employment and HR matters are subordinated to these objectives. Accordingly, business is mostly involved with hiring and firing, evaluation and training, whereas working time, health and retirement plans tend to be regulated centrally.

Given the recent emphasis on personnel reductions and 'downsizing'[2] – the result of a very deep recession between 1992 and 1994 – this means that firms employ fewer, but in general more qualified, personnel because of the technical and professional knowledge that is required to compete effectively. One example of the problems associated with this slow but irreversible shift is the big banks. When in state ownership they used to be big employers for modestly qualified personnel (occasionally, they may have been requested by the relevant authorities to hire personnel in order to lessen the regional unemployment problems). Now privatized, they need to become 'lean and mean' with well-trained personnel to serve increasingly sophisticated and demanding clients in henceforth unprotected markets. Until now, the transition has been managed sensitively, probably also because of state intervention in delaying the onset of substantial competition in the home market. But big reorganizations, such as those which have taken place in the automobile industry, cannot to be excluded if market conditions become too difficult, and if strategic and competitive conditions require them.

The capacity to lay off personnel relatively freely was granted to business to a large extent in 1989. Relieved from stringent employment obligations, firms were expected to be ready to hire more liberally. This has not been the case, however, mainly due to labour costs. Firms have been as cautious as ever in hiring, and the trend has been predominantly towards temporary contracts. So called CDDs (*contrats à durée déterminée*) fixed on a yearly basis, with the possibility of one renewal, are extensively used (over 80 per cent of new recruitments). Firms' attitudes towards the labour force are illustrated even more crudely by an analysis of lay-off patterns. Both in terms of seasonal adjustments and the number of contracts being terminated there appears to be a close correspondence with the frequency of board meetings, and the losses made by a firm. According to some commentators, a profit reduction or loss of 193,000 francs will on average translate into a job cut (Dure and Chevalier, 1994). It seems that manpower reductions may be more to do with reassuring shareholders and financiers than with strategically driven reorganization measures. Firms' social discourses invoke outside determinism – loss-making in this instance – to require cutbacks and render them legitimate.

Finally, business HRM is reflected in the objectives of professional training: people are made to fit firm structures and procedures rather than the reverse. To some extent, this priority is attributable to the popular belief that acquiring knowledge is more important than actually using it. More time is being spent in preparation than in acquiring the benefits of previous investments. To refer to professional training, the French commonly talk about *formation permanente*. The spirit and the importance of such education is crucial for competitiveness, as is expressed by Yves Cannac, director of the influential CEGOS consulting firm (1985).

The bottom line is that French firms have indeed become more competitive; the new form of partnership with the state is fairly successful. However there remains a clear dilemma. The economy generates unemployment, so that the new ideology of giving more autonomy and more initiative to business is confronted with general social problems (such as renegotiating job-grading systems) in which the state cannot help being heavily involved. Such difficulties have appeared recurrently with nurse's working conditions in the public sector where controversial salary differentials have created strong resentment. Other groups of public sector employees also resist, at times vigorously, attempts to privatize institutions such as Renault and the RATP (the Parisian public transport system). Even the Banque de France, despite its hallowed institutional status, experienced industrial conflict when its independence was being implemented. As for the currently high unemployment level, radical cures have to be found, probably along the lines of extensive worktime reduction and more training.

Leaders of business HR opinion

Business opinion leaders belong to various groups such as consultants, journalists and directors of large firms, who have achieved visibility through their publications or their position. They contribute to the maintenance of social consensus through their discourse and their writings, particularly at a time when a new ideology leads business and the state – as we have seen – to be less active on the social front. A degree of tacit co-ordination is achieved among policy makers and opinion leaders through the remarkably strong French 'old boy' network to which top-level managers and civil servants belong (Hamdouch, 1989). The effectiveness of this co-ordination via networks of élites is furthermore enhanced by the considerable attention that orthodox statements on HR are accorded. Though criticisms do exist and are voiced, they are often less influential when coming from academics or trades unions. As a result, the tendency to bolster a policy with strong 'publicity', almost producing the effect of a self-fulfilling prophecy, goes almost unchallenged.

At the executive levels of large firms and of the administration, positions are held by the alumni of prestigious educational institutions, the *grandes écoles* – people who belong to an elite network (Bourdieu, 1989). This has the effect of making implementation and diffusion of new 'theories' swift and effective. The fairly regular rotation of the members of this elite between public and private positions reinforces still more the tendency to collaborate. Privatization of some major organizations – in banking, insurance and industry – has not changed things much. There is still a very substantial level of control through the network involving friendly shareholders of the *noyau dur* ('hard core', see Hamdouch, 1989) and through alumni networks. In their leadership-of-opinion role, managers publicly express the new orientations, thus providing additional credibility to state initiatives. The case of apprenticeship described above is one example of the dual role of executives as both early adopters of innovations and proselytizers of these schemes.

A few representative and influential examples of managerial discourse will give the flavour of this opinion leadership. To begin with we can take the case of a manager being requested officially by a member of the government, or by a political leader, to produce a report of 'public interest'. Antoine Riboud, CEO of Danone (once known as BSN) the large food conglomerate with a strong reputation for its constructive HR policies, was formally invited in 1987 to provide an analysis and a series of proposals to face up to the deep changes new technologies would bring about in working life and employment. The report was published as a book with an intriguingly ambiguous title – *Modernisation, mode d'emploi.* This can be translated both as 'modernization – instructions for use' and as 'modernization, a road to employment'. The book criticizes the arcane complexities of business information and public business services in France (paving the way for administrative reform), and popularizes the idea of strategic human resources planning. The possibility of saving jobs and creating new ones with the introduction of modern technologies is illustrated with many examples.

A second example illustrates the social democratic strain of the new ideology. Michel Albert, another CEO, this time of AGF the major insurance company, in his best-selling book *Capitalisme contre capitalisme* (1991) develops the idea that the social cost of Anglo-Saxon capitalism would be unbearable even for most liberal minded French. In his words, the lower performing system wins out paradoxically because of its consensual basis, because of its long-term perspectives, and because of its emphasis on collective rather than individual success. The comparison of American and French health care systems provides specific arguments in favour of this version of controlled liberalism, and legitimates the high level of taxes on employment.

A third example of opinion influence and consensus building comes from consulting, and is more directed toward business people and professionals. Cannac's book *La bataille de la compétence* was published in 1985. Its objective was to develop the idea of a firm as a place of learning as much as a place of working, with the aim of developing a high level of professionalism and hence a capacity to integrate change and to achieve renewed competitiveness. Apart from a very pragmatic approach to the problem, the book also contains the accounts and the views of a number of CEOs of prestigious firms. Typically, the principal author Yves Cannac is a former high-level civil servant who has also been at the helm of one of France's major advertising agencies.

In this context, a sociologist such as Michel Crozier occupies an unusual position. Known for his conception of sociology as a generalized (liberal) political economy, he recently authored, in collaboration with the research arm of the *patronat*, a pamphlet titled *L'entreprise à l'écoute* (1991) based on a variety of qualitative case illustrations, and purporting to emphasize the key importance of HR in post-industrial society. The exclusive focus on the firm in this fairly normative text is very reminiscent of the American school of Human Relations (an influence to which we will soon return) and is disconnected from most of Crozier's wider sociological analysis. The message is directed towards a more popular readership and advocates strictly liberal ideas resting on the management principles of professionalism, autonomy, simplicity and so on. A more elaborate version, with a more sophisticated argument, taking employees' interpretations of the social protection system into account, which does better justice to Crozier's work is his publication *Etat modeste, état moderne* (1987).

A critical perspective on these normative views of HR and on work organization is given by Jean-Pierre Le Goff (1992). He argues that whatever the efforts to make work meaningful and creative, as in the case of the 'Action Principles' of Lafarge Coppée, a firm at the forefront of social innovation, the organization itself, salary and social benefits will remain the central elements of motivation in business firms. Therefore, the efforts to render jobs meaningful beyond their actual contents is suspect. Le Goff sees here manifestations of a typically French paternalism. Examples of this include Olivier Lecerf (retired CEO of Lafarge Coppée) with a strong catholic ethic and Jacques de Fouchier founder of the Compagnie Bancaire (subsequently merged with Paribas) with a very paternalistic stance (Lecerf, 1989; de Fouchier, 1989). The exemplary role generally attributed to 'the manager and his investment in the collective good' in this discourse is reminiscent of Barnard's long-standing precepts for good management. The problem with this type of analysis is that the demand for ethical behaviour competes in an uncontrolled fashion with the requirements of accepted institutions, the representatives of employees, and other agreements reached through negotiation with trades unions.

To summarize this section we can say that the state, business firms and opinion leaders have together recently modified the characteristically French way of thinking about personnel and employment issues. The new orthodoxy, dominant since the 1980s, is (like many ideologies) ambiguous and often internally contradictory. As conceptions of the state's roles and responsibilities have changed so have those of the business firm, but if the latter has taken on a newer, more 'heroic' social role in France it is unclear whether the managerial community will, in the future, be ready to assume the social obligations that many still expect. (Nor is it clear, as we shall see below, that companies have developed internal HR policies that are in tune with the ideology itself.)

Ultimately the new view may well be frustrated by the strength of long-standing notions of rights and duties held by professional groups in French occupational culture. The point is made very well by d'Iribarne (1989) in his contrast of French and American ideas of duty at work: 'a French employee doesn't need to be assigned a responsibility to feel responsible. This term does not have in the first place for him the American meaning, but emphasizes what he considers to be important to monitor' (pp. 22–3).

In the next section we turn from the representation of HRM in the discourse of 'opinion leaders' to that which dominates the academic world.

HRM – The View from French Academia

As in most other countries the academic perspective on HRM in France is almost impossible to separate from views of management *per se*. Although specialists in the teaching and research of HRM now exist in the universities and the ESC (*écoles supérieures de commerce*), their existence is a recent phenomenon. More long-standing is a tradition of analysis of management and organizations with its roots in the social sciences, particularly psychology, sociology, economics and the like. These disciplines – and here we must confine the discussion to the first two – have traditionally considered management with a detached and critical view; much as one would expect in a country so marked by the evolution of Marxism and psychoanalysis.

Within sociology two traditions stand out, on the one hand that of the *sociologie du travail* associated with the name of Friedmann and strongly linked to the journal of that name, and on the other that of *l'analyse stratégique* developed by Michel Crozier and Erhard Friedberg. The former shares certain affinities with the concerns of British 'Labour process theory' (Thompson, 1989) in focusing on management as, above all, an activity of employee control and consensus manipulation. The latter on the other hand, since its birth in a critical appreciation of North American organizational research (in particular the work of Herbert Simon – Crozier and Friedberg, 1977) has maintained a more nuanced view of management activity – it is for empirical work to determine what is the content and fate of managerial policies because they will be inevitably influenced by the 'play' of interaction between the interests and strategies of different organizational actors, both individual and collective.

During the 1980s both traditions, alongside other currents in industrial relations (Reynaud, 1983) and organizational research (Sainsaulieu, 1987) had to come to terms with, and indeed contributed to, the ideological and social changes which have been sketched above. The strong wave of company interest in participative management, however complex its cause, brought with it forms of workplace experimentation (such as quality circles, employee expression groups, etc.) which, despite their 'faddish' nature, were eventually taken seriously, and sometimes championed by, academics. Their coincidence with union decline and a redrawing of some aspects of the industrial relations landscape subsequent to the Auroux legislation, the 'imperatives of flexibility' and national industrial policies on quality and competitiveness, all saw to this. The world of work and organizations was clearly in mutation: both schools set about charting some of the developments through empirical research.

HRM as such is rarely the main object of concern in this work. In focusing on organizational reactions to technological change, or to new forms of communication and interaction, for example, this research examines the 'playing out' of a broad set of management policies, bringing in HRM when necessary for interpretation. Training and job evaluation have thus, quite naturally, been a focus of work which has examined skill adjustments provoked in French firms by social and technical innovation. Moreover it is often the 'inertia' of French organizations and the rigidities of the traditional French 'model of management' which come under the microscope – over-centralized leadership, a strict separation between *cadre* (manager) and non-*cadre*, over-complex systems of job classification and grading and personnel administration as opposed to human resources planning and development (Linhart, 1991). Managerial innovation and analysis remains in the background while the conditioning role of societal and micro-organizational struggles comes to the fore. Rationalities and representations – their diversity, their continuity and their confrontation – are essential objects of analysis. Work by the LEST at Aix-Marseille (Maurice et al., 1986) by IRESCO (Borzeix, 1987), the CNAM (Linhart, 1991) and the CSO (Pavé, 1994) – these latter all Parisian – illustrates this clearly.

As for French psychology, we find a similar complexity, with the contrast between empirical work psychology (Jardillier, 1986) and psychoanalytically inspired work structuring the field. The former draws much of its inspiration from the well-known Anglo-Saxon 'Human Relations' work associated with Herzberg, Maslow and others, and questions of motivation, appraisal and development are naturally of central importance here (Lévy-Leboyer, 1990). This literature often aims, as it does in the UK, to clarify the psychological grounding of HR systems for personnel practitioners. French work psychology at the same time builds on a specifically gallic tradition in ergonomics. The latter has produced much original work on working conditions and the influence of information technologies (particularly software) on them (see Montmollin, 1986).

Psychoanalytically informed work on management has also recently appeared in France and has, interestingly, tried to confront the claims and ambitions of HRM directly. The resulting critiques (Collectif Dauphine, 1988; Aubert and de Gaulejac, 1990), although empirically rather limited, none the less hit at the heart of some of the most modern techniques used in HR, and at some of their central assumptions. Focusing on the HR practices of 'strong culture' companies the latter two authors, for example, combine a functionalist 'socialization' problematic with Freudian elements to show how the internalization of organizational values by young managers can involve a perverse and dangerous appeal to 'self-realization'. A battery of HR systems (appraisal and MBO being the most crucial) are used by these firms to encourage a high level of fit between the objectives of the firm and the personal ideals of young *cadres*. Yet in creating 'cultures of excellence' the effects for some individuals can be severe with high levels of stress, 'burnout' and even complete nervous breakdowns reported. Aubert and de Gaulejac (1990) force home the general point about a central danger in modern HR thinking – trying to make the realization of company objectives coincide with the realization of the self – which in European cultures invites a whole series of excesses in personnel management which in turn can entail cynical surveillance and manipulation. In this they share much with the work of Le Goff (1992) mentioned earlier. Such concerns have only relatively recently emerged in the view of HRM that dominates the naturally rather different perspectives of Management Science (*les sciences de gestion*) taught in the ESC and the University Business Schools, the IAE (*institut d'administration des entreprises*).

Naturally the management perspective is far more normative, concerned as it is with teaching skills and principles to potential future practitioners, and this shows in the extensive text book literature available (see Peretti, 1994; Martory, 1992; Bournois and Poirson, 1989; Graphe, 1994). The growth in publication of this material corresponds with the emergence of the national HR ideology we have described above, with the transitions in industrial relations set in motion by the Auroux laws (greater direct worker representation, etc.) and with the view that the personnel function in the firm should move away from its traditionally purely administrative role and support business goals – in particular 'flexibility' – more directly.

Throughout the early to mid-1980s there was a proliferation of education and training programmes built around this literature and offering the new, optimistic (and even 'heroic') image of personnel (now HR) managers as 'architects and strategists' on an equal footing with production and finance directors. For the most part this work presents HRM conventionally by considering the discrete constituent domains of personnel management from recruitment through to appraisal, training and so on. A further preoccupation here – apart from the obvious one of clearly presenting HR responsibilities and systems – is the vaunting of the 'strategic' role of HR in the firm, and in this the American work of the mid-1980s (Beer et al., 1985; Fombrun et al., 1984) is the clear and direct inspiration (see for example Besseyre des Horts, 1987). The resulting French approach places the emphasis on three types of company behaviour: (1) broad attempts to manage and change organizational culture (Thévenet, 1993); (2) implementation of specific projects for the *mobilisation* of employees (*projets d'entreprise*, see d'Almeida and Nutkowicz, 1993); and (3) development of more sophisticated HR *planning (la gestion prévisionnelle de l'emploi et des compétences – GPEC)* in order to match employees to the strategic needs of the organization (see Thierry, 1992).

Only relatively recently has French work in this stream shown the desire to examine *critically* the assumptions and concepts at the *roots* of the American (and Japanese) models of HRM. Through the forum of the *Association française pour la gestion des ressources humaines* (AGRH, an annual colloquium which began in 1989, using study workshops and publications) and also the increasing amount of empirical work linking the mainstream social sciences with management, this has now begun (Brabet, 1993), albeit timidly. Both epistemological questions and those concerning the sociocultural relativity of management models are now being posed, but the compartmentalization of research in France is still very strong. It is curious for example, as Didier Cazal has noted, that it took an Anglo-Saxon publication (*The Academy of Management Review*) to provoke French interest in the relevance of the work of Michel Foucault to the evolution of management practices! There is no doubt that this lack of cross-fertilization of research is due to the complex and rigid structure of French higher education and also to the relative absence of a strong institutional presence of industrial relations as a fully accepted academic field. Progress is being made, and it is understandable that it is somewhat slow, but the contrast with the dynamic world of 'popular' management debate and discourse that we sketched above, with its business opinion leaders, 'intellectualization' and fashions is striking and somewhat paradoxical.

HR Problems and Their Treatment in Contemporary French Firms

The complex re-evaluation of the firm during the France of the 1980s sketched above reveals an ideological dynamic, a movement of re-appraisal of management and organizations, that testifies to an intellectual energy in French society of some force. Its discursive expression has been very diverse as we have seen – from new legislative programmes to the explosion of publications by consultants, '*patronal*' pressure groups, 'think tanks' and management theorists. Concrete organizational experimentation has interacted with this trend in a dialectical manner – as stimulus but also as effect. But apart from the claims and clamour associated with managerial fashions and the ideological evolution we have sketched above, what of the evidence of this experimentation and innovation in the human resources domain? What does empirical research tell us? To what extent has the recent period constituted one of real rupture with traditional French managerial practices? Has personnel administration become subordinated to a more ambitious, comprehensive and 'strategic' HRM?

It is to these issues that we turn next in this section. Given the enormity of the question and the limited space available, we choose to focus on changes in the organizational status of HR and in companies' investment in human resources planning – both, we would argue, central to the issue of the strategic role of HRM.

Human resources – a 'strategic' position in the hierarchy?

To begin with it is important to determine whether the change in terminology which has taken place in France – from personnel management to HRM – has coincided with a real change in the organizational rôle of personnel/HR specialists and with their inclusion in the process by which company strategies and business policies are formulated.

The evidence here is clear on at least some levels. First the domain grew in numerical significance throughout the 1980s as its identity became modified. Rioux (1989) cites an APEC study showing clearly the doubling in the percentage of personnel posts (in proportion to other management posts) advertised in the press between 1984 (1.5 per cent) and 1988 (3.0 per cent). Secondly, the results of the Price-Waterhouse/Cranfield study, which obtained data on the HR practices of 1400 French companies (all with more than 200 employees, it should be noted), show that a very large number of HR directors play a rôle in the *comité de direction* – 84 per cent – and are also involved in the formulation of company strategy at an early stage – 65 per cent – (Bournois and Versaevel, 1993). Furthermore 91 per cent of companies in the study consider that they have an 'HR strategy' although in 52 per cent of these cases it was regarded as unwritten and non-formalized (ibid.). These findings are supported by another study which reported (from a sample of 190 firms) that 81 per cent of HR directors were members of the *comité de direction* (Gautier and Salzman, 1992).

Human resources planning and performance management

Over and above the issue of titles and hierarchical positions is the incidence and sophistication of co-ordinated human resources planning. This is often seen as an index of the degree to which personnel issues have actually become strategic in a firm – in other words, to what extent its 'critical success factors' have become linked with a coherent, integrated, and planned set of HR policies aimed at specific performance objectives.

Human resources planning (HRP) in France can be analysed, as elsewhere, in terms of the extent to which it is used by a number of exemplar firms in the automobile, electronics and financial services sectors who have recently restructured their operations. These sectors are at the leading edge of HR sophistication and in France Renault is probably the most well-known and best-documented example. The company's progressive economic recovery through total quality control and product innovation (Midler, 1989, 1994) was matched by sensitive and imaginative HR management with an unfavourable workforce age pyramid and skill level (Praderie, 1990).

However, it is also interesting to examine the use of HRP by a broad range of companies in terms of financial assistance from the state. Between 1988 and 1989 the French government set up – exemplifying the interventionist role described above – the LIGE

(*Ligne d'innovation pour la gestion de l'emploi*) programme in order to encourage better anticipation of skills changes and employment needs in small companies. Analysis of how this money was used is revealing.

Detailed studies by Uan (1992) and Gadille (1992) considered those developments which occurred in a total of seventy-five firms participating in the scheme. Uan examined the motives which lay behind fifty-two companies seeking help, the methods they used and their various impacts within these organizations. In 90 per cent of these companies she found a primarily 'defensive' approach to HRP. In other words, it was a new way of tackling already existing problems, whether these be related to product quality or workforce skills. Therefore she found evidence of a proactive and truly anticipatory HRP approach in only 10 per cent of these companies. The most popular method of adaptation was the programming and provision of training – in only 20 per cent of the sample was a more radical reappraisal of the work system undertaken as part of the HRP process of interrelating jobs and employees. In summary, this study found little evidence of workforce involvement in the planning process.

Gadille (1992) dealt also with this question of participation. She differentiated between the companies in her study according to their position on two axes. The first sought to determine their degree of anticipation of adaptation needs in a specific 'niche'. The second sought to identify their ability and willingness to engage employees in HRP. Four groups emerge in relation to these axes, each using the LIGE according to a specific logic. Therefore, each groups saw HRP in a different way.

1. The first group of firms, with the 'lowest score' on each of the two axes, has an HRP logic of 'mobilization'. These firms were largely Taylorist in management style and segmentalist in structure (Kanter, 1989; Linhart, 1991). Their dominant concern is reaching certain productivity and quality targets and for this the LIGE is used to develop training plans considered by top management to be the solution to problems of motivation. The traditional organization structure and personnel practices are not questioned in any radical way although 'parallel structures' (quality circles for example) are envisaged. Tensions between such organizational innovations and their context were evident (and were somewhat inevitable) during this 'first step' towards a more comprehensive HRP approach. (Such

problems have been amply traced and documented in French firms by Chevalier (1991).

2. In the second group Gadille identifies two subgroups. In the first one (Group 2) the companies were struggling to articulate a strategy which linked restructuring to HRP while in the second subgroup (Group 3) the dominant concern was to analyse and co-ordinate the evolution of jobs and skills. The former subgroup (all SMEs of less that 300 employees) was comprised of dynamic and expanding firms with the consequence that HRP was used to tackle the reorganization of their work system resulting from their industrial strategies (new technologies, redistribution of jobs and creation of new ones, etc.). These firms used consultants – (a) to assist with the process of developing job definitions and employee specifications for new managerial rôles – particularly cross-functional and quality orientated ones; and, (b) to reformulate the very rigid grading schemes (*les classifications*) typical in many French firms governed by sector-level agreements (*conventions collectives*) between employer's associations and employee representatives.

3. In the second subgroup (Group 3), reorganization was not the central HRP issue. Rather these firms were attempting to achieve the effective redeployment of staff in order to avoid redundancies by anticipating future changes in the nature of skills and jobs. These larger and more complex firms had less decision making autonomy than the first subgoup since they were often divisions of larger entities. Consequently, HR techniques were sometimes 'parachuted' in from the divisional HR departments. Skill profiling and the assessment of employee potential were frequently used but their organizational meaning was not always well communicated.

4. The fourth and final group of companies married HRP with a logic of constant innovation and learning. HRP tools were used as part of a quest for better and better adaptation of both the individual and the organization as a whole (i.e. they were innovators). This was often expressed concretely in the form of a *projet d'entreprise* (or mission statement) which typically formulated a new vision of the firm and included the organizational objectives. Additionally in a number of cases – and this is a very important innovation for all groups involved – the works' council (the *comité d'entreprise*) received training in HRP so that they could analyse and negotiate the changes to

come on a more equal footing with those managers seeking to implement changes. In other instances an *observatoire des emplois* was created. This was composed of actors at all levels of the hierarchy and was used to brainstorm and anticipate future needs. As a result HRP, and HRM in general, had high legitimacy in the eyes of actors at all levels of the hierarchy in these firms.

Burdillat (1993) examines five organizations in order to reconstruct the thinking behind HRP practices in such large firms. She also, like Merlin (1993), uses the 'accords' signed by them to highlight the 'public' framework of strategy. In addition to her five examples the following organizations have all been seeking to forge new and stronger links between their business policies and HRM: Bull, Thomson CSF, Usinor-Sacilor, EDF-GDF (*Electricité* and *Gaz de France*), the ANPE (*l'Agence nationale pour l'emploi*), Renault (the *accord à vivre*, see Praderie, 1990) and the GAN insurance group. In order to achieve this, innovation has been necessary in a number of different managerial processes. While increased use at head office of better information systems has made possible a balancing of employee numbers across different subdivisions in the medium term, more sophisticated 'strategic job analysis' at the local level has provided a clearer view of the potential horizontal mobility and skill transfers within job types or families. This latter move away from a focus on 'one person – one job' to job families and clusters appears to be common to all of these companies. In demanding mobility and flexibility in skill use – crucial for business strategy – they have had to attain a new sophistication in establishing career paths at all hierarchical levels. As a consequence, both management and employees have had to focus on issues of potential 'employability' and development. At the same time, and (quite logically), more sophisticated processes of appraisal and assessment have become more widespread at the managerial level in order to provide data necessary to achieve and support these changes.

These firms have therefore been struggling towards the proactive and adaptive approach characterized by Gadille's fourth group of companies (the innovators). Through tough negotiations these companies have obtained union agreement to (and in some cases involvement in) HRP and have thereby institutionalized relatively new processes such as the systematic use of 'job observatories'. As Merlin (1993) points out, this in itself marks the emergence of a new form of negotiation in French industrial relations, albeit one shot through with ambiguities. For instance, neither side seems sure of the precise contribution that unions and worker representatives can make to HRM (what skills, what weight to attribute to counter proposals?) and thus the very terms of these agreements often remain unclear.

For a similar detailed view of small to medium-sized enterprises (SMEs) Bertrand et al.'s (1993) study, while not representative, provides essential information, particularly with regard to the elements of HRP. In their sample of twenty-five organizations both the techniques used and the quality of involvement of employees were much more modest than in the examples just considered (that is, the innovators). The five dominant practices used by these twenty-five organizations to clarify and take stock of present and medium-term skill needs were as follows: (1) job analysis focusing on *métiers* and on clusters of skills and crafts (96 per cent); (2) development of better training plans (64 per cent); (3) development of better performance appraisal (54 per cent); (4) adaptation of grading systems (40 per cent); and (5) analysis of employee skills and potential (34 per cent).

The dominance of job analysis and training reveals the worry in these firms of the poor 'fit' between job demands and employees' skills. We should note that HRP here rarely starts from the reverse process, the inventory of employees' skills and potential and then the deduction of how work-system design might evolve strategically. Furthermore, the participation of non-managerial employees in the definition and use of techniques was relatively limited. This provoked, particularly among senior employees, the fear that restructuring would ultimately result in redundancies. Line managers and foremen, for their part, participated (essential for any significant result) but not without a certain degree of scepticism and mistrust. These findings would suggest that these SMEs are somewhere between Gadille's (1992) 'mobilizers' and his 'innovators' (Group 4).

If we turn specifically to consider performance management in France and examine the wider evidence of its use we find that this is inconclusive. On the one hand the statistics of the Ministère du Travail (Hassoun, 1990) show clearly that towards the late 1980s an increasing number of companies were paying non-managerial employees according to their individual performance or merit. In 1987 the proportion was 43 per cent of firms surveyed. By 1989 it the proportion had grown to 49 per cent. Linhart (1993) argues convincingly that this is no mere managerial fashion and that the 1991 recession (which continued, and to a depth misunderstood by many in the country, through 1994) only served to accelerate the use of a practice hitherto confined mainly to engineers and *cadres*. On the other hand when we look for evidence of practices of performance appraisal, which are of course essential to the process of rewarding individual merit, the picture becomes very unclear. Naturally a detailed picture of the proportion and types of firms embedding this practice in the reformulation of the jobs of both the first line supervisor and middle manager would be ideal, but it is precisely this which is lacking.

Managerial work is, as would be expected, more clearly subject to performance appraisal (PA). Dany et al. (1991) in their poll of 1,081 managers (a representative sample) show that 63 per cent consider PA to be well established in their companies although 40 per cent consider its use to be 'unsystematic' and 37 per cent view career management as being too low an HRM priority. The picture that emerges from this study is that while performance management tools and indicators have increased in their sophistication there has been little change in managerial behaviour nor have they been fully integrated into career development strategies.

This image of 'hesitant innovation' is also shown in the domain of vocational training. This is an area in which firms have been particularly active as a result of legislation on minimum investment in training. Overall spending, expressed as a proportion of the total wage bill, has not stopped climbing since a legal minimum was first introduced over twenty years ago. Even during the recent recession the proportion rose from 3.2 per cent in 1991 to 3.3 per cent in 1992 (Bentabet, 1994). Behind the spending statistics there is of course a complex stratification with regard to who spends the most, how and for what purposes. An unskilled worker in a large French company still has more possibilities for training than an engineer or manager in a small one. Indeed, firms with over 2,000 employees spend over three times as much on training as those with fewer than 50. Sectoral and regional disparities are also considerable (Jenkins, 1993).

Yet alongside this French training effort a considerable number of companies have continued to complain of skill deficiencies and to perceive their employees as lacking in technical knowledge and human relations expertise in particular (Serfaty, 1992). (French companies still look longingly across the border at the German example of skill development.) In Serfaty's study two-thirds of the sample of 638 firms expressed this concern. These problems appear most acute in industry (where on average 79 per cent of the workforce were considered to lack the necessary skills) and in the construction/building sector in particular (65 per cent).

Dealing with this skills gap has often, as we have seen above, led companies to sharpen their HRM polices or to innovate in training. This has to be viewed as a positive sign. Yet all too often, as has been vividly shown in the recent very sharp recession, as soon as the economic conditions worsen companies adjust by making employees redundant through poorly conceived and implemented 'downsizing' programmes. Serfaty (1992) shows this clearly. In his study one-third of those firms reporting skills deficiencies were also considering implementing a redundancy plan. This figure rose to two-thirds for firms with over 2,000 employees. Small wonder that some commentators have been tempted to see in the recent waves of lay-offs evidence of a real lack of a profound penetration of strategic HR policies in French management practice. As much was suggested in 1994 in criticisms of the *patronat* made by the then Prime Minister Edouard Balladur. He was responding to the continuing vertiginous climb in unemployment statistics produced by this behaviour.

Conclusion

The last remark brings us back to the central theme that has structured this chapter – the institutional conditioning of the 'hesitant innovation' within which HRM has emerged in France. HRM takes on a complex form in France because of the continuing role of the state and other collective actors in determining the legal and institutional frameworks within which it has emerged. As state-led liberalism has gradually gained ground and the oppositional role of the unions declined, innovation in HRM – often clearly inspired by American, German and Japanese examples – has taken place in a number of sectors and in a whole range of firms.

Nevertheless, the evidence from empirical studies, as we have seen, reveals the halting and hesitant nature of this innovation. It appears that it may be confined to a small and select group of large employers. It has therefore not yet had a major impact on the employment procedures of the majority of French firms. Despite enormous advances in some of the large industrial groups, the formidable and admirable French capacity to theorize and debate innovation has not always been followed by deeds and by the investments in time, finance and reorganization necessary to create new managerial norms and paradigms. It seems almost as if faith in the basis and future of a more 'strategic' practice of HRM is lacking in the fibre of French management; an intellectual and emotional doubt befitting Descartes undermines its very principles whenever the economic pressures reach a certain level. The recent history of HRM in the country appears to support this assertion.

However, this idea should perhaps not be taken too far. The ambiguity of HRM principles themselves and the relative organizational precariousness of the personnel/HR function – recognized by many commentators as an international phenomenon – perhaps makes 'hesitant innovation' and pragmatism an increasingly likely response to a widening range of uncertainties in the contemporary management of employee relations in France. HR transition is indeed under way in France, but its final destination is still far from clear.

Notes

1 The Auroux legislation transformed a third of existing labour law. Three objectives were central to this legislative programme: (1) stimulate more regular and systematic collective bargaining; (2) extend worker representation in the firm (in works councils, *comités d'entreprise*), and open new channels for worker influence and direct expression; (3) accord new rights of worker representation on boards in the public sector.

2 An empirical indicator of this is the rise in the number of individuals being granted higher state aid to tackle redundancy and outplacement problems. The 1993 total was 58 per cent higher than that of 1992 (Tesnière et al., 1994).

References

Albert, M. (1991), *Capitalisme contre capitalisme*. Paris: Seuil.
Aubert, N. and de Gaulejac, V. (1991), *Le coût de l'excellence*. Paris: Seuil.

Beer, M., Spector, B. Lawrence, P. R., Quinn Mills, D. and Walton R. E. (1985), *Managing Human Assets: A General Manager's Perspective*. New York: Free Press.

Bentabet, E. (1994), 'La formation continue des salariés dans les régions', *Cereq Bref,* **94**, January, pp. 1–8.

Bertrand, H., Lamoureux, J.-L. and Vermel, N. (1993), 'La gestion prévision-nelle des emplois et des compétences dans les PME', *Travail et Emploi,* **57**, pp. 67–78.

Besseyre des Horts, C.-H. (1987), *Vers une gestion stratégique des ressources humaines*. Paris: Editions d'organisation.

Bourdieu, P. (1989), *La noblesse d'état*. Paris: Editions de minuit.

Bournois, F. and Poirson, P. (1989), *Gérer et dynamiser ses collaborateurs*. Paris: Eyrolles.

Bournois, F. and Versaevel, B. (1993), 'Gestion stratégique des ressources huamines. Une approche contingente à travers une typologie des grandes entreprises françaises', *Gestion 2000,* **3**.

Borzeix, A. (1987), 'Ce que parler peut faire', *Sociologie du Travail,* **2**, pp. 65–83.

Brabet, J. (ed.), (1993), *Repenser la gestion des ressources humaines?* Paris: Economica.

Burdillat, M. (1993), 'La gestion prévisionelle de l'emploi. Les conceptions des directions', *Travail et Emploi,* **57**, pp. 21–31.

Cannac, Y. (1985), *La bataille de la compétence*. Paris: Editions Hommes et Techniques.

Cazal, D. and Peretti, J. M. (1992), *L'Europe des ressources humaines*. Paris: Liaisons.

Chevalier, F. (1991), *Cercles de qualité et changement organisationnel*. Paris: Economica.

Collectif Dauphine (1988), *Organisation et management en question(s)*. Paris: Harmattan.

Crozier, M. (1987), *L'entreprise à l'écoute*. Paris: Interéditons.

Crozier, M. (1991), *Etat modeste, état moderne*. Paris: Fayard.

Crozier, M. and Friedberg, E. (1977), *L'acteur et le système*. Paris: Seuil.

d'Almeida, L. and Nutkowicz, T. (1993), *Les projets d'entreprise dans la tourmente*. Paris: Liaisons.

de Fouchier, P. J, (1989), *La banque et la vie*. Paris: Editions Odile Jacob.

d'Iribarne, P. (1989), *La logique de l'honneur*, Paris, Seuil.

Dany, F., Livian, Y.-F. and Sarnin, P. (1991), 'La gestion des carrières des cadres en France, vue par les cadres'. In *Pour une vision de la GRH*, Actes du 2ème Congrès de l'AGRH, Cergy-Pontoise, France.

Delmas, P. (1992), *Le maître des horloges*. Paris: Editions Odile Jacob Economie.

Dure, J. and Chevalier, J. M. (1994), *Les mécanismes du licenciement*. Paris: Mémoire Ecole des Mines.

Fombrun, C. J., Tichy, N. M. and Devanna, M. (1982), *Strategic Human Resources Management*. New York: Wiley.

Gadille, M. (1992), 'L'apprentissage par l'entreprise de la gestion prévision-nelle de l'emploi', *Travail et Emploi,* **51**, pp. 70–85.

Gallie, D. (1985), 'Les lois Auroux; the reform of French industrial rela-tions?'. In H. Machin and V. Wright (eds), *Economic Policy under the Mitter-rand Presidency, 1981–84.* London: Frances Pinter.

Gautier, M. and Salzman, C. (1992), 'Enquête CEGOS sur la fonction ressources humaines', *Personnel,* 332, pp. 54–7 and 333, pp. 80–4.

GRAPHE (1994), *L'année ressources humaines.* Paris: Editions Maxima.

Hamdouch, A. (1989), *L'etat d'influence.* Paris: Presses du CNRS.

Hassoun, M. (1990), 'Salaire au mérite. Les ouvriers aussi', *L'Usine Nou-velle,* **2286**, 11 October.

Jenkins, A. (1993), 'France: training innovation, social strategies and organ-izational change'. In J. B. Shaw and P. Kirkbride (eds), *Research in Person-nel and Human Resources Management, Supplement 3.* Connecticut: JAI Press.

Kanter, R. M. (1989), *The Change Masters.* New York: Irwin.

Lecerf, O. (1989), *Au risque de gagner. Le métier du dirigeant.* Paris: Edi-tions de Fallois.

Le Goff, J. P. (1992), *Le mythe de l'entreprise.* Paris: Editions La Décou-verte.

Lévy-Leboyer, C. (1990), *La crise des motivations.* Paris: Editions d'Orga-nisation.

Linhart, D. (1991), *Le torticolis de l'autruche.* Paris: Seuil.

Linhart, D, Rozenblatt, P. and Voegele, S. (1993), 'Vers une nouvelle rému-nération scientifique du travail', *Travail et Emploi,* **57**, pp. 30–47.

Martory, B. (1992), *Les tableaux de bord sociaux.* Paris: Nathan.

Maurice, M. (1993), 'Les nouveaux systèmes productifs. Entre "taylorisme" et "toyotisme" ', *Sociologie du Travail,* **1**, pp. 1–19.

Maurice, M., Sellier, F. and Sylvestre, J. M. (1986), *The Social Foundations of Industrial Power.* Cambridge, Mass.: MIT Press.

Merlin, L. (1993), 'Les accords de GPE. Une coopération ambivalente', *Tra-vail et Emploi,* **57**, pp. 41–9.

Midler, C. (1989), 'De l'automatisation à la modernisation: les transforma-tions dans l'industrie automobile', *Gérer et Comprendre*, March, pp. 4–16.

Midler, C. (1994), *L'auto qui n'existait pas.* Paris: Interéditions.

Montmollin, M. (1986), *L'ergonomie.* Paris: La Découverte.

Morville, P. (1985), *Les nouvelles politiques sociales du patronat.* Paris: La Découverte.

Moscovici, P. and Hollande, F. (1991), *L'heure des choix.* Paris: Editions Odile Jacob Economie.

Pavé, F. (1994), *L'analyse stratégique.* Paris: Seuil.

Peretti, J.-M. (1994), *Ressources humaines* (4th edn). Paris: Vuibert.

Praderie, M (1990), ' "L'accord à vivre" à Renault. Un exemple, pas un modèle', *Droit Social*, June.

Raynaud, J.-D. (1983), *Sociologie des conflits du travail.* Paris: PUF.

Riboud, A. (1987), *Modernisation, mode d'emploi.* Paris: Seuil.

Rioux, O. (1989), 'L'ascension des DRH', *Liaisons Sociales Mensuel,* **36**, February.

Rojot, J. (1992), 'Flexibilité de la main d'oeuvre dans les entreprises, expériences nationales'. In M. Durand (ed.), *Politiques economiques et sociales en Europe,* Paris: Harmattan.

Sainsaulieu, R. (1987), *Sociologie de l'organisation et de l'entreprise.* Paris: Dalloz.

Serfaty, E. (1992), 'Les entreprises face aux manques de compétences de leur main-d'oeuvre', *Cereq Bref,* **76**, May, pp. 1–8.

Tesnière, M. O., Durand, P. and Tixier, P. (1994), 'Les mesures d'accompagnement des restructurations en 1993', *Premières Synthèses,* **62** (3), August.

Thévenet, M. and Vachette, J.-L. (1993), *Culture et comportement.* Paris: Vuibert.

Thierry, D. and Sauret, C. (1993) *La gestion prévisionnelle et préventive des emplois et des compétences.* Paris: Harmattan.

Thompson, P. (1989), *The Nature of Work.* London: Macmillan.

Uan, F. (1992), 'La GPE dans tous ses états', *Lettre de l'ANACT,* **175**, June.

Villette, M. (1988), *L'homme qui croyait au management.* Paris: Seuil.

4 Spain in the Context of European Human Resource Management

JOSEP BARUEL

Introduction

To date there has been little academic discussion in Spain as to the nature and incidence of human resource management (HRM). Although the limited number of previous attempts to describe HRM in Spain have given some idea of what it constitutes (see Filella and Soler-Vicente, 1992; Flórez-Saborido et al., 1992) none of them has made a clear distinction between personnel management and HRM. In general these studies do not attempt to define the term HRM with any precision, although they still use it. This perhaps indicates the need to give 'personnel management' a more modern ring. It may also reflect what many companies have done: replace the term personnel management with that of HRM without doing much to change the content. This chapter attempts to shed a little more light on the difference between personnel management and HRM in Spanish companies.

In order to achieve this the chapter is organized as follows. It begins by defining the central features of HRM. We then examine whether large Spanish companies are in the process of, or have already adopted, an HRM approach to employee relations. We then look at the key activities of the HR function in relation to recruitment and selection, employee education, training and development and redundancy. In the final sections of the chapter the impact of the Single European market on Spanish companies is examined and the contribution of HRM is considered.

Three Characteristics of HRM

If we are to examine whether there has been a shift in the employee-relations practices of Spanish companies towards something which may be termed HRM we first have to define the term. At present there is no clear definition of Spanish HRM. It may however be possible to identify the nature of HRM by examining the policies and techniques actually being put into practice by organizations throughout Europe, including Spain. This task is facilitated by the European survey sponsored by the European Association for Personnel Management (EAPM) and carried out by the Institute of Management Development in Lausanne (IMD, 1992).

The survey findings indicate that central to the shift from personnel management to HRM in Europe is the devolvement of responsibility for HRM issues and policies such as recruitment and selection, training and development, to line management. As an organization moves towards an HRM approach to employee relations the HR manager becomes an adviser to line management, assisting with the development of HR policies which seek to harness and direct the abilities and skills of employees in such a way that they make a significant contribution to the organization's goals, objectives and competitive position. In addition, the HR manager becomes a line manager and occupies one of the highest positions on the senior management team.

This concept of HRM requires that at least the following three conditions be met:

1. HRM should be represented on the senior management board of the company. Companies moving away from traditional personnel management and towards HRM assign their HR managers a high rank in the corporate hierarchy that is commensurate with the importance of HR issues to corporate decision- and policy-making. In these companies one of the members of the board of directors, or its equivalent, will have responsibility for HR issues.

2. In addition to being members of the board, HR managers should have line authority and responsibility for making decisions on business issues, in particular in relation to the company's human resources. This means that HR managers should occupy very high positions, preferably close to that of CEO, within the organization.
3. The HR function and HR managers should participate in the strategic planning and decision-making processes of the company.

HRM in Large Spanish Companies

We now turn to consider the extent to which these three central features of an HRM approach to employee relations, as identified by the IMD (1992) study, are present in Spanish companies. The following discussion draws on data collected by the International Organization Observatory (termed hereafter IOOE) (see Baruel, 1992; Baruel and Rucabado, 1992). This was a survey of 105 of the largest 1,000 companies in Spain. Before proceeding it should be noted that this data was *not* collected with these specific issues in mind, but nevertheless represents the best attempt yet to examine the incidence of HRM among Spanish companies.

Representation on the board of directors

As mentioned earlier in the chapter the first characteristic of an HRM approach to employee relations is the appointment of an individual with special responsibility for HRM issues to the main policy-making body of the company. This means that one of the members of the board of directors should carry the title 'Director of Human Resource Management'. Some evidence for this is provided by the Price Waterhouse/Cranfield (1992) survey of personnel directors (PWC). This survey asked if the head of the human resource function had a place on the main policy-making forum of the company. To date the survey has been conducted three times in Spain – 1990, 1991 and 1992. On each occasion over seven out of ten of the organizations surveyed reported that the head of human resources was represented on the main board of directors. Out of the seventeen countries surveyed by the PWC team, Spain ranks third on this measure, with Sweden scoring highest and France scoring second highest. These results are confirmed by a study conducted by Rodriguez-Porras et al. (1990) which reported that in 75 per cent of the companies they surveyed the HR function was represented on the board of directors or its equivalent.

However, these two surveys give a very broad picture of HRM representation on the boards of directors of Spanish companies. They may therefore tend to exaggerate the extent to which HRM is represented on the board of directors since this may take any one of the following forms:

1. There is a director of HRM on the board of directors who is responsible solely for HR matters and reports directly to the CEO.
2. HRM is the responsibility of a member of the board of directors but in addition to HRM this person is also responsible for public relations, general services, legal matters, information systems, administration, etc.
3. A member of the board of directors has responsibility for reporting on HRM matters but the head of HRM reports directly to them and not to the CEO.

In each of these cases HRM can be considered to be represented on the board of directors. The IOOE study found that only 21 per cent of the sample of firms had a first-level director (who usually was a member of the board of directors) who was solely responsible for HRM matters (the first case above). In addition, 23 per cent of companies had a first line manager (usually on the board) with a broad set of responsibilities of which HRM was one (the second case above). Furthermore, in 31 per cent of the sample of companies the head of the HRM function reported to a first line manager – usually a member of the board of directors (in other words, HRM was a second-level position – see (3) above). Finally, 25 per cent of the companies in the sample did not have anybody responsible for HRM at either the first or second levels of the corporate hierarchy.

These figures show that in 75 per cent of the sample of 100E companies a member of the board of directors had responsibility for HRM. However, in view of this analysis it cannot be concluded that HRM is of such importance in Spain that 75 per cent of the companies appoint a director of HRM to their board of directors as the PWC and Rodriguez-Porras studies imply. More frequently HRM is one part of a general portfolio where the incumbent has responsibility for a range of organizational activities. In these instances the Director of Legal Affairs, Director of General Services or some other director is also the 'Director of HRM'. Thus, while there is still somebody on the board of directors with responsibility for HRM it is not viewed as important, or strategic, enough to warrant a separate appointment. According to the company titles these individuals hold they are first and foremost the Director of Legal Affairs or Director of Administration in addition to being also the Director of HRM. In this sense HRM is a 'second order' activity within these organizations. In those organizations where the head of HRM reports to a first line manager, who may or may not be a member of the board of directors, it is considered even less important and less strategic.

The above discussion indicates that some companies have full HR departments run by HR directors who sit on the board of directors. In other companies, personnel-related activities are dealt with by different positions at different levels of the corporate hierarchy and are often included in departments other than personnel. In some companies, these personnel jobs may not even be grouped together in a single department but are spread out among a number of different departments with each one doing all or part of the personnel work necessary for that particular department. The IOOE data reveals that the position of the HR function and the way in which it is organized, is related to the size of the company. Tables 4.1 and 4.2 show that whether one takes turnover or number of employees as a measure of a company's size, the larger the company the more likely it is to have a Director of HRM on the board of directors. Conversely, the smaller the company the more likely the head of HRM is to be a second- or third-level position or somebody answering to a department other than that of HR management.

In summary, it cannot be assumed that HRM representation on the board of directors equates with the appointment of a Director of HRM. Thus, while the PWC study indicates that Spain is one of the more advanced countries in Europe on this measure of HRM, the more detailed analysis provided by the IOOE data indicates that HRM would appear to be in its nascence within large Spanish companies.

Table 4.1 The location of HRM in different-sized organizations by turnover

Turnover (millions of pesetas)	HR department run by an HR director who is on the board of directors (%)	HR department run by an individual who reports to a member of the board of directors (%)	HR department run by an individual who reports to a second-level director (%)
1000,000–499,999	90	10	0
10,00–99,999	41	24	35
1,000–9,999	28	33	39

Source: IOOE

High-status line management

As mentioned above, HRM must have: line authority to make business and personnel decisions that can affect first line managers; and therefore a position that is close to that of the CEO, perhaps with even higher status than other first line managers. As a result, companies developing HRM will tend to: (1) promote the people in charge of HR management to important line management positions and not just use them as advisers; and (2) include personnel management specialists among their highest-ranking managers.

Table 4.2 The location of HRM in different-sized organizations by number of employees

Number of employees	HR department run by an HR director who is on the board of directors (%)	HR department run by an individual who reports to a member of the board of directors (%)	HR department run by an individual who reports to a second-level director (%)
5,000 and over	83	17	0
3,000–4,999	71	0	29
1,000–2,999	59	29	12
less than 1,000	29	32	39

Source: IOOE

In terms of the first point the IOOE study indicates that only 7 per cent of the senior managers in the sample of companies came from the personnel area. When selecting executives with line authority Spanish companies have tended to promote managers from technical and marketing areas rather than from personnel. The data indicate that 34 per cent of the senior management positions were occupied by people with technical backgrounds and 29 per cent with marketing backgrounds. It would appear that few HR managers are promoted to senior management positions outside the HR department.

The second point highlighted above (personnel managers with a status close to that of the CEO) may be analysed by using the IOOE data relating to the speciality of the managers ranked in the four positions immediately below the CEO. Only 6 per cent of them came from the personnel area.

To summarize, few Spanish companies have promoted HR managers to senior management positions and even fewer have given HR managers a higher status than the company's other senior managers in technical and marketing areas, for example.

Participation in corporate decisions

According to the IMD study (1992), if organizations are moving towards an HRM approach to employee management then the HR function and senior HR managers should participate in the development of the corporate strategy and major organizational or strategic decisions (such as when considering whether to enter a new market and produce a new product and so on). To determine the role of the HR function in the wider decision-making process of the company the IOOE study analysed 429 decisions made in the areas of personnel, production and marketing. The analysis of this data reveals that the members of the HR function rarely have an input into production, and marketing decisions. This is the case even where HR issues are particularly relevant, such as entry into a new foreign market. HR managers were consulted on these issues in only 2 per cent of the instances.

The IOOE study further reveals that the HR function has greater input into decisions falling within its natural ambit of control. Consider the decision to recruit a new employee. Where the person to be recruited was a senior manager in 35 per cent of the decisions analysed the HR function was not consulted. In these instances the decision to recruit an employee was taken by the CEO, another senior manager or by the parent organization. In the 65 per cent of cases where the personnel function was involved its role varied from sharing mid-level decisions (3 per cent of the cases) or final decisions (6 per cent) with line managers, to total responsibility in mid-level decisions. The HR department is never alone in making the final decision. In contrast, where the decision concerned the recruitment of a middle manager the HR department was involved in 80 per cent of cases.

In summary, the evidence from the IOOE study indicates that the HR function has little input to decisions outside its locus of control. Furthermore, even in those areas which fall within its boundary of expertise there is considerable interference and delegation to other parts of the organization.

Conclusions

Having considered the three criteria established as indicative of a HRM approach to employee management, it is possible to state that Spanish companies do not appear to have moved substantially towards such an approach to employee relations. A little over one-fifth of the companies in the IOOE study appointed a specialist, stand-alone, HR director. More commonly the responsibility for HR issues was diluted since it was often included in a 'catch-all' category on the board of directors, or was a second-or third-level position within the organization. As a consequence, HR, in the majority of companies, was unable to demonstrate a strategic impact. Moreover, few HR managers have been promoted to any high position.

Why is it that Spanish companies have not made a clearer move towards HRM? It appears that one of the main reasons is that many executives perceive personnel management as a low-status function – essentially an administrative activity. Personnel managers will only be able to overcome this if they are able to convince the dominant coalition (senior management team) that their task makes an identifiable contribution to organizational or strategic objectives. Until they do, personnel/HR managers will continue to have few opportunities to occupy influential positions from which they can seek to change these views. The HR function is therefore stuck in a vicious circle. It has a low status and so is unable to demonstrate its relevance to organizational goals; until HR managers are able to demonstrate a clear linkage between their activities and organizational outcomes HR will continue to be viewed as a low-status function. Until this circle is broken, HRM will continue to have a hesitant start in Spain.

HRM as a Corporate Necessity

So far in this chapter we have considered whether Spanish companies have moved from a personnel management to a HRM approach to employee management. We must now answer a question which the IMD study suggests but leaves open to discussion: do companies really have to shift to HRM? Is this change truly necessary or is it only a reflection of personnel managers' desires to make themselves more important? We will attempt to clarify this question by illustrating it with the example of the current situation in Spanish companies.

Given that the personnel function is generally an administrative activity within Spanish companies we now turn to consider the methods used by Spanish companies to procure the required corporate workforce – recruiting, selecting, developing and dismissing employees. This does not mean that we are ignoring the fact that in many companies the HR function also takes care of a number of other activities. However, as the nature of these activities varies enormously between companies (and space in this chapter is, in any case, limited) we will not discuss them here. But it is necessary to make a short digression and consider a number of important labour market characteristics which impact on the 'employment cycle', if we are to understand how the HR function is obliged to operate in many companies.

Some characteristics of the labour market

The rate of unemployment is a serious and alarming problem in Spain. Between 1983 and 1992 the average rate of employment was around 19 per cent (Ministry of Labour, 1992). However, by the last quarter of 1992 the rate of unemployment had crept above 20 percent. In November 1993 3,500,000 people were out of work in Spain. Unemployment was particularly high among school leavers: in 1992 the unemployment rate for young people between 16 and 19 was around 39 per cent. For those aged between 20 and 24 the unemployment rate was about 33 per cent. Unemployment is perhaps Spain's greatest social problem.

One aspect of the high rate of unemployment in Spain has been the oversupply of labour. Despite an economic boom in Spain between 1985 and 1989 not enough jobs were created. As a consequence, this boom did not make a serious impression on the rate of unemployment. The continuing high rate of unemployment has been supported by the large number of redundancies as indicated by 'workforce adjustment plans'. The 123,116 workforce adjustment plans registered between 1983 and 1992 affected 4,144,978 employees. Therefore, each plan affected on average approximately 34,500 people.

In summary, the rate of unemployment is very high in Spain (the highest in Europe). Many companies are reducing the size of their workforces, but for those seeking to take on new employees there is an abundant supply of labour. It should be noted that, as a result of so many adjustment plans, there is a much greater supply of less qualified job-seekers; highly qualified job-seekers are much rarer. This situation strongly influences the HR practices related to recruiting and selecting new personnel. In what follows we examine the HR practices being adopted by Spanish companies within the constraints detailed above. We have arranged the material in the order of a 'life cycle' which begins when employees are located, selected and enter the company. Then education and training are considered, followed by employee departures.

Recruitment and selection

Table 4.3 shows the sources of new middle-managers and workers in Spain. When companies hire new employees candidates are drawn from two main sources: (1) recommendations by company employees, or (2) unsolicited applications. This is particularly true of unskilled workers. The figures may indicate that people with jobs are assisting unemployed relatives and friends to find work. When they become aware of a vacancy they either recommend a friend or relative to their employer or they encourage the person to submit an early application to the company.

Competitors have been an important source of supply for technical staff. This source is listed under 'other sources' in table 4.3. In a market with a large number of job-seekers who are not necessarily what employers are looking for it is easier for companies to fill their vacancies by luring employees away from other companies rather than embarking on a lengthy process to select

Table 4.3 Source of new middle managers and workers

Source	Middle managers (%)	Workers skilled (%)	unskilled (%)	Total (%)
Recommendation	11	12	57	35
Unsolicited application	17	30	29	29
University	21	27	3	14
employment agency	28	15	1	8
Internal candidate	4	4	2	3
Other sources	19	12	9	11

Source: IOOE

a suitable candidate from among the army of unemployed. Employees who receive an offer that includes an increase in earnings do not generally pass up the opportunity. Instead, they quit their jobs for the better-paid position.

The low use of employment agencies (8 per cent) reflects a legal obligation to use the National Employment Service (Instituto Nacional de Empleo). This is purely a formal obligation and in the great majority of cases the company simply submits the name of the person they want to employ to the local office of the National Employment Service.

Candidates are usually selected via interviews (36 per cent of the IOOE sample companies used these) or some kind of work or performance test (35 per cent of the IOOE sample companies used these). These tests often consist of a brief trial period in the job for which the candidate is applying. Psychometric tests were used by 22 per cent of the IOOE sample companies. These became increasingly popular in Spain during the 1970s but have recently declined in popularity (see Flórez-Saborido et al., 1992).

Employee education, training and development

Employers in Spain are seeking to develop a highly educated workforce in order to take full advantage of modern technological innovations. The overall quality of the workforce can be enhanced in three ways. (1) The existing human resources of a company may have particular levels of education. (2) Employers may recruit new employees with higher qualifications. (3) Employers may devote resources to the training and development of their employees.

Each case is considered in turn below.

Qualifications of existing employees The IOOE study revealed that 66 per cent of senior managers of companies participating in the survey had a university degree. Most of the remaining 34 per cent had completed some sort of shorter university programmes. Moreover, 56 per cent of senior managers had some kind of postgraduate qualification. Table 4.4 shows the educational background for the rest of staff. Over half the middle managers had a university qualification.

Recruiting employees with higher qualifications   Table 4.5 shows that employers generally seek the most highly qualified individuals in the labour market. This probably indicates their desire to develop a high quality workforce. However, according to a *Coyuntura laboral* survey (1991), 66 per cent of the companies feel that the manpower available in the labour market has insufficient training and 80 per cent underscore the need for specialized training in the new technologies.

Training and development   Because of its impact on the work done by HR managers, special mention should be made here of the importance of training for executives, regardless of their past

Table 4.4 Educational background of different types of staff

Level of education[a]	Middle managers (%)	Skilled workers (%)	Unskilled workers (%)	Total (%)
Primary school	21	57	74	59
Secondary school	13	20	7	15
Occupational training	15	3	17	9
University short programmes	26	11	1	9
University studies	25	10	1	9
Total	100	101	10	101

[a] Primary school is compulsory until the age of 14; secondary school is completed at age 18, occupational training takes three or more years; university short programmes take three years; university studies take five or more years.

Table 4.5 Level of education sought by employers

Level of education	Employers hiring staff at different educational levels (%)
College or university	50
Occupational training (advanced level)	42
Occupational training (elementary level)	44
Occupational training (apprenticeship)	14

Source: *Coyuntura laboral*, 1991

education. According to the results of the *Coyuntura laboral* survey (1991) shown in table 4.6, this is principally due to the increased pace of technological and organizational change resulting in a need to continuously update managers' skills and knowledge. Similarly, the survey reports that middle managers and technical personnel primarily require training to keep abreast of technological and organizational changes.

In 53 per cent of the IOOE sample of companies, managers had received some kind of training during the year. Table 4.7 shows that most of the training for top managers was supplied in

Table 4.6 Reasons for training different types of staff

Reasons for training	Executives (%)	Technical personnel and middle management (%)	All staff (%)
Technological improvement	24	29	23
Permanent education	25	23	22
Organizational improvement	27	23	15
Underqualified employees	3	8	14
Improve employee flexibility	5	5	11
Employee recycling	2	5	6
Others	3	2	2

Source: *Coyuntura laboral*, 1991

courses given outside the company. In contrast, administrative people received their training in in-house courses. The increase in training activity in Spain has resulted in an enormous expansion of external providers. Executives and middle management are most commonly trained by external providers (see table 4.8). For all other types of staff in-house training is the most popular option. It should be noted that the majority (53 per cent) of the companies with more than 500 employees have their own training facilities. This is a positive situation. However, the smaller the company the lower the percentage of those equipped to provide their own training.

A detailed analysis of the training courses by the IOOE sample of companies reveals that 35 per cent of companies provided for some training for their employees. It also reveals that the more senior the employees the more likely they are to receive training. These people also tend to be the most qualified. Thus, on average in these companies 60 per cent of middle managers received some kind of training. This compares with 32 per cent for skilled personnel and 26 per cent for non-skilled personnel, which suggests that in practice the training efforts of many large companies are centred on specific groups of employees, particularly senior and middle managers and skilled/technical personnel.

Despite the lack of comparative figures and of a study of specific corporate training needs, it would nevertheless appear safe

Table 4.7 Areas in which executives receive training

Areas	In house		External	
	hours per person	%	hours per person	%
General management	33	12	49	22
Administration	12	13	4	21
Commercial	5	17	5	32
Financial	5	13	5	35
Technical	5	16	4	36
Organizational	3	12	4	25
Total	5	20	4	48

Source: IOOE

Table 4.8 Source of training for different types of staff

Sources	Executives (%)	Technical personnel and middle management	Administrative (%)	Maintenance (%)	Production (%)
Courses taught by private institutions	33	30	22	15	12
In-house courses	17	27	27	21	28
On the job training (contract)	2	2	3	4	6
On the job training (without contract	2	3	5	4	5
National employment agency (INEW)	2	6	9	9	16
Courses taught by public institutions	3	4	3	3	3
No training	18	13	13	19	12
Training not available	21	11	14	22	14

to say that Spanish companies provide little training, particularly if we recall that the percentages indicating the amount of training provided referred only to those companies which had actually furnished some sort of training during the year. If we also take into account the fact that the figures provided refer only to the largest companies and that, as mentioned earlier, smaller companies provide less training, our conclusion that Spanish companies provide little training would appear to be confirmed.

Managing the downsizing of the workforce

In a labour market characterized by considerable oversupply and little demand we might expect few voluntary resignations. But the figures in table 4.9 appear to indicate just the opposite. In 1987 24 per cent of IOOE respondents indicated that resignation was almost the main reason for employees leaving their jobs. In the 1989 the figure had risen to 29 per cent. Much of the explanation for these percentages is to be found in the recruiting system used by many companies in recent years, hiring experienced employees from other companies rather than recruiting from among the unemployed.

Under the terms of current Spanish legislation, employers cannot simply fire employees they consider unsatisfactory. Arbitrary dismissal is against the law. Apart from collective dismissals, which were infrequent prior to 1993 but are now becoming increasingly common, there are a number of other ways in which companies are able to rid themselves of undesirable employees. Under Spanish law employees may be dismissed on an individual basis for two kinds of reasons:

1. **Objective reasons** (technical, economic or *force majeure*) – in this instance the employer has to pay the employee an indemnity of twenty days' wages for every year of employment, with a ceiling equivalent to one year's pay. However, in practice it is very difficult for employers to build a convincing case with the consequence that this form of dismissal is rare.
2. **Disciplinary reasons** (the employee is habitually late to work, badly behaved towards other employees, etc.) – however if this is judged as unjustified by the labour magistrate the employer has to offer employees their old job back or pay them the equivalent of forty-five days' pay for each year of employment with the company. The maximum compensation a company

Table 4.9 Reasons for employees leaving their employer

Reasons	Year	Middle managers (%)	Personnel Skilled (%)	Personnel Non-skilled (%)	Total (%)
Voluntary	1987	25	34	14	24
resignations	1989	38	25	31	29
Transfer	1987	4	2	0.3	0.3
	1989	1	1	2	2
Retirement	1987	9	3	9	6
	1989	6	6	2	5
Early	1987	27	26	29	27
retirement	1989	33	39	31	35
Induced	1987	21	11	30	20
resignation	1989	10	17	23	19
Individual	1987	3	13	6	9
dismissal	1989	4	5	5	5
Collective	1987	0	0.3	0	0.1
dismissal	1989	0.1	0.1	1	0.3
Disability	1987	11	11	11	11
or death	1989	7	6	6	6

Source: IOOE

has to pay to an employee who is considered to have been unjustifiably dismissed is forty-two months' pay.

Table 4.9 refers to *induced resignation*. By this we refer to a situation in which an employee is dismissed and then sues for wrongful dismissal. The company and the employee then agree on a financial settlement which is less than the amount the company would have to pay if found guilty by the labour magistrate. Employees generally accept their dismissal in exchange for a negotiated level of compensation.

In Spain *retirement* is a right, not an obligation, except for some civil servants. Full pensions are paid to employees who have made social security payments for thirty-five years and have reached the age of 65. Employees are eligible to take early retirement (technically known as *jubilación de coeficiente reductor*) at the age of 60, providing they have made social security payments since 1 January 1967. In this case, they are eligible for 60 per cent of the retirement pension, or as much as 92 per cent if the employee retires at age 64. Early retirement can also be taken before the age of 60. In this case, employers and employees usually make an agreement whereby employees are paid a supplement to their unemployment benefits until they reach the age of 60.

It should be emphasized that reducing the workforce, apart from voluntary resignations and retirement, is considerably more expensive in Spain than elsewhere in Europe. According to the fifth European Commission report on unemployment, severance pay in Spain 'amounts to more than 40 weeks' salary, a figure considerably higher than the average in other Single European Market (SEM) countries, which stands at around 22 weeks'. The increase in early retirement between 1987 and 1989 could indicate an attempt on the part of employers to reduce the costs associated with reducing the size of the workforce.

The Impact of the Single European Market

Having discussed the current situation and the way HR managers presently operate in order to procure a suitable workforce, it is now time to consider the future. Following the Accession Treaty in 1986 and the advent of SEM in 1993, Spain now faces a number of unanswered questions about the years remaining until the Economic and Monetary Union becomes a reality in 1997 (Viñals, 1992). No one really knows the circumstances in which companies will be operating within the next few years and it is even less clear what the situation will be in each industry. Some authors have attempted to sketch scenarios, generally painting a fairly bright picture for all the industries examined in IOOE (Baruel and Rucabado, 1992). According to these authors, production costs will drop, employment will increase, although relatively little, exports will also rise (Collado et al., 1992). On the whole this report, which was inspired by the Cecchini Report, suggests that the future is very promising, although the latter report contained very few figures on the Spanish economy. However, since publication of this study, certain things have happened that appear to contradict some of its conclusions. Because of the recession the situation is now being viewed from a very different angle.

In order to obtain the views of industry as to the likely impact of the Single European Market we surveyed the opinions of managers in thirty-seven of the largest companies in Spain. The results are summarized in table 4.10. The respondents see the following advantages accruing from Spain's participation in the SEM:

- an improvement in banking services, greater access to capital and lower borrowing costs;
- the potential for greater foreign sales;
- improvements in productivity resulting from greater competition; and
- increased investment in research and development.

The survey respondents also indicated a number of problems for Spanish companies seeking to operate successfully in the emerging SEM:

- Many companies will have to downsize in order to compete.
- Many companies have out-of-date equipment.
- Domestic sales may fall as a result of increased competition from foreign companies.
- Setting competitive prices may be difficult.
- In many cases middle management is not well developed.

Table 4.10 Perceived advantages and problems of membership of the Single European Market

Subjects	Advantage (%)	Problem (%)	Both (%)	Indifferent (%)
Costs	30.6	33.3	16.6	19.4
Prices	27.8	41.7	11.1	19.4
Productivity	42.9	31.4	5.7	20.0
Banking services	82.9	8.6	2.9	5.7
Spanish sales	8.3	48.2	8.3	36.1
European sales	54.5	18.2	3.0	24.2
Size:				
Number of employees	12.5	53.1	6.3	28.1
Number of plants	15.2	45.5	15.1	24.2
Equipment	30.3	42.4	6.1	21.2
Technology, R&D				
Technical development of				
executives	47.1	23.5	11.8	17.6
middle management	31.4	37.1	11.4	20.0
technology, R&D	38.2	26.5	11.8	23.5

As a result of these perceived problems respondents indicated that they would have to undertake a number of specific 'projects' if they were to compete effectively and successfully in the SEM. These are:

1. **Downsizing**, which includes: (a) reducing the size of the workforce and (b) reducing the size or number of factories in order to improve overall profitability.
2. **Restructuring**, which also involves two major actions: (a) modernizing or replacing existing facilities and equipment and (b) undertaking a structural reorganization.
3. **Promoting and improving R&D**. This involves: (a) fostering research, (b) training research personnel and (c) acquiring new technology from other companies through purchase or other bilateral arrangements.
4. **Improving sales** by: (a) creating or developing sales networks and contacts in major European markets, (b) developing suitable logistics systems and (c) undertaking the marketing studies required by the new conditions.
5. Involves plans for **training and making corporate personnel more cohesive**. This necessitates: (a) a change in outlook, (b) greater employee involvement and (c) encouraging and making use of employee initiatives, corporate aggressiveness, improvement projects and employee creativity in general.

According to the survey respondents, if Spanish companies are to compete successfully by producing at low cost, selling at low prices, attaining high quality and high margins in order to secure a solid future they will have to undertake one or a combination of the above projects. According to Fuentes Quintana (1993) the three 'battle horses', as he put it, that can make Spanish companies competitive, are technology, marketing and human resources. This brings us to the subject of the work which HR managers will have to undertake in order to acquire, develop and maintain a workforce that contributes to the company's competitiveness in the emerging SEM (Fernández, 1992).

HRM in the Single European Market

In the final section of this chapter we examine the contribution that an HRM approach to employee relations could make to the competitiveness of large Spanish companies in Europe. The following paragraphs represent a personal view on what is a very complex issue and about which there are a myriad of different opinions. In general we wish to suggest that with regard to the five projects listed in the previous section:

1. It will be impossible or at least extremely difficult to correctly implement them: (a) unless the implications for the human resources of an organization are taken into consideration from the very outset of any decision process; and (b) without some awareness that it is this factor that will have to implement any decisions made.
2. It is very likely that the success of each project will in part be determined by the introduction of suitable (i.e. supporting and complementary) personnel policies and that their effective introduction will require painstaking preparation, monitoring and evaluation.

We would further suggest that the pursuit of any one of these five projects will be made easier if a company moves to an HRM approach to employee relations in contrast with a personnel management approach. There are two main reasons for this:

1. Personnel analyses should be made from the very start of any of the five projects described above. Decisions to implement these projects must take previously made personnel analyses into account. This is a standard procedure in HRM but not in traditional personnel management.
2. Authority is needed to implement personnel policies. This is facilitated by the presence on the board of directors of a HR director whose status is close to that of the CEO. This is a characteristic of HRM, as explained earlier.

In what follows we give our personal opinion on certain points of the aforementioned five projects that we feel can best be handled through HRM:

1. Before either of the first two projects – downsizing and restructuring – can be implemented a thorough analysis of the workforce is required in order to determine the number and type of employees that will ensure the future competitive strength of the company.
2. The third project, which involves strengthening R&D, suggests that companies should develop their own R&D capacities rather than attempting to imitate and therefore live a scavenger existence off the research successes of other companies.

Companies that are to compete successfully in a technologically intensive industry must be equipped to use innovation as a weapon when fighting for a share of the market. The companies that opt to live off the technology of the pioneers in the field or use it to enhance their own technologies may be making the correct decision in some cases, but they will naturally be permanently relegated to the second rank. The fact that the advent of the Single European Market has made R&D increasingly necessary provides an opportunity to silence once and for all the nerve-wracking refrain so often heard in different areas of Spain that 'inventing is for others'. The determination to conquer the research challenge must originate with the human team and if so HRM is more likely to foster this determination.

3. The commercial development proposed in the fourth project could naturally be achieved with traditional personnel management. However, we would like to point out that extensive sales networks in companies organized in business units generally cause considerable problems in terms of co-ordination and communication. Purely commercial problems can and should be solved by the commercial organization itself. But many of the problems that also involve most of the most important units, such as production, R&D, marketing, sales and customer services, are usually at least partially rooted in human attitudes and in endemic shortcomings in communication. The CEO has the power to co-ordinate and solve these problems and a much-used means of doing this is through contact among senior managers in each of the aforementioned units. However, this is frequently impractical. The extremely large number of details involved sometimes make it advisable that a senior authority, ranked just below the CEO, deals permanently with a subject which is as much a part of human relations as it is of communication. This would be the responsibility of the HR director or manager.

4. The final project, training and making the team cohesive, is directly and almost exclusively related to the human factor. In our opinion, it is the most ambitious of the five projects because if it is implemented all the other projects will be likely to follow. But trying to attain this objective through traditional personnel management is scarcely feasible, if at all, particularly if management personnel are to be involved.

It must be remembered that whatever work is to be done by HRM or personnel management will start from the current situation. This complicates matters tremendously because, as we have seen, HRM currently has little room to manoeuvre due to rigid legislation, the shortage of resources because of the economic situation, etc. It is to be expected that the recently enacted measures to reform the labour market will facilitate the task of HRM to some extent. In December 1993, the government embarked on a campaign to deregulate the labour market. According to employers associations the measures are insufficient; according to Unions they are excessive. Spanish labour legislation, has been altered with a Decree-Law. Among the changes likely to be introduced are greater freedom for companies to bypass the public employment office when hiring employees, new kinds of contracts that will make hiring easier, particularly in terms of contracting young people, and the acceptance of organizational and production-related reasons for dismissal.

The example of the situation in the largest and most important Spanish companies appears to point to the advisability of HRM. Naturally, this can be established in many ways, depending on the particular requirements of each case, and can, as we have stated, range widely in degree, from bordering on pure traditional personnel management to full HRM. A thousand different circumstances can affect the decision on what must be done. But in our opinion, continuing with traditional personnel management that forms part of other departments and does not provide the human vision necessary for designing general corporate policies is too risky given the current circumstances. Continuing as before will make it extremely difficult to shape competitive companies.

Conclusion

This chapter began by examining the extent to which Spanish companies have moved towards an HRM approach to employee relations. Three key features of HRM were initially identified: (1) representation of the HR function or the senior management team of the organization; (2) line authority for HR managers with respect to business decisions; and (3) the participation of HR managers in the strategic planning process. Data drawn from a study conducted by the author, in addition to the results of a number of other studies, indicates that these features of HRM are not yet present in Spanish companies. Spanish companies appear not to have moved towards an HRM approach to employee management. This may be the result, in part, of importing an external (non-Spanish) model of HRM into the Spanish context. This was necessary because to date the debate on the nature of HRM in Spain has been very limited. Consequently, one conclusion may be that Spanish companies have simply failed to adopt a foreign conception of HRM. Future work should therefore seek to ascertain the special features of a Spanish approach to HRM and whether Spanish companies show any signs of moving towards this.

The chapter further argued that a HRM approach to the employment relationship was critical if Spanish companies were to succeed in and benefit from the emerging SEM. However, the extent to which they are able to develop a HRM approach is constrained by the context within which they are currently operating. The HR function is currently viewed primarily as an administrative activity concerned with the regulation or 'through flow' of the workforce. It is a low-status function. The role of the HR function and its contribution to future organizational goals and objectives has to be ascertained and determined more clearly if Spanish companies are to compete effectively in the SEM. Indeed, until the HR function is able to elevate its organizational status any moves towards HRM will be hesitant and short-lived in Spain.

References

Baruel, J. (1992), *La estructura organizativa de las empresa*. Barcelona: ESADE.

Baruel, J. and Rucabado, J. (1992), *Observatorio organizativo 1992*. Barcelona: ESADE.

Baruel, J., Rucabado, J. and Serrano, I. (1988) *Observatorio organizativo 1988*. Barcelona: ESADE.

Collado, J. C., Tomba, M. and Werling, J. (1992), *Efectos del Mercado Unico sobre los sectores productivos españoles*. Madrid: Instituto de Estudios Económicos.

Coyuntura laboral, **31** (1991), Madrid: Ministerio de Trabajo y Seguridad Social.

Dirección General de Estadistica (1993), *Boletin de estadisticas laborales*. Madrid: Ministerio de Trabajo y Seguridad Social.

Fernández, S. (1992), 'Algunas reflexiones sobre la competitividad empresarial y sus causas'. In *Información comercial española,* **705**. Madrid: Ministerio de Comercio.

Filella, J. and Soler, C. (1992), 'Spain'. In C. Brewster, A. Hegewisch, T. Lockhart and L. Holden (eds), *The European Human Resource Management Guide*. London: Academic Press.

Flórez-Saborido, I., González-Rendón, M. and Alcaide-Castro, M. (1992), 'Human resource management in Spain', *Employee Relations*, **14**, pp. 39–61.

Fuentes Quintana, E. (1993), 'La competitividad de la industria española'. Address given at ESADE on the occasion of the presentation of *Papeles de economia*, **56**, November.

IMD (1992) *The Emergent Role of the HR Manager in Europe*. Lausanne: IMD.

Ministerio de Trabajo y Seguridad Social (1992), *Boletín de estadísticas laborales*.

Proyecto Price Waterhouse Cranfield (1992), *Informe de Conclusiones*. Barcelona: Price Waterhouse-ESADE.

Real Decreto-Ley 18/1993, 3 December, de 'Medidas Urgentes de Fomento de la Ocupation'. In *Boletin oficial del estado*, 7 December 1993.

Recio, E. (1991), *La direccion de personal en España*, Papers ESADE, **53**, May.

Rodriguez-Porras, J. M., Chinchilla-Albiol, M. N, Casanova-Martí, A. and Reuter de Cabo, J. M. (1990), *La dirección de personal en España, 1989*. Aedipe, Barcelona: IESE, Hay Management Consultants.

Serrano, I., *Estrategias empresariales, relaciones industriales y cultura organizativa. MILCO 1978–1988*. Chapter 2. Thesis dissertation. In progress.

Soler-Vicente, C. (1993) 'Human resources management in Spain: strategic issues, the economic and social framework'. In S. Tyson, P. Lawrence, P. Poirson, L. Manzolini and C. Soler (eds), *Human Management in Europe*. London: Kogan Page.

Viñals, J. (1992), 'La economia española ante el mercado único. Les claves del proceso de integración en la Comunidad Europea'. In J. Viñals (ed.), *La economica española ante el Mercado Unico Europeo*. Madrid: Alianza Editorial.

5 Human Resource Management in Germany

CHRISTIAN SCHOLZ

Introduction

Human resource management is now a well-established academic subject in many management schools on German universities. However, trying to communicate to a foreign audience what is meant by HRM in Germany is very difficult. We come to understand the special features of countries other than our own through different types of encounter. One type of encounter is when a foreigner becomes acquainted with another country as a manager of a local subsidiary of a foreign organization, as a scholar on a sabbatical, as an immigrant, or as a consultant conducting an assignment in a foreign country. However, frequently the pictures painted by these strangers are not recognized (or at least not enjoyed) by the members of the culture they seek to depict. In part this is because the special features they seek to highlight are often contaminated by their cultural viewpoint. As a consequence, these foreign observers tend to overemphasize those aspects which appear strangest to them and underemphasize, or ignore, a number of features which do not appear peculiar but are nevertheless important to the members of the 'foreign' culture. An example of this occurring in the field of HRM is the article by Lawrence (1993) entitled 'Human resource management in Germany'. This bears little resemblance either to the human resource management curricula being taught in German universities or the academic debates being conducted within management schools.

This chapter is an example of another type of encounter. It is written by a researcher from Germany who has had the opportunity to work abroad and observe his own country from the viewpoint of strangers. But the writer is not a complete stranger in that he is familiar with the special features of the German situation. With this in mind the purpose of this chapter is to convey the nature of HRM in Germany. To achieve this I begin by examining the German terminology with respect to HRM. I then consider a number of features of the German context which impact on HRM – for example, economic factors, labour market situation, education system, co-determination, trades unions and partnership. I then examine the historical development of HRM in Germany in terms of the work of 'first generation researchers', 'second generation researchers' and 'contemporary researchers'. Four contemporary approaches to HRM in Germany are then outlined: the 'Stuttgart'. 'Mannheim, 'Zurich' and 'Saarbrücken' approaches. HRM in a number of German companies (VW, Bertelsmann, BMW) is examined. This is followed by a report on some the empirical findings from a study of HRM excellence in German companies. Finally, a number of the future challenges facing HRM are highlighted.

What is Meant by HRM?

In seeking to describe the nature of German HRM to an English-speaking audience it has to be appreciated that in the German language there are a number of terms which while they may appear similar have different meanings and which do not have any equivalents in English (Wächter, 1992). Therefore, to begin to understand what is meant by HRM in Germany the reader needs to be aware of the meaning of the appropriate terminology. In Germany, Austria and the German-speaking part of Switzerland, four different basic labels are used, each representing one specific concept of HRM:

1. *Personalverwaltung* (personnel administration) refers to the practice of personnel management in German organizations. It implies the efficient administration of personnel. This is often seen as a burdensome task.

2. In academia, the traditional term for HRM is *Personalwesen* (personnel affairs). It implies an administrative and bureaucratic view of personnel. It focuses on the tasks of the personnel function and neglects the active role of the other parties to the employment relationship.

3. Often used in theory is the term *Personalwirtschaft* meaning the economically oriented administration of personnel. Being similar to the German term for the science of business management (*Betriebswirtschaft*), it implies that personnel programmes can have important financial impacts with the consequence that the management of employees can make a distinctive contribution to organizational performance and the 'bottom line'.

4. *Personalmanagement* is a term generally accepted and used among more advanced HRM-managers. This describes a management approach which considers the management of human resources as an active part of the whole management process – not the preserve of the personnel function but the responsibility of all managers. This implies a professional and integrated approach to the management of employees. This integration has two aspects: (a) HR policies should be integrated with the strategic needs of the organization; (b) the HR policies themselves should be integrated such that they mutually reinforce each other.

Thus, when the Anglo-American literature refers to the shift from 'personnel administration' or 'personnel management' to 'human resource management' the equivalent shift in the German literature is from the traditional *Personalverwaltung* to *Personalmanagement* (see table 5.1). Although the Anglo-American and German literatures use different terms the ideas and practices underlying both shifts are virtually identical.

The National Context

In order to convey the nature of HRM in Germany it is important to explore some special features of the German corporate environment which impact on HRM. These include economic factors, the labour market situation, the education system, co-determination, trades unions and partnership. Despite the growing importance

Table 5.1 The changes in terminology in the Anglo-American and German literature relating to personnel issues

	Key term in the 1960s	Key term in the 1970s	Key term in the 1980s
Anglo-American	Personnel	Personnel management	Human resource management
Germany/ Austria/ Switzerland	*Personalwesen* (2)	*Personalverwaltung* (1) *Personalwirtschaft* (3)	*Personalmanagement* (4)

and impact of the European Union they remain of primary importance.

Economic factors

Some important environmental factors for HRM arise from the economic situation including:

- The emphasis on a social market philosophy which stresses the need for free markets and competition. This results in strong competition in the domestic marketplace from national and foreign companies which encourages companies to become as efficient as possible.
- Germany is an export-oriented nation with limited natural resources, with the consequence that it is very dependent upon its human resources as a key source of competitive advantage.
- Employee costs are very high with the consequence that these have to be paid for by high levels of productivity.

As a result of the above any employee management system in Germany has to provide a skilled and highly productive workforce.

Labour market situation

Currently there are two seemingly contradictory trends. Unemployment is historically (in the last thirty years) high with four million people unemployed, but at the same time there is also a growing shortage of skilled workers and professionals. A further very important demographic factor is the shift in average age. As a consequence of the declining birth-rate and increasing life expectancy the proportion of elderly people in German society is rapidly increasing. The education and development of the German workforce are widely regarded as a key solution to these problems. This is clearly one of the major future problems facing Germany.

Educational system

The German educational system, the so-called *Duales System* (dual system), is characterized by a general education system and a vocational training system. The state is responsible for the school and university system. School attendance is compulsory between the ages of 6 and 18. School education divides into the following: *Hauptschule* (basic secondary school); *Realschule* (intermediate school); and *Gymnasium* (high school). These stages are the precursor to a university education.

Universities, senior technical colleges and business schools complete the German educational system. While the *Fachhochschulen* (senior technical colleges) and the MBA programmes of business schools offer a shorter and far more vocationally oriented education, universities have a more scientific orientation. The duration of education in business schools is on average two years, in senior technical colleges on average three to four years and in universities on average four to seven years. Thus, a 'typical' German university graduate is around 28. Companies regard university graduates as good abstract thinkers, while the more practically educated graduates from the senior technical colleges and the MBAs specializing in management are considered to be better prepared for jobs as specialists.

According to Conrad and Pieper (1990, p. 128) more than 90 per cent of those who end their general schooling go into vocational training. These students choose a practical apprenticeship which incorporates on-the-job training in companies with theoretical learning in vocational schools (*Berufsschulen*), which they attend part-time. In 1991 there were approximately 1,650,000 apprentices undergoing official vocational training (Randlesome, 1994, p. 46). The *Lehre* (apprenticeship) is the main formal method of manual-worker skill formation. For special on-the-job training, larger companies often have their own training facilities, whereas smaller companies send their trainees to inter-company training centres. There are more than 400 programmes which lead to a formal degree (for example *Facharbeiter*). The German chambers of commerce (*Industrie und Handelskammern*), craft chambers (*Handwerkskammern*) and companies offer additional training programmes which lead to a *Meister* (foreman qualification). Thus in Germany responsibility for the education of workers is a joint responsibility of government and private enterprise.

Co-determination

The system of co-determination (*Mitbestimmung*) is a key determinant of the nature of HRM in German organizations. Joint stock companies in Germany (those with AG after their name) have 'two-tier' boards. The higher-level board is the *Aufsichtsrat* (i.e. supervisory board). The members of this board are elected for five years and often include representatives from the organization's bank, customers, suppliers and employees in addition to a number of senior executives from other organizations. While this board is potentially influential – it appoints the management board (*Vorstand*), it can reject management strategic decisions and block the reappointment of managers it believes to be incompetent – it does not have the legal power to force the adoption of alternative strategies (Lane, 1992). The *Vorstand* is composed of senior executives who are in the full-time employ of the company concerned. Warner and Campbell (1993, p. 98) have pointed out that senior managers in German organizations are generally well qualified, with many board directors having doctorates. The distinction between the *Aufsichtsrat* and the *Vorstand* is important for understanding the operation of the co-determination system.

Co-determination in Germany operates at three levels: supervisory board, management board and works' council. First, there are elected worker-representatives on the supervisory board (*Aufsichtsrat*). Depending on the size of the company or the type of industry in which it operates these can make up a third or a half of the *Aufsichtsrat* members. Second, there is the *Arbeitsdirektor* (personnel director) on the *Vorstand*. The *Arbeitsdirektor* is required to devote their full time to employee relations matters. In the *Montanindustrie* (iron, steel and coal) the appointment of the *Arbeitsdirektor* has to be confirmed by the majority of the worker-representatives sitting on the *Aufsichtsrat*. The Co-determination Act of 1976 extended the labour director system to other branches of industry, but without the above electoral provision.

The third level at which co-determination occurs is that of the *Betriebsrat* (works' council). Virtually all companies with more than twenty employees are legally obliged to establish a works council. These councils have been in existence since the early 1950s and are regarded as an *Ordnungsfaktor*, an element of national stability. The elected works council has three sets of rights:

1. *Mitbestimmungsrecht* (co-determination right) gives workers the right to be consulted on certain aspects of organizational life such as dismissals, setting the start and end of the working day, job descriptions, internal transfers, health and safety, recruitment and selection systems and so forth.
2. *Mitwirkungsrecht* (right to be consulted) refers to planning problems such as the decision to close a plant, open a new plant.
3. *Informationsrecht* (information right) enables workers to obtain information on the company's performance and prospects.

Trades unions

Germany has a strong trades union system which has played an important part in the economic regeneration of the country since the 1940s – the *Wirtschaftswunder* (economic miracle). However, since the 1970s trades union membership has been declining. In 1990 approximately 42 per cent of German employees were members of a trades union (Lecher and Neumann, 1991, p. 97). German unification has stemmed much of the recent decline in trades union membership. Jacobi et al. (1992, p. 231) suggest that union density is higher in the east than in the west and that IG Metall has gained 900,000 new members from the east. The largest trades unions, such as IG Metall, IG Medien and the Public Services and Transport Union, are affiliated to the Deutscher Gewerkschaftsbund (DGB). There are additionally two other main union confederations: the Christian Federation of Trades Unions (Christlicher Gewerkschaftsbund or CGB), with around 300,000 members, and the German Salaried Employees' Union (Deutsche Angestellten-Gewerkschaft or DAG). More than 80 per cent of union members belong to a union which is affiliated to the DGB. These unions are each responsible for one industry or an economic sector. The biggest unions are industrial unions, as opposed to being craft, general enterprise or professional unions. Membership of any one of these unions is open to anyone in a given industry who wishes to join a union whatever their particular skill level or status: manual labourer, blue- and white-collar worker and the works supervisor. Lane (1992) writes that 'union organization on an industry basis, together with strong central organization, results in solidaristic rather than sectional demands and facilitates the formulation of social demands, going beyond shop-floor concerns' (p. 74).

A large percentage of employees in Germany are covered by collective bargaining agreements. According to the Collective Agreement Act the parties to a collective agreement must be the unions on the workers' side and single employers or employers' associations on the other. Such agreements are primarily industry-based although bargaining may occur at a regional level in some industries. The agreement set in the engineering sector exerts considerable influence on all other negotiations and agreements. According to Jacobi et al. (1992, p. 248) other industries generally settle wage increases within one per cent of the engineering agreement.

Three kinds of collective agreements are usually distinguished: wage and salary agreements (*Lohn- und Gehaltstarifvertrag*) affect only pay; framework conditions agreements (*Rahmentarifvertrag*) affect additional matters such as working hours, holidays, benefits dismissals and redundancy provisions; and 'umbrella' agreements (*Manteltarifvertrag*) regulate all other conditions of employment. With the exception of a few companies (such as Volkswagen, and the large chemical and oil companies, which often negotiate single employer agreements) company-level agreements follow those of their sector with some minor modifications. Once signed these agreements are legally binding on all employers and employees within an industry or sector. The HRM function in German organizations has to take account of the content of these agreements since the federal or state minister of labour can declare them to be *allgemeinverbindlich* (generally binding) regardless of whether an employer has signed the agreement or whether employees are union members. Roughly 90 per cent of all employees are covered by a collective agreement – almost three times the number of union members. This indicates an important feature of German industrial relations: the impact of collective agreements is much wider than the immediate union membership.

Partnership

A further important German attribute is that of *Betriebsverbundenheit* (the feeling of belonging to the company) which is associated with long-term employment. Employees are generally proud to work for their companies. Employers in turn view this strong identification with the organization as an important source of commitment and motivation. This is beginning to change as Germany becomes a more individualistic society and rates of personnel turnover increase.

Closely related to this is the concept of *Partnerschaft* (partnership). This refers to the constructive co-operation of different interest groups such as trades unions and employers' associations. The idea of partnership was a historic necessity for the post-war reconstruction and has also proven to be an important factor in the reunification of the former East and West Germanies. The idea of partnership consists in two components which are found in organizations in different degrees:

1. **The immaterial component** refers to the outcomes of changes in the corporate decision making structure (described earlier) which permit greater employee participation.
2. **The material component** refers to the outcomes of changes in the ownership structure and profit distribution in order to permit employees a greater access to profits or capital. Materially oriented partnerships are encouraged by law.

As a consequence of partnership German companies tend to display a uniquely 'German business culture' which is often overlooked by non-German commentators who tend instead to stress such stereotypes as the Germans being technically oriented or extremely bureaucratic.

HRM in Academia

In this section we consider the development of HRM in Germany by elaborating in turn the work of the 'first-generation researchers', the 'second-generation researchers' and the 'contemporary researchers'.

First-generation researchers

In examining the historical roots of contemporary German HRM the basic elements originated in the ideas and work of a number individuals who may be termed first-generation researchers. According to Drumm (1993, pp. 678–9) the following roots can be identified:

1. The empirical foundations were laid initially by Kosiol (1959) who identified a number of fundamental empirical questions which were subsequently applied specifically to the area of personnel by Witte (1972).
2. The identification and description of the practice of personnel management is closely related to the work of Goossens (1981) who for many years edited the *Personalleiter-Handbuch*, a handbook for personnel managers, which in spite of a lack of theoretical sophistication answered all kinds of administrative questions related to personnel work.
3. Marx (1963) was appointed the first German professor for personnel issues in 1963 at the University of Mannheim. He introduced the importance of manpower planning, personnel development, motivation and leadership to the subject of personnel management.
4. Hax (1969) initiated the research into the co-determination system.
5. The values of social responsibility central to Roman Catholic teaching strongly influenced the normative aspects of HRM (von Nell-Breuning, 1950). While Hasenack (1961) unsuccessfully tried to start the field of anthropological economics, Fischer (1935, 1955, 1962) introduced a concern for an ethically oriented corporate personnel policy.

In addition to the above, the behaviouristic approach of organizational psychology and the theoretical base of business administration are two further influences on the nature of contemporary HRM in Germany.

Second-generation researchers

Since there is more than one approach to the topic of HRM in Germany there are a large number of systematizations which have been developed to show the various orientations of researchers (see, for example Staehle and Karg 1981; Ende 1982; Röthig 1986). In this chapter, the so-called 'second-generation researchers' represent the link between the historical roots of HRM and the contemporary HRM researchers. The work of five researchers is especially important since they have had a considerable influence on the development of contemporary notions of HRM in Germany (Krulis-Randa, 1985; Drumm, 1992; Staehle, 1991; Reber, 1987; Gaugler et al., 1974).

Contemporary HRM in Germany

We distinguish five general approaches to contemporary HRM in Germany. Each of these has a different focus. These are (1) on management; (2) on controlling; (3) on development'; (4) on information; and (5) on planning/administration. Figure 5.1 summarizes the different historical roots and theoretical orientations which are discussed below and in so doing synthesizes current approaches to HRM in Germany.

Focus on management   This approach stresses the Anglo-American meaning of the term 'management' which is characterized by a broad and action-oriented perspective. These researchers do not limit their activities to a single discipline area; on the contrary, for them the management of people is seen as a broad subject area in which the theories and ideas from a range of disciplines are relevant. Thus, traditional personnel issues are complemented by concerns with system design processes and corporate culture, for example. Authors like Ackermann (1986; 1987), Berthel (1991) and Scholz (1993; 1994a; 1995) represent this approach in Germany.

Focus on controlling   Authors such as Potthoff (1974; Potthoff and Trescher, 1986) and Wunderer (Wunderer and Kuhn, 1993) represent the tradition of a controlling-oriented approach to HRM in Germany. They point out that employees have to be managed because of their cost to organizations. As a consequence,

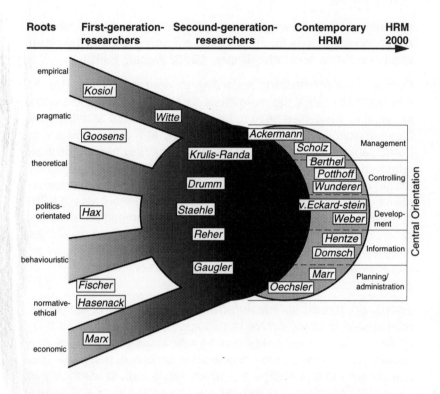

Figure 5.1 The historical development of HRM in German academia

they argue that the realization of strategic goals and organizational objectives is only possible via a continuous evaluation of the strengths and weaknesses of the workforce in terms of the needs of the organization. Of particular importance is the cost implications of workforce programmes to the organization. Thus, the focus on control means at its simplest the management of the workforce as a cost factor (like any other factor of production). In a more sophisticated form this focus leads to an evaluation of the added value the HRM function is able to create via its various activities.

Focus on development This approach regards personnel development as the central issue of personnel policy. The advocates of this approach concentrate on training and development programmes and integrating personnel development into the development process of the organization as a whole. For these researchers developing employees that are motivated to learn and then providing them with the resources to do so are the nec-essary preconditions for establishing a learning organization (see von Eckardstein and Schnellinger, 1978; Weber, 1985).

Focus on information   According to Hentze (1991a; 1991b) and Domsch (1980) the main basis for HRM is information. Com-munication processes need to be carefully reviewed to make sure they are adequate. These authors argue that if employees are to participate in organizational decision making they need to be well-informed about key-business issues. They also need information that enables them to do their job effectively. Thus,the represent-atives of this approach investigate the informational basis of HRM by focusing on identifying the type of information and the mechan-isms of communication which will enable management as well as employees to work effectively. They seek to establish a more har-monious and power-balanced work environment on the basis of greater informational transparency.

Focus on planning/administration   The employer–employee relationship is at the centre of this approach. In addition to this, all fields of personnel policy dealing with strategic issues as well as with its implementation in operative actions appear. The spe-cial concern of this approach – which exists almost identically in most other countries – is with issues concerning legal and partici-pational restrictions. The main representatives of this branch of writing in Germany are Marr (1987) and Oechsler (1994).

Contemporary Approaches to HRM

Below we consider in a little more detail the four main contempor-ary approaches to HRM in Germany. These are termed the Stutt-gart, Mannheim, Zurich and Saarbrücken approaches.

The Stuttgart approach

On the basis of an empirical study of HRM in practice, Ackermann (1986, 1987) conceptualized his so-called 'Stuttgart approach'. The purpose of the research, derived from empirically tested hypotheses, was to identify the range of alternative personnel strategies available to German organizations. For Ackermann a personnel strategy refers to the intended or unintended patterns which follow from HRM decisions. More specifically he wanted to find out:

- how to identify and measure personnel strategies;
- which types of personnel strategies were being used;
- which factors determined the choice of a particular personnel strategy;

He identified four different types of personnel strategy:

1. The **personnel development strategy** is characterized by intensive training and development, long-term personnel planning, sophisticated recruitment and selection practices.
2. The strategy of **personnel appraisal** gives a key role to appraisal schemes. These serve as a base for determining the performance of employees and underpin schemes such as performance related pay.
3. In the **personnel administration** strategy all personnel activities are performed with equal emphasis. Except for short-term personnel planning, HRM issues are neglected. Sophisticated personnel selection takes place only to a minor degree. This is traditional personnel management.
4. The strategy of **personnel research** is mainly characterized by intensive research of the labour market and regular employee interviews. Scanning the environment indicates the strengths and weaknesses of the personnel policy being pursued relative to competitors. External applicants are primarily selected through the use of strict criteria.

Each of these strategies was related to specific environmental conditions, specific corporate strategies and formal structures. While larger, diversified and risk spreading companies tended to adopt the personnel development strategy (1), the personnel appraisal strategy (2) was chosen by fast-reacting companies in heterogeneous environments. In a stable and non-dynamic environment the personnel administration strategy (3) was frequently pursued, whereas the personnel research (4) strategy was used in large divisionalized companies. Ackerman argues that in each set of circumstances each strategy is equally capable of providing a basis for organizational success. In other words, each strategy is suited to particular environmental circumstances and not others.

The Mannheim approach

Gaugler, a disciple of Fischer (1935, 1955), shows a strong anthropological orientation. The theme which pervades most of his writings is the humanization of working life under economic limitations and restrictions. For example, he has analyzed the impact of increasing workforce flexibility and the reduction of working time on employees (Gaugler, 1983). Indeed, he was one of the first people in Germany to encourage employers to implement such policies.

His general position becomes evident when we summarize his nine fields of HRM. These primarily focus on the employee in the working process (for example 1993, pp. 3146–52):

1. **Personnel policy** should be part of corporate policy with the consequence that the impacts of corporate decisions on personnel are considered.
2. **Personnel planning** covers all strategic, long-term activities in personnel work.
3. **Recruitment** covers the overall planning of the workforce which, together with labour market research, is an important precondition for the optimization of the workforce.
4. **Personnel assignment** applies to both the short term and long term: in the short term the task involves the co-ordination of employees and positions; in the long term, it covers all measurements to reach the intended number of employees, i.e. even personnel displacement (redundancy).
5. **Leadership** informs the employees about the tasks resulting from the division of labour and the integration of their results to reach the corporate objectives.
6. **Compensation** is regarded as central because it is an important corporate cost as well as being the basis for the employment of the workforce.
7. **Corporate social policy** aims to reconceptualize work in modern thinking companies to overcome the idea of employees as simply objects in the work process. This is assisted by corporate communications, employee development, long-term contracting and the paternal orientation of working conditions.
8. **Personnel development** mainly deals with individual training for personal job-related advance.

9. **Personnel administration** covers administrative tasks such as settling of wage claims and controlling the number of employees.

The Zurich approach

In the mid-1980s Krulis-Randa (1985, 1986, 1988) and Rühli and Wehrli (1986) developed the so-called Zurich approach with the intention of establishing a framework for strategic HRM. This approach takes a holistic view of management which aims to integrate the social and technocratic aspects of leadership while emphasizing the importance of developing a corporate policy which considers the implications of particular decisions on the workforce. The main features of the Zurich approach are:

- the central position of people (*anthropocentrizm*);
- people being *part* instead of the *object* of HR strategy;
- problem-solving in multipersonal teams;
- social relationships.

To integrate HRM into general management three basic **dimensions** are stressed:

1. The **structural dimension** is differentiated into planning, decision, organization and control on the three levels of actors, processes and tools.
2. **Corporate culture** is seen as a system of values and basic assumptions. It directly influences the recruitment and selection of personnel.
3. **Corporate policy** or strategy is reviewed or changed by the senior personnel and influences the development of the corporate culture.

A further development of the Zurich approach is conceptualized by Staffelbach (1986, 1988). His system of strategic HRM postulates a narrow integration of HRM strategy with general management strategy. The main characteristics of this approach are, in addition to the holistic view of management, a strict orientation on organizational success factors, an orientation towards individuals, and an HRM-oriented scan of the environment. Covering almost all HRM issues, Staffelbach suggests that an HRM strategy varies according to the intended impact, the qualitative and quantitative changes of the workforce and/or the changes in values and attitudes.

The aim of the Zurich approach is the implementation of its ideas in reality. Undoubtedly this approach has influenced the development of HRM in Germany from a management tool for control to HRM as an integral component of the strategic planning process. In a recently published book (Krulis-Randa et al., 1993) the implications of these ideas for practising managers are explicitly considered.

The Saarbrücken approach

According to Scholz (1993), successful HRM has to address three basic dimensions

The first dimension covers the different **fields** of HRM. The following are some of the main HR fields relevant to German organizations and their managers:

- The **analysis of the workforce** develops the informational base for HRM. The size and quality of the workforce to meet current and future organizational needs is determined.
- The **personnel requirement analysis** determines the characteristics of the current workforce. Shortcomings in terms of organizational needs are noted.
- By internal and external **recruitment** the workforce is adapted to meet actual organizational needs.
- To adapt the existing workforce to actual organizational needs personnel **training and development** policies are instituted. Meaningful training programmes are designed and implemented to enable each employee to meet the changing work standards, either in their current job or in a new work assignment.

In order to integrate these HRM fields a number of 'sectional functions' become important including personnel marketing (the acquisition of future employees and the motivation of present ones), personnel controlling (integrates the HRM fields with business and strategic issues thus ensuring the effectiveness of HRM) and international HRM (faces the challenges of increasing European integration and the globalization of the marketplace).

The second dimension refers to the three managerial **levels** at which each of these fields operates: (1) operational – the level of every-day operations; (2) tactical – the interface between the operational and strategic; and (3) strategic – the level of formulating plans and visions. Operational issues which are of most relevance to the lower hierarchical levels focus on the short term and on individuals. Tactical issues concentrate on groups within the company, and thus their time horizon is longer. Strategic issues are found at the top management level, they tend to concern the whole organization and have a long-term perspective.

In the third dimension, two *orientations* are identified: (1) information, and (2) behaviour. The main objective is to optimize the information base while at the same time ensuring that this is relevant to the needs of individual employees and the organization.

Figure 5.2 illustrates the 'three-dimensional approach' to HRM. It has been developed to establish a framework within which a HRM approach can be implemented which fits the challenges of a market orientation, individualization, flexibility, professionalization and the need for ensuring acceptance of leadership and change.

HRM in Practice

Having examined in some detail the various theoretical approaches to HRM in Germany our discussion now turns to consider HRM in practice. The development of HRM as practised in Germany can be described as a series of steps in which the objectives of HRM have changed. HRM has moved from an administrative orientation towards a participative employee orientation (Wunderer, 1990; Scholz, 1993). Table 5.2 shows that in the 1950s personnel administration was of central importance. Personnel issues came to the fore in the 1960s when a certain degree of professionalization and specialization in personnel affairs developed. During this period the formalization of the

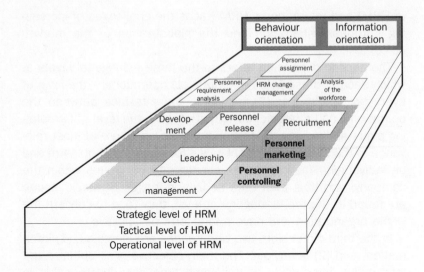

Figure 5.2 Three-dimensional HRM

organizational structure was regarded as an important precondition for the development of a personnel planning system. In the 1970s, under the influence of 'humanization of working life-programmes' leadership issues became important. In the 1980s the idea of strategic HRM was developed. Future issues can only be guessed at, but it seems likely that the devolution of responsibility for HRM to line management will become increasingly important. This is based on the view that personnel issues are too important to be the exclusive preserve of a specialist department; they are of importance to all managers.

Some examples of the contemporary practice of HRM in German organizations are discussed below in order to show how these companies connect traditional ideas with the theoretical approaches outlined above in order to meet the challenges of today.

The Volkswagen model

In recent years the Volkswagen group (VW) has been faced with a very difficult economic situation with the consequence that it has had to take the unprecedented step of reducing the workforce. After years of success, the worldwide recession of the early 1990s led to a major decrease in the volume of sales with the consequence that car production had to be reduced. As a result, fewer workers were needed. In order to avoid dismissing any employees VW invented the idea of the 'four-day week'. The works' council agreed to a reduction of the working week to 28.8 hours for the whole workforce (Hartz, 1995, p. 52). This has been connected with the reduction in wage levels, though monthly incomes remain unchanged because the wage cuts are realized by cancelling or reducing annual bonuses. In return VW promised not to make any of its 30,000 employees redundant. While the scheme experienced some initial difficulties it is now generally viewed as a success since levels of worker motivation appear not to have declined noticeably.

The reduction in the working week only produced about two-thirds of the required labour savings. Therefore, VW developed a number of additional schemes in order to obtain the needed savings such as the 'courier model' (young workers after apprenticeship start with shorter working hours and then gradually work longer hours) and 'leisure in blocks' (three or more months off work for employees to pursue individual development and training).

A more holistic approach towards strategic personnel development can be found in the notion of the 'M4–employee' (Hartz, 1994, pp. 113–27). This approach attempts to develop a more flexibly oriented type of employee. At the same time employees have a chance to influence their work environment as well as their personal development and VW is able to realize its lean structure and release the innovatory capacities of its employees. The central aim of this programme is to secure and improve VW's chances of future success.

In detail, the components of the 'M4–employee' are as follows:

- Employees should be encouraged to gain additional competencies to enable them to cope with new functions and skill demands in their complex working situation. Thus they should become *multifunctional*.
- Employees should become more *mobile* due to the growing importance of international assignments within the global VW group. The reasons for this include the individual transfer of experience, the growing importance of foreign markets and the irregularity of labour supply.

Table 5.2 Steps in the development of HRM in practice

		Wunderer (1990, p. 21)	Scholz (1993, pp. 22–3)
Until about 1960	I. Bureaucratization		I. Personnel administration
	Central functions	Administration, execution of decisions in personnel affairs	Primary task: Personnel administration deals with the settlement of payment of wages and salaries and a rudimentary personnel assignment
	Responsibility	Head of staff	
	Philosophy	Mercantile care for personnel accounts	Secondary task: Controlling
From about 1960 on	II. Institutionalization		II. Organization of labour
	Central functions	Professionalization, centralization, specialization	Primary task: The personnel function is organized bureaucratically: co-ordination through organizational charts and highly structured controlling reports, first approaches to personnel development, personnel administration
	Responsibility	Personnel head in large and partly in middle sized companies	
	Philosophy	Adaptation of personnel to organizational demands	Secondary task: Industrial law
From about 1970 on	III. Humanization		III. Leadership
	Central functions	Humanization, participation, employee orientation, organization of work	Primary task: Leadership becomes one of the central orientations, focusing on development and attendance of employees and on industrial law
	Responsibility	Personnel staff, employee representation	
	Philosophy	Adaptation of organization to employees, efficiency	Secondary task: Controlling, administration

From about 1980 on	IV. Economization		IV. Strategic HRM	
	Central functions	Flexibilization, rationalization, substitution of personnel by assets	Primary task	Finding a long-term conception for the personnel function by formulating a personnel strategy
	Responsibility	Personnel department, line management	Secondary task	Controlling, marketing, industrial law, development, leadership, administration
	Philosophy	Adaptation to changed environment, effectiveness		
From about 1990 on	V. Intrapreneuring		V. Interfunctional HRM	
	Central functions	Corporate co-knowing, co-thinking, co-acting and co-responsibility	Primary task	The personnel function is broadly spread over all corporate functions, so that each department head deals with certain HRM tasks and the personnel department concentrates on integrating the activities into the strategic frame
	Responsibility	Top management, line managers, employees		
	Philosophy	Employees are the most valuable and sensitive resource	Secondary task	Marketing, industrial law, controlling, administration

- Employees should be more participative (*mitgestaltend*) through involvement in such aspects as job design.
- The idea of humanization (*menschlich*) refers to the possibility of employees moving from being co-workers to being co-managers. This is combined with the chance for them to develop both in terms of their personality and career.

When examining this model in more detail the vision of a new kind of employee becomes clear: an employee with new responsibilities, but also with chances for individual development. However, there remains the continuing need to develop and improve the existing organizational system to create and support the emergence of these new employees. The crucial issue for the VW group is how to utilize these employees who have been, to a certain degree, 'saturated' by individual leadership and development schemes, for the long-term creativity, innovation and success of the organization.

The partnership model in Bertelsmann Corporation

The basic idea underpinning the notion of the 'partnership corporation' is the recognition that there are common interests between all of the organization's major stakeholders – shareholders, management and employees. It is when these different groups of stakeholders focus on their common interests that the continued prosperity of the company can be best guaranteed (Mohn, 1986). As a result of this the active co-operation between shareholders, the senior management team and employees is central to Bertelsmann's corporate culture.

The notion of partnership in Bertelsmann AG encompasses both the 'material' and 'immaterial' dimensions referred to earlier in this chapter. With regard to the 'material' dimension an employee share-option scheme was introduced in 1980 and in 1986 participation certificates were issued on the stock exchange. The 'immaterial' components of partnership are based on the notion of co-operative leadership. Employees in all areas and at all levels are integrated into the corporate decision process through communication systems, information, team briefing arrangements and the formulation of corporate objectives reflecting both co-operative and participative ideas. In addition, managerial responsibility is spread throughout all levels of the hierarchy (Bieker, 1992). Thus the interests of employees are recognized and supported through the decision-making system and at the same time employees are motivated by being accepted as partners in the decision-making system (and by participating in the company's financial success). Moreover, Bertelsmann tries to behave as a socially responsible organization through long-term job protection and subsidiary maintenance payments.

The main leadership instruments in Bertelsmann are:

- annual interviews with each employee in order to monitor individual career aspirations;
- annual meetings between supervisors and subordinates both to improve the vertical dialogue between employees at different levels in the hierarchy and for managers to receive feedback in the sense of upward appraisal (i.e. by subordinates);
- annual talks at a corporate level between the corporate works council and corporate management about general issues;
- a staff opinion survey every five years;
- a suggestion system;
- employee talks at the work place to facilitate communication and the flow of information between supervisors, employees and the works' council.

This example shows that at Bertelsmann AG strategic thinking in HRM has for a long time been understood to be a central factor affecting the future competitive success of the company.

The scenario analysis of BMW

In 1983, BMW, one of the leading German car manufacturers, initiated a 'value-oriented personnel policy'. The aim of this was to achieve a closer fit between corporate HRM and the values of employees in order to increase commitment and motivation. In a first phase, different values and other factors influencing HRM were identified. In a second phase beginning in 1990, BMW started to examine its HRM strategy by using the scenario-analysis technique. The following five steps were undertaken (see Scholz, 1993, pp. 119–27):

1. The main future factors influencing HRM were evaluated. A number of internal factors were identified including the production process, products, administrative processes and computer-aided technology. In terms of the external factors political change, societal change, labour costs, demographic trends and the education system were found to be of relevance.

2. For each of these factors a group of BMW employees developed a separate scenario.
3. These separate scenarios were integrated into two scenarios for the year 2000: (a) the 'probable' scenario; (b) the 'contingency' scenario.
4. On the basis of the probable scenario six key issues were identified as critical to the development of the HRM strategy up until the year 2000.
5. In a final step these key issues were specified in order to support the execution of the main goals and objectives of the organization.

The six key issues emanating from the last point were the following:

1. The qualified employee will become a self-confident entrepreneur of his own labour potential.
2. The key to efficiency and productivity lies in developing a corporate and leadership culture.
3. Qualifications will become the key factor relevant to success for both the employees and the company.
4. The time for revolutionary changes in production is over. In the future, evolutionary developments in the structuring of labour and the organization will occur.
5. Older employees will become a central challenge for HRM activities and policies.
6. The attractiveness of BMW as an employer depends more and more on its role as leader in the field of ecologically-oriented innovation in the car industry.

By using the results from the scenario-analysis HRM concepts and policies can then be evaluated in terms of their relevance to organizational objectives and those issues essential to a strategic and long-term personnel policy become clear.

Empirical Findings for 'Excellent Companies'

In the discussion that follows we report on research conducted by the author (for detailed results see Scholz, 1994b) to discover on

HRM excellence in German companies. The German business journal *Manager Magazin* ran a competition to find out which companies in Germany had the most professional and innovative approach to HRM. In the discussion which follows we report on research conducted by the author to discover which German companies had the most progressive HRM practices. This is based on a detailed analysis of HRM in fifty-three German companies.

In order to obtain a ranking of the companies with respect to their HRM activities, the PRISMA score (named after the research group which conducted this study) was developed. Each company which participated in the research was given a score between 0 and 100 for ten HRM practices (see table 5.3). These were then summed and an aggregate score was given for each company ranging between 0 and 1000. The scores were derived by comparing the HRM practices of the fifty-three companies that participated in the research. The company that was considered to have the best HRM practice with respect to recruitment, for example, established the upper limit (100). In contrast the company considered to have the worst practice with regard to recruitment set the lower limit (0). The PRISMA score is therefore a dynamic scoring system. Each new entry in the data base may move the benchmarks up, making it more difficult to reach high values. Thus a company which set the top score may have its score reduced as the HRM practices of other companies are included.

Table 5.3 shows PRISMA scores for the industries which were the focus of the research. This shows that the automobile industry has the highest PRISMA score. In this respect it sets the standards for HRM. In most of the ten HRM fields it is very close to the maximum score of 100 points. It is likely that strong international competition has forced this industry to improve its HRM practices. The management consultancy and computer industries rank second and third. The engineering and electronics industries have the lowest PRISMA scores indicating that HRM is least developed in these industries.

The table also shows that smaller companies score better than their larger counterparts. Yet it is commonly assumed that the larger the company the better its HRM practices. This study contradicts this commonly held assumption. These results perhaps suggest that HRM practices may be viewed as a key source of competitive advantage by smaller companies. Furthermore, this study may show that smaller companies are more innovative in

Table 5.3 The PRISMA scores for a sample of German companies in selected industries

	Sum score	Analysis of work force	Require-ment analysis	Recruit-ment	Develop-ment	Displace-ment	Assign-ment	Leader-ship	Cost manage-ment	Informa-tion manage-ment	Other HR functions
All	534	53	43	50	59	58	49	44	70	65	42
Car industry	741	70	88	72	85	77	67	54	81	68	60
Consultants	623	72	37	72	66	67	70	47	71	60	60
EDP industry	622	60	39	68	70	63	57	66	70	72	57
Metal working industry	550	51	57	35	54	77	65	21	73	77	39
Other services	533	27	27	58	64	47	50	45	70	62	48
Others	499	40	40	51	57	46	44	44	69	56	42
Banks, insurances	488	45	45	43	50	52	47	43	64	67	28
Engineering industrial	483	40	40	43	51	58	36	44	73	61	35
Electrotechnical industry	470	46	46	28	59	64	35	34	71	62	32
Small companies	567	61	28	64	66	54	55	51	69	59	59
Medium sized companies	451	46	42	30	47	57	38	37	70	59	25
Large companies	550	50	56	49	62	60	51	42	70	72	37

their HRM practices than larger firms. Thus, it may be amongst these small firms that HRM is at its most advanced.

The table also shows that the most developed areas of HRM in this sample of German companies were cost management, HR information management, development and displacement. In contrast leadership and requirement analysis have the lowest scores. Further analysis of the data suggests that four factors underpin whether an organization has a highly developed approach to HRM (shown by a high PRISMA score). These are:

1. The company sees itself as a global player with fast product changes in an environment in which technology is changing rapidly.
2. The top HR managers do not undertake additional tasks such as controlling, financing or accounting. This means that they do not have additional responsibilities.
3. The HR function places considerable emphasis on the development of a corporate culture.
4. The HR managers and their teams are well-qualified in such areas as organizational development, leadership and strategic HRM.

The study also sought to determine those factors which were at the top of HRM agenda for the sample of companies. What aspects of HRM were these organizations prioritizing? Figure 5.3 shows that the main areas of HRM which these companies believed were important included motivating employees, seeking quality employees, developing a corporate culture and image and changing employees' values. This does not imply that these companies were having problems motivating staff, for example, but that they considered it a priority when it came to devoting time and resources to HR activities.

In developing a more strategic approach to HRM, companies have to make use of HR planning techniques. There are a great variety of planning techniques which have been known and used for some time (Scholz, 1982). Figure 5.4 shows those HR planning techniques used by the sample of companies. This demonstrates that a large number of techniques exist such as scenario analysis, trends analysis, HR portfolio planning, simulation models and so on. This plethora of HR planning techniques may indicate the increasing importance of a strategic approach to HRM. Indeed, the survey results indicate that each company used an

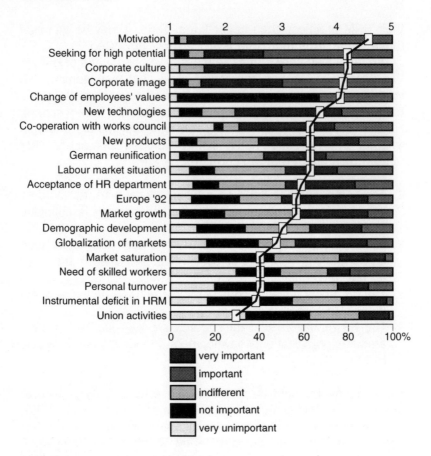

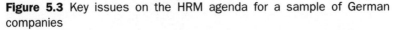

Figure 5.3 Key issues on the HRM agenda for a sample of German companies

average of eleven techniques and that almost all companies use at least three of the techniques listed in the table.

The study also reveals that German companies use a wide variety of HRM programmes (see table 5.4). This may be a result of the co-determination law and other strict laws, for instance those dealing with working hours, which require the adoption of certain HR practices, which are discussed with and monitored by the works' councils. This puts greater pressure on these companies to introduce certain programmes. At the top of the list in table 5.4 are programmes for part-time work, seminars, flexible work hours and exit interviews. Each of these programmes either promotes

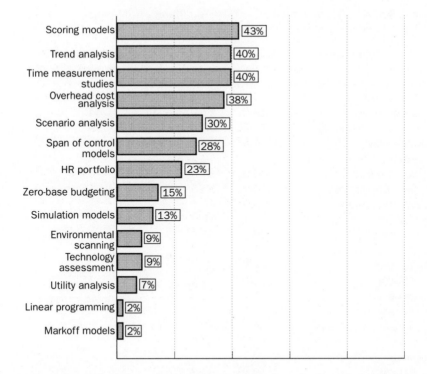

Figure 5.4 The range and frequency of use of different HR planning techniques by a sample of German companies

or deals with the effects of measures for adjusting current patterns of work. The table shows that these particular programmes often impact on a large proportion of the workforce. In contrast, sabbaticals and dual-career-systems (job sharing) for couples are not common and seem to effect only a few employees.

In summary, this research suggests the following:

1. These companies are tending to stress the soft, people-related issues such as the motivation of employees, the development of a corporate culture, and corporate image as their key priorities. These issues will become increasingly important sources of competitive success in the future. It may be that by putting these aspects at the top of their list of priorities these German companies may have obtained a head start in the race for global competitiveness, and equally important, in the race for competitiveness in a more united and more integrated Europe.

Table 5.4 The range and frequency of use of different HRM programmes by a sample of German companies

HRM programmes	Yes (%)	No (%)	Percentage of employees concerned (%)
Part-time work	84.9	13.2	15
In-house seminars	83.0	17.0	44
Flexible working hours	73.6	26.4	39
Exit interview	69.8	30.2	40
Job rotation	69.8	30.2	15
Limited contracts	66.0	34.0	6
Trainee programmes	64.2	35.8	1
Flexible retirement	50.9	49.1	16
Computer-based training	49.1	50.9	8
Management games	49.1	50.9	< 1
Individual guidance system	45.3	54.7	9
Quality circles	41.5	58.5	7
Job sharing	39.6	60.4	< 1
Coaching	37.7	62.3	10
Earlier retirement	37.7	62.3	3
Outplacement advisory	34.0	66.0	3
Lernstatt (self-structured learning)	17.0	83.0	< 1
Sabbatical	13.2	86.8	< 1
Dual-career systems for couples	7.5	92.5	< 1

2. These companies use an impressive range of HR planning techniques. These are usually integrated into the decision making structure in accordance with the regulations covering co-determination. This may mean a direct input from the works council and employee representatives into the development of an HR strategy resulting in greater acceptance of the policy outcomes by employees.

Current Challenges and Trends for Corporate HRM

Finally in this chapter we examine a number of challenges arising from the internal environment of companies and the external environment to the future of HRM. It is important to note that HRM in Germany is regarded as one of the mainstays of national competitive advantage. In this context, it is not important whether academic theory reflects practice or whether practice is initiated by academic theory. Both are needed to complement each other. Thus, the challenges to HRM emanating from both the external environment and from within the organization are highlighted below.

Challenges emanating from the external environment

The following environmental challenges are considered to be important for the future development of HRM in Germany:

- There are important political changes resulting from the ongoing process of European integration (see Scholz, 1994a) and especially with respect to developments in Eastern Europe. New markets are growing which provide huge potential for sales. In terms of German national politics there are the continuing difficulties associated with the difficult task of reunification. Success in working life will be one of the major determinants for the success of the gradual 'growing together' of the formerly divided Germany. In addition, the general orientation towards ecological issues will continue. This is likely to influence future legislation affecting all areas of production.
- As for societal change, attitudes continue to change. People are tending to emphasize the importance of ecological and ethical values. They are planning their lives increasingly around their individual interests. This results in growing demands for flexible work and working conditions. Thus the employees of the future will have much clearer ideas of what they expect and want and will be more critical of what they receive.
- As the average age of the German workforce increases, it will be necessary to improve the recruitment and marketing functions of the organization in order to ensure that the workforce continues to meet the strategic needs of the organization. These demographic trends are widely expected to increase the competition for skilled workers. This is likely to worsen as the economic situation in key export markets improves.

- The high costs of wages and salaries in Germany and new legislation covering such areas as health and safety will continue to
drive up the costs of employee benefits and thus necessitate
labour cost reductions. Pay increases for most employees will
continue to be lower than in recent years because of modest
inflation and difficult business conditions. Viable pay-for-
performance programmes coupled with lower employee
expectations are one of the possible solutions to these circumstances.
- Trades unions – many of them facing declining memberships –
will be looking to increase their memberships. They will try to
increase their level of influence on employers directly (i.e.
works' councils) and through the legislative process.

Challenges emanating from within the organization

The relevant factors arising from within the organization are summarized below:

- It is becoming more and more common to view personnel as a
strategic resource. Indeed, HRM itself is increasingly becoming
a top management priority. However, the strategic relevance of
HRM can only be demonstrated if its contribution to corporate
value added is proven.
- The manager's role will change significantly as a consequence
of the introduction of various employee participation programmes. It is likely that responsibility for HR issues will
increasingly shift from the personnel function to line management. As a consequence, HR managers will concentrate on the
co-ordinating and integrating tasks while line management will
focus on the operational and tactic
- Technological and social changes will encourage a greater level
of employee involvement. This will result in a more self-directed
and committed workforce better able to achieve gains in productivity.
- Cultural and communication factors can be expected to
become more and more important for HRM. (1) The development and maintenance of strong corporate cultures will
become a major priority for the HR function; (2) the establishment of a constructive relationship between the company and
its employees via works' councils and union representatives

will continue to be important; (3) as the attitudes of employees change and the knowledge of experts increases, new working forms based on communication and co-operation will become more important.

Conclusion

This chapter has sought convey the nature of HRM in Germany. It has demonstrated that HRM has a long academic and practical tradition. HRM has not arrived pre-formed but rather developed out of, and fused together, a number of previously independent strands in the personnel management literature. It has come to represent a distinctive approach to employee relations which emphasizes the value and importance of human resources to competitive advantage and seeks to integrate HR strategies with corporate strategies and integrate the HR policies themselves so that they are mutually reinforcing.

The growing interest in HRM has occurred at a time when Germany has been undergoing fundamental change. German organizations have had to respond to increased levels of competition in the European marketplace, a recession and the reunification of the two Germanies. This combination of events has perhaps been unprecedented. In order to compete German firms have been putting considerable emphasis on ascertaining and then supporting the contribution of employees to the strategic objectives of the organization. This is in part driven by the high employment costs in Germany. Although firms are introducing new employment practices, we examined those in Volkswagen, Bertelsmann and BMW, these are being implemented within a context of co-determination, partnership, strong employee representation both at the central and local level and centralized collective bargaining procedures. Therefore, the outcomes are to a large extent consonant with this institutional context. For example, Volkswagen radically restructured its operations in the early 1990s without making a single employee redundant. Bertelsmann and BMW both sought to increase employee participation.

The future development of HRM in Germany will be determined by a variety of factors emanating from the external environment and within the firm. Changes in the expectations of employees, the institutional environment (via legislation), the role of management, etc. will all influence the future character of HRM. Thus

HRM is not a static concept in Germany but one which is constantly evolving.

References

Ackermann, K.-F. (1986), 'A contingency model of HRM-strategy: empirical research findings reconsidered'. *Management Forum*, **6**, pp. 65–117.

Ackermann, K.-F. (1987), 'Konzpetionen des Strategischen Personalmanagements für die Unternehmenspraxis'. In H. Glaubrecht and K. Wagner (eds), *Humanität in Personalpolitik und Personalführung. Beiträge zum 60.* Freiburg/Brsg: Geburtstag von Ernst Zander, pp. 39–68.

Berthel, J. (1991), *Personalmanagement. Grundzüge für Konzeptionen betrieblicher Personalarbeit.* Stuttgart: Poeschel.

Bieker, J. (1992), 'Managemententwicklung bei Bertelsmann'. In H.-C. Riekhof (ed.), *Strategien der Personalentwicklung* (3rd edn). Wiesbaden: Gabler.

Conrad, P. and Pieper, R. (1990), 'Human resource management in the Federal Republic of Germany'. In R. Pieper (ed.), *Human Resource Management: An International Comparison.* Berlin: Walter de Gruyter, pp. 109–39.

Domsch, M. (1980), *Systemgestützte Personalarbeit.* Wiesbaden: Gabler.

Drumm, H.-J. (1992), *Personalwirtschaftslehre* (2nd edn). Berlin: Springer.

Drumm, H.-J. (1993), 'Personalwirtschaft. Auf dem Weg zu einer theoretischempirischen Personalwirtschaftslehre?' In J. Hauschildt and O. Grün (eds), *Ergebnisse empirischer betriebswirtschaftlicher Forschung. Zu einer Realtheorie der Unternehmung.* Stuttgart: Schäffer-Poeschel, pp. 673–712.

Ende, W. (1982), *Theorien der Personalarbeit im Unternehmen.* Königstein/Ts.: Hanstein.

Fischer, G. (1935), *Betriebswirtschaftslehre. Eine Einführung.* Heidelberg: Quelle and Meyer.

Fischer, G. (1955), *Partnerschaft im Betrieb.* Heidelberg: Quelle and Meyer.

Fischer, G. (1962), *Politik der Betriebsführung.* Stuttgart: Poeschel.

Gaugler, E. (1983), 'Flexibilisierung der Arbeitszeit', *Zeitschrift für betriebswirtschaftliche Forschung,* **35**, pp. 858–72.

Gaugler, E. (1988), 'HR management: an international comparison', *Personnel,* **65**, pp. 24–30.

Gaugler, E. (1993), 'Personalwesen'. In W. Wittmann et al. (eds), *Handwörterbuch der Betriebswirtschaft* (5th edn). Stuttgart: Schäffer-Poeschel, pp. 3140–58.

Gaugler, E. Huber, H. and Rummel, C. (1974) *Betriebliche Personalplanung. Eine Literaturanalyse,* Göttingen: Schwartz.

Goossens, F. (1981), *Personalleiter-Handbuch. Kompendium des betrieblichen Personal- und Sozialwesens* (7th edn). Landsberg am Lech: Moderne Industrie.

Hartz, P. (1994), *Jeder Arbeitsplatz hat ein Gesicht. Die Volkswagen-Lösung.* Frankfurt: Campus.

Hartz, P. (1995), 'Kreative Wege zur Kostenentlastung und Beschäftigungs-sicherung'. In C. Scholz and M. Djarrahzadeh (eds), *Strategisches Personalmanagement. Konzeptionen und Realizationen.* Stuttgart: Schäffer-Poeschel, pp. 51–9.

Hasenack, W. (1961), 'Mensch im Betrieb. Inwieweit kann oder muß die Betriebswirtschaftslehre den Menschen in ihre Untersuchungen einbeziehen?', *Zeitschrift für Betriebswirtschaft,* **31**, pp. 577–96.

Hax, K. (1969), *Personalpolitik und Mitbestimmung.* Köln-Opladen: Westdeutscher Verlag.

Hentze, J. (1991a), *Personalwirtschaftslehre,* Band 1: *Grundlagen, Personalbedarfsermittlung, -beschaffung, -entwicklung, -bildung und -einsatz* (5th edn). Bern, Stuttgart: Haupt.

Hentze, J. (1991b), *Personalwirtschaftslehre, Band 2: Personalerhaltung und Leistungsstimulation, Personalfreistellung und Personalinformationswirtschaft* (5th edn). Bern, Stuttgart: Haupt.

Jacobi, O., Keller, B. and Muller-Jentsch, W. (1992), 'Germany: codetermining in the future'. In A. Ferner and R. Hyman (eds), *Industrial Relations in the New Europe.* Oxford: Blackwell, pp. 218–69.

Kosiol, E. (1959), *Gundlagen und Methoden der Organisationsforschung.* Berlin: Duncker and Humblot.

Krulis-Randa, J. S. (1985), 'Fundsätzliche Überlegungen zur strategischen Unternehmensführung', *Management Forum,* **5**, pp. 91–112.

Krulis-Randa, J. S. (1986), 'Strategie und Personalmanagement', *Management Forum,* 6, pp. 3–12.

Krulis-Randa, J. S. (1988), 'Personalführung und -entwicklung im veränderten gesellschaftlichen Umfeld', *Schweizerische Zeitschrift für Volkswirtschaft und Statistik,* **124**, pp. 349–63.

Krulis-Randa, J. S., Staffelbach, B. and Wehrli, H.P. (1993), *Führen von Organisationen. Konzpete und praktische Beispiele aus privaten und öffentlichen Unternehmen.* Bern, Stuttgart, Vienna: Haupt.

Lane, C. (1992), 'European business systems: Britain and Germany compared'. In R. White (ed.), *European Business Systems: Firms and Markets in their National Contexts.* London: Sage, pp. 64–97.

Lawrence, P. (1993), 'Human resource management in Germany'. In S. Tyson, P. Lawrence, P. Poirson, L. Manzolini and C. Soler-Vicente (eds), *Human Resource Management in Europe: Strategic Issues and Cases.* London: Kogan Page, pp. 25–41.

Lecher, W. and Neumann, R. (1991), 'Zur aktuellen Lage der Gewerkschaften'. In W. Däubler and W. Lecher (eds), *Die Gewerkschaften in den 12 EG-Ländern.* Köln: Bund, pp. 15–97.

Marr, R. (1987) (ed.), *Arbeitszeitmanagement. Grundlagen und Perspektiven der Gestaltung flexibler Arbeitszeitsysteme.* Berlin: Erich Schmidt.

Marx, A. (1963), *Die Personalplanung der modernen Wettbewerbswirtschaft.* Baden-Baden: Verlag für Unternehmensführung.

Mohn, R. (1986), *Erfolg durch Partnerschaft. Eine Unternehmensstrategie für den Menschen.* Berlin: Siedler.

Oechsler, W.A. (1994), *Personal und Arbeit. Einführung in die Personalwirtschaft unter Einbeziehung des Arbeitsrechts* (5th edn). Munich, Vienna: Oldenbourg.

Potthoff, E. (1974), *Betriebsliches Personalwesen.* Berlin: Walter de Gruyter.

Potthoff, E. and Trescher, K. (1986), *Controlling in der Personalwirtschaft.* Berlin: Walter de Gruyter.

Reber, G. (1987), 'Führungsforschung, Inhalte und Methoden'. In A. Kieser, G. Reber and R. Wunderer (eds), *Handwörterbuch der Führung.* Stuttgart: Poeschel, pp. 397–411.

Röthig, P. (1986), 'Zum Entwicklungsstand der betriebswirtschaftlichen Personalplanung', *Die Betriebswirtschaft,* **46**, pp. 203–23.

Rühli, E. and Wehrli, H.P. (1986), 'Strategisches Management und Personalmanagement', *Management Forum,* **6**, pp. 35–46.

Scholz, C. (1982), 'Zur Konzeption einer strategischen Personalplanung', *Zeitschrift für betriebswirtschaftliche Forschung,* **34**, pp. 979–94.

Scholz, C. (1993), *Personalmanagement. Informationsorientierte und verhaltenstheoretische Grundlagen* (3rd edn). Munich: Vahlen.

Scholz, C. (1994a), 'Strategisches Euro-Management'. In C. Scholz and J. Zentes (eds), *Strategisches Euro-Management.* Stuttgart: Schäffer-Poeschel, pp. 31–55.

Scholz, C. (1994b) *Human Resource Management in Germnay.* Working Paper No. 33, Lehrstühl für Betriebswirtschaftlehre, Insb. Organisation Personal- und Informationsmanagement, University of Saarland, Saarbrücken.

Scholz, C. (1995), 'Strategisches Personalmangement als Konzept zwischen Fata Morgana und aufkommender Morgenröte (Überblick)'. In C. Scholz and M. Djarrahzadeh (eds), *Strategisches Personalmanagement. Konzeptionen und Realisationen.* Stuttgart: Schäffer-Poeschel, pp. 3–18.

Scholz, C. and Baumann, H. (1989), *Die Verbreitung des Personal Computers in der Personalabteilung. Eine empirische Bestandsaufnahme.* Munich: Hampp.

Staehle, W. (1991), *Management. Eine verhaltenswissenschaftliche Perspektive* (6th edn). Munich: Vahlen.

Staehle, W. H. and Karg, P. W. (1981), 'Anmerkungen zu Entwicklung und Stand der deutschen Personalwirtschaftslehre', *Die Betriebswirtschaft,* **41**, pp. 83–90.

Staffelbach, B. (1986), *Strategisches Personalmanagement.* Bern, Stuttgart: Haupt.

Staffelbach, B. (1988), 'Skizzen strategischer Personalpolitik'. In C. Lattmann (ed.), *Personal-Management und Strategische Unternehmensführung.* Heidelberg: Physica, pp. 47–63.

Von Eckardstein, D. and Schnellinger, F. (1978), *Betriebliche Personalpolitik* (3rd edn). Munich: Vahlen.

Von Nell-Breuning, O. (1950), 'Der Mensch im Betrieb', *Zeitschrift für Betriebswirtschaft,* **20**, pp. 257–66.

Wächter, H. (1992), 'Vom Personalwesen zum Strategic Human Resource Management. Ein Zustandsbericht anhand der neueren Literatur'. In W. H. Staehle and P. Conrad (eds), *Managementforschung 2*. Berlin: Walter de Gruyter, pp. 313–40.

Warner, M. and Campbell, A. (1993), 'German management'. In D. J. Hickson (ed.), *Management in Western Europe*. Berlin: Walter de Gruyter, pp. 89–108.

Weber, W. (1985), *Betriebliche Weiterbildung. Empirische analyse betrieblicher und individueller Entscheidungen über Weiterbildung*. Stuttgart: Poeschel.

Witte, E. (1972), *Das Informationsverhalten in Entscheidungsprozessen*. Tübingen: J.C.B. Mohr.

Wunderer, R. (1990), 'Szenario. Personalmanagement der 90er Jahre', *Personalwirtschaft Sonderheft DDR*, pp. 18–21.

Wunderer, R. and Kuhn, T. (1993), *Unternehmerisches Personalmanagement. Konzepte, Prognosen und Strategien für das Jahr 2000*. Frankfurt: Campus.

6 The Dutch Business System and Human Resource Management

MARIËLLE HEIJLTJES,

ARJEN VAN WITTELOOSTUIJN,

SEBASTIAAN VAN DIEPEN

Introduction

In recent years the nature of the personnel function has been changing in the Netherlands. This is in part due to the decentralization and deregulation of the employee-relations system which has resulted in an increasing level of autonomy for employers over the employee management practices and systems in their own organizations. In addition, the impact of technological developments and increasing international competition have changed the principles upon which the workforce was previously controlled and managed. To deal with the aforementioned changes, and inspired by the researches and writings of distinguished management scholars, human resource management (HRM) is often sought as a part of the solution (Kluytmans, 1989; Samson and Brongers, 1993). Fundamental to HRM is the claim that the human resources of an organization are its most precious asset and that competitive advantage comes from making the most of the human potential within the organization. This should be developed and encouraged rather than constrained and stifled. The purpose of this chapter is to discuss and ascertain whether Dutch management commentators and practitioners have embraced something called 'HRM', and if so to identify its central features.

To achieve this the chapter begins by examining a number of features of the Dutch context which impact upon the employment relationship. These include the nature of the Dutch national culture, decision-making power within Dutch companies, the industrial-relations system and the nature of Dutch labour and product markets. The meaning of HRM is then considered within the Dutch context. Four features of HRM are identified. These are derived, in the main, from the Anglo-American literature. As a consequence their relevance to the Netherlands, given the previous discussion of the Dutch context, is considered. In the final section of the chapter we report the results of a study of seven Dutch food and drink companies and five Dutch chemical companies in order to determine whether there has been any noticeable shift towards HRM in these companies. This data is drawn from the Dutch part of the International Organizational Observatory (IOO) study.

The Dutch Context

National culture

National culture is an important context variable for management in general and HRM in particular. According to Laurent (1986), HRM is particularly sensitive to cultural diversity since it is designed by 'culture bearers in order to handle other cultural bearers' (p. 97). However, the concept of national culture has been a matter of controversy, even among anthropologists. It is one of those concepts which has as many definitions as users, with the consequence that a consensual definition has yet to emerge. Yet the concept of national culture only becomes useful when we have some idea of what it means. For the purposes of this discussion we use the definition proposed by the Dutch researcher Hofstede (1980, 1991). He defines national culture as 'the collective programming of the mind which distinguishes the members of one group or category of people from another' (1991, p. 5). This definition implies that culture is learned and derived from the societal setting. Since the societal setting within a nation is likely to be fairly homogeneous – due to that nation's education system, laws, religious affiliation, political system and so on – people in different nations are, by and large, programmed differently. Hofstede (1980), on the basis of a study of work-related attitudes within the American multinational corporation IBM in fifty-three countries, identified four basic dimensions of the differences between national cultures which he termed power distance, individualism versus collectivism, uncertainty avoidance and masculinity versus femininity. Although these are already specified in Chapter 1 we consider the nature of each of these cultural dimensions in a little more detail in order to determine the character of Dutch culture as identified by Hofstede:

1. The first dimension, power distance, refers to the extent to which it is expected and accepted that power is unequally distributed among people. In a high power distance culture inequality is accepted. In contrast, in a low power distance culture superiors and subordinates consider each other to be colleagues, both agreeing that inequality in society should be minimized. An example of how this is reflected in the functioning of organizations, is the degree to which authority stemming from position in a hierarchy is accepted without question. When the power distance is small, a superior is more likely to discuss a task before assigning it to a subordinate, while in a high power distance country it is more accepted that a superior simply orders that a specific task is to be performed.
2. The individualism dimension refers to the degree to which the culture encourages individual as oppozed to collectivist group concerns. In an individualistic society identity is based on the individual. The emphasis is on individual initiative and achievement and one is supposed to take care of oneself plus only one's immediate family. A collectivist culture is characterized by a tighter social framework, where people are members of extended families or clans which protect them in exchange for loyalty. The emphasis is on belonging and the aim is to be a good member – whereas in the individualistic culture the ideal is to be a good leader. An example of what this means for organizations is the design of the reward system. In a society that underscores the individual, rewards can be based on personal achievement. In a country where collectivism prevails, rewards are more likely to be related to the accomplishments of the group, occasionally to such an extent that individual performance appraisal is regarded negatively.
3. The third dimension is the degree to which the culture copes with novelty and encourages risk taking. In a society where uncertainty avoidance is strong, people feel threatened by uncertain situations, and high anxiety and stress are experienced. In these societies people feel most comfortable in

work situations that are well structured and minimize uncertainty. In societies where uncertainty avoidance is weak, the uncertainty inherent in life is more easily accepted – and each day is taken as it comes – which means that less stress is experienced. In strong uncertainty avoidance cultures members agree that rules should not be broken and look forward to staying with the firm until they retire.

4. The fourth, and final, dimension – masculinity versus femininity – describes the degree to which values associated with masculine and feminine gender roles are dominant within a particular culture. In masculine societies masculine values – such as assertiveness, toughness and competition – dominate. In feminine societies values such as the quality of life, modesty and concern for relationship play a larger role. The degree of masculinity or femininity of a country is reflected in, for example, the way in which labour relations are organized. In a masculine country conflicts between trades unions and company management tend to be resolved by a good fight, while in feminine countries the tendency is towards negotiation (Hofstede, 1991, p. 92). A further example is the structure of the reward system of companies. In a masculine culture performance-based reward schemes will be present, even dominant, whereas in a feminine culture employees will tend to be rewarded on the basis of equality according to needs.

Table 6.1 shows the score on these four dimensions for the Netherlands compared with the USA and the UK. In addition, the table shows the ranking of each country in relation to the fifty-three nations studied by Hofstede. The table reveals that the scores for the Netherlands, the USA and the UK on three of the dimensions are similar. All three countries are characterized by low power distance, high individualism and weak uncertainty avoidance. The only dimension on which the Netherlands differs from the USA and the UK – the latter two having similar scores on this dimension – is masculinity versus femininity. In comparison to the Netherlands, the USA and the UK are masculine societies. Indeed, the Netherlands is one of the most feminine countries in Hofstede's sample.

In summary, Hofstede classifies the Dutch culture as reflecting individualism, 'femininity', egalitarianism (low power distance) and relatively weak uncertainty avoidance. These characteristics

Table 6.1 Scores and rankings on Hofstede's four culture dimensions for the USA, UK and the Netherlands

Hofstede's dimensions of culture	USA Score	Rank n = 53	UK Score	Rank n = 53	The Netherlands Score	Rank n = 53
Power distance	40	38	35	42/44	38	40
Individualism versus collectivism	91	1	89	3	80	4/5
Masculinity versus feminity	62	15	66	9/10	14	51
Uncertainty avoidance	46	43	35	47/48	63	35

Source: Based on Hofstede (1980)

of the Dutch culture are reflected in the Dutch business system and the industrial relations system which are discussed below.

Decision-making power within Dutch companies

The business system is the social-institutional environment within which organizations are embedded. White (1992) suggested that 'business systems are particular arrangements of hierarchy-market relations which become institutionalized and relatively successful in particular contexts' (p. 6). The fact that the Netherlands, according to Hofstede, is a highly egalitarian and feminine culture is reflected in the way decision-making power within Dutch companies is organized. There is a strong emphasis on consensus, negotiation and consultation between employees, top management and shareholders/owners, which is institutionalized by a number of laws.

The Works' Council The first of these interest groups – employees – is represented through the works' council (*Ondernemingsraad*). The precise competencies and duties of the works' council are specified in the Work's Councils Act (*Wet op de Ondernemingsraden*, 1979). Every organization in the Netherlands with more than 100 employees is obliged by law to install a works' council. Smaller organizations with more than thirty-five employees also have works' councils but their authority is more restricted. The works' council is an independent body within the company. The members of the works' council – all non-management employees – are elected by the entire workforce and cannot be dismissed while they are a member of the works' council. The works' council meets six times a year and has the legal right to be consulted on all major company decisions, such as corporate restructuring, mergers and acquisitions and other major investments. After a reasonable period allowing for consultation, the works' council issues its advice on the matter under consideration to management. If its advice is ignored, management is required to explain why they disagree with the view of the works' council. If the works' council still does not agree, management is unable to make a final decision on the matter for a month thus permitting time for further consultation. There are, however, a number of decision-making areas where management needs the explicit consent of the works' council, such as personnel policy and fringe benefits.

Top management The second interest group, top management, in large companies is divided into two different bodies. As in Germany large Dutch public companies have a two-tier board structure. According to the Structure of Corporations Act (1971) large companies are defined as firms with a turnover of over 225 million guilders, more than 100 employees and a works' council. The higher-level board is termed the *Raad van Commissarissen* (supervisory board) while the second board is termed the *Raad van Bestuur* (executive board). Although both of these boards are concerned with the general interests of the company and have to consider the interests of all the stakeholders – banks, management, employees, suppliers and customers – they have different functions. The members of the executive board are appointed by the supervisory board and can be removed from office by the same board, although this is an extreme measure. The executive board is concerned with the day-to-day management of the company. This board has to obtain consent from the supervisory board on matters affecting the long-term policy of the company, such as mergers and acquisitions. In general, the control of the executive board by the supervisory board is minimal with the latter only intervening in non-routine circumstances such as a collapse in the share price, a crisis of confidence in the senior management or a take-over bid. As Lawrence notes (1986, quoted in Iterson and Olie, 1992, p. 101) the supervisory board is a 'prestige barometer' often comprised of former politicians, former senior company executives and leading dignitaries. A vacancy on the supervisory board is filled by co-opting – the members of the board elect new members. Their choice, however, is subject to the consent of the works' council and the general assembly of shareholders (*Algemene Vergadering van Aandeelhouders*). At this level interlocking directorships are common. According to van Dijk and Punch (1993) 'the Dutch business elite is frequently filled by lawyers from Leiden University, economists from Erasmus University Rotterdam, or engineers from Delft. It is characteristically small, intimate, intertwined, and self-recruiting' (p. 177). They report that there is a clear concentration of power in the boardrooms of Dutch companies with eighteen businessmen holding 156 of the most senior posts in Dutch industry. This is also supported by a study by Stokman et al. (1985) which reported that two-thirds of the 1,200 cross-directorships in 250 large Dutch companies were accounted for by only sixty-eight individuals.

Shareholders The third interest group, the shareholders or owners of the organization, meets once a year at the general assembly of shareholders to evaluate the performance of the executive board. This assembly has ultimate authority over the composition of the supervisory and executive board. Thus, in managing a large corporation the executive board has to consult and cooperate on the one hand with the employees' representatives (the works' council) and on the other hand with the supervisory board on all major decisions. The outcomes of this careful balancing act are then evaluated by the shareholders once a year. It is important to note that the consultation structure described above also impacts on the management of smaller organizations, those with fewer than 100 employees. Although the authority of the works' council is less extensive and a supervisory board is absent, the influence of shareholders or owners is generally somewhat larger.

An important consequence of the structure of decision-making power described above on the Dutch approach to management is the emphasis on consensus. On the one hand, the manager's role is a problem-solving and task-oriented one (which tends to fit a masculine culture); yet, on the other hand, subordinates expect a manager to be considerate and to nurture group relations (which suits a feminine culture). The importance of this second aspect for employee relations and the associated Dutch tendency for modesty and avoidance of glamour and showiness is captured in the following Dutch saying: 'Act normally, that will be extraordinary enough' (*Doe maar gewoon, dan doe je al gek genoeg*). Indeed, according to Hampden-Turner and Trompenaars (1993, p. 270), in Dutch society 'no one is permitted to rise too high – no political party, no religion, no industry, and, certainly, no individual'. This emphasis on consensus is manifested in the structure of the reward system in Dutch companies. It was argued previously that in a feminine culture rewards tend to be distributed primarily on the basis of equality according to need. Evidence from our study of Dutch companies confirms this. When all categories of personnel are averaged, an individual bonus based on results was present in only 33 per cent of the companies in our sample. If the management level is excluded this percentage drops to 23 per cent.

Dutch industrial relations

The tendency towards consensus and stable relationships is also present in the Dutch industrial-relations system. Table 6.2 reveals that in 1991 the Netherlands lost fewer working days to industrial disputes than did the USA and the UK. In the European Union (EU) only Germany (excluding the former East Germany) and Luxemburg lose fewer working days to industrial disputes (CBS, 1994). This may arise from the Dutch tendency to make 'extensive efforts to negotiate among principled positions' (Hampden-Turner and Trompenaars, 1993, p. 283). These writers argue that the Dutch make strenuous efforts to listen to minority opinions in the belief that disharmony impacts upon an organization's ability to achieve its objectives and create wealth.

Trades unions in the Netherlands are industrial unions, as opposed to being craft, general or enterprise unions. That is to say that membership of these unions is open to anyone in the given industry. However, according to Sorge (1992) the ideological segmentation within the Dutch trades union movement is particularly high. There is a general union movement and a Protestant one. This reflects the typically Dutch phenomenon of *verzuiling* (literally, pillarization). However, since the 1970s a number of mergers between unions have taken place which have reduced

Table 6.2 The number of working days lost through industrial disputes in the USA, UK and the Netherlands in 1991

Countries	Working days lost through disputes per 1000 employees
USA	40
UK	34
The Netherlands	17

some of the ideological segmentation and so led to a process of *ontzuiling* (de-pillarization). In 1976 the Roman Catholic union movement joined the general union confederation (Federatie Nederlandse Vakverenigingen or FNV). There are nineteen unions affiliated to the FNV covering 60 per cent of the unionized workforce, of which the largest is ABVA/KABO with approximately 300,000 members. The second largest grouping of unions is the CNV (Christelijk Nationaal Vakverbond), with 18 per cent of the unionized workforce in 1993 and incorporating twelve unions. Although originally a Protestant organization the Protestant Public Servants Union merged with the Catholic Civil Servants Union to form the Algemeen Christelijke Federatie van Overheidspersoneel (CFO) which has joined the CNV. This is a further example of depillarization. Union membership in the Netherlands is not high in an international context, having declined from 41 per cent in 1977 to 25 per cent in 1993 (CBS, 1994).

Employers in the Netherlands are represented by a number of employers' associations. The largest associations are the VNO (Verbond van Nederlandse Ondernemingen – Federation of Dutch Enterprises) and the NCW (Nederlands Christelijk Werkgeversverbond – Christian Employers' Federation). Small and medium-sized firms have their own employers' associations, the largest one being the KNOV (Koninklijk Nederlands Ondernemers Verbond). These employers' associations can be viewed as umbrella organizations for a number of strong industry associations such as banking, construction, engineering and printing. Some of these industry associations are members of both the VNO and NCW, for example the Engineering Federation (FME) and the General Employers' Federation (AWV), which encompasses several industries and has most multinational corporations (such as AKZO, DSM and Shell) among its members. Philips is a member of the

FME and is represented on the executive councils of both the VNO and NCW.

The negotiations between this limited number of employers' associations and trades unions are centralized, with the government actively participating. Since Dutch trades unions have a tradition of 'broad unionism', the unions tend to focus on broader social and economic issues rather than simply the interests of their members. These broader issues are often part of the consultation process in which trades unions and employers' associations meet in two public institutions: the Labour Council (Stichting van de Arbeid) and the Social and Economic Council (SER: Sociaal-Economische Raad). These public bodies consist of employers, employees and government representatives who regularly meet to confer and to settle a large range of issues. Generally, these meetings establish the bargaining framework within which the two parties negotiate. Since the employers' associations and the trades unions operate in a broader context than just on behalf of the 'capitalists' and the 'workers', management and the unions are not necessarily adversaries in these negotiations but often co-operating partners. The legally prescribed collective bargaining process between trades unions and employers' associations usually results in (industry- or company-specific) collective labour agreements (CAO: *Collectieve ArbeidsOvereenkomst*). These agreements not only deal with wages but also with vocational training and early retirement procedures. These agreements function as minimum standards that apply to entire industries, and they are formally sanctioned by the Dutch Secretary of Social Affairs for all workers in an industry. They therefore establish a base upon which companies build their HRM policies. Approximately 750 different agreements were set in 1986, covering 84 per cent of the Dutch employees, of which 191 agreements were industry-wide while the remainder applied to single companies only (Albeda and Dercksen, 1989).

The Dutch labour market, education system and business structure

The Dutch labour market has a number of paradoxical features. This is clear from the following 1993 figures. The population of the Netherlands is currently 15.3 million. The size of the workforce is 7.2 million people, which represents 1.3 per cent of the world workforce. The unemployment rate in 1993 amounted to

7.7 per cent of the Dutch workforce. After the recession in the early 1980s (with an unemployment rate of 10.4 per cent at the low point of 1984) and the recovery at the beginning of the 1990s (unemployment fell to 6.6 per cent in 1991) the rate of unemployment has begun rising once more. In addition, the structural unemployment rate and the percentage of long-term unemployed in the workforce are both increasing (Kerckhoffs et al., 1994). For those that are employed 72 per cent of the working population work in the service sector, 26 per cent in the manufacturing sector and 2 per cent in agriculture and fisheries (CBS, 1994).

Dutch labour costs are above the average European level. In 1991 the average hourly wage in industry was 22.80 guilders, while total hourly wage costs amounted to 41.78 guilders (CBS, 1994). Of the total labour cost per company, 74 per cent is spent on gross wages, 14 per cent on social security and the remainder, 12 per cent, on fringe benefits and externally hired personnel (Coopers and Lybrand/Berenschot, 1994). The net income of the workers, however, is relatively low. This is partly due to the relatively extensive Dutch welfare system (including social security benefits). In 1992 around 35 per cent of the national income was devoted to the social security system.

The Dutch education system from which companies recruit new employees is very stratified. After completing primary school at the age of twelve the following choices of secondary school are available:

1. The lower vocation school (*Lager BeroepsOnderwijs* – LBO) mixes general education and basic education and training in vocational areas such as metal work and domestic work, and takes four years to complete.
2. Middle secondary education (*Middelbaar Algemeen Voorbereidend Onderwijs* – MAVO) offers general education for at least four years.
3. Higher secondary education (*Hoger Algemeen Voorbereidend Onderwijs* – HAVO) takes one year longer than MAVO.
4. The grammar school (*Voorbereidend Wetenschappelijk Onderwijs* – VWO) takes at least six years and provides access to a university education.

Unlike Germany, but like France, apprenticeships are for those who do not make it into 'proper' secondary and subsequently vocational or university education. In this sense the Dutch education system is concentrated on the period before an individual enters the workplace.

The contemporary structure of the Dutch business sector resembles the shape of an hour-glass (van Iterson and Olie, 1992, p. 98). Table 6.3 shows the size distribution (in terms of the number of firms per employment class) for a number of industry sectors in 1993. This 'waisted' structure is characterized by a large number of very small enterprises, such as small farms, breeding and greenhouse operations and a highly concentrated sector of large, multinational, companies, such as AKZO, DSM, Philips, Shell and Unilever (with the latter two being Anglo-Dutch enterprises). There are roughly 500,000 registered companies in the Netherlands of which half are one-person enterprises, and 90 per cent of the other half have fewer than ten employees (van Dijk and Punch, 1993). Thus the typical Dutch company is small and tends to be smaller than its counterparts in neighbouring countries such as Belgium and Germany. However, the 'big five' (the five multinationals referred to above) account for 55 per cent of all people employed by joint-stock companies in the Netherlands. These five companies also dominate the activities of the Amsterdam Stock exchange and control much of the country's R&D activities (van Iterson and Olie, 1992). Furthermore, although not shown in table 6.3, there is a skewed sectoral distribution in the Netherlands with a strong focus on agro-related, trade, service and chemical industries.

Future developments

Changes in industrial relations and HRM are occurring only gradually in the Netherlands. The Dutch labour market is generally viewed as extremely inert. However, it is now widely agreed that the trend toward further decentralization of collective agreements to the company level is structural. According to Visser (1989, 1992) the firm has been rehabilitated as the central theatre of labour relations, although the extent and effect of this trend towards greater decentralization differs between economic sectors. It is in those sectors which are subject to intense international ˙ competition – such as chemicals or consumer electronics – where the most advanced changes in employee relations have occurred and are continuing to occur. Indeed, it is in these sectors that the decentralization of labour relations is most

Table 6.3 Size distribution of organizations in selected Dutch industries, 1993

Industry	Number of employees							
	1–5	*5–10*	*10–20*	*20–50*	*50–100*	*100–200*	*200–500*	*500+*
Building & construction	12,2414	4,704	3,642	2,543	728	267	96	30
Trade, catering, and equipment	85,361	15,229	8,268	4,738	1,119	457	228	102
Transport and communication	6,648	2,134	1,717	1,335	415	161	69	41
Banking, insurance and professional services	31,638	4,851	2,778	1,740	616	297	193	117
Food and drink	2,605	1,279	688	460	192	125	106	37
Textile	349	124	108	121	49	36	18	4
Paper and pulp	51	27	35	45	37	30	34	9
Chemicals	181	64	72	92	64	55	48	32

advanced. Thus, it is the professional personnel managers and the works' council which play the dominant role in determining working conditions and personnel policy; not the employers' associations or trades unions. In these sectors companies will have greater flexibility to determine company-specific arrangements.

In sectors that operate within more stable markets and/or more domestically oriented markets – examples are building and construction and retailing – it is unlikely that the traditional labour relations system characterized by collective bargaining between the employers' associations and trades unions will change dramatically in the short term. Additionally, no change (such as decentralization of collective bargaining) is likely to occur in the collective and subsidized sectors where union membership is at its highest.

What does HRM Mean in a Dutch Context?

In the Anglo-American literature HRM cuts across a number of distinct academic disciplines and subject areas including economics, organizational behaviour, organizational psychology, industrial relations and the sociology of work and organizations (Storey, 1992). Similarly, the Dutch literature on HRM also has an interdisciplinary character. One consequence of this is that there is considerable argument and confusion surrounding the notion of HRM since academics approach the topic from different viewpoints. To convey the meaning of HRM in a Dutch context is therefore not an easy task. This problem is exacerbated by the uncertainty over the extent to which the concepts and practices advocated by HRM have been translated into management action. For example, one of the leading Dutch text books on the subject (Kluytmans, 1990) describes a growing trend away from the administration and control of employees towards an emphasis on their development linked to the achievement of organizational ends. Kluytmans writes that 'if one desires to attach the term human resource management to this trend one may. This, however, does not mean that the promising premises of this school are realized in practice' (1990, p. 38).

An analysis of the publications by some of the leading Dutch writers on HRM suggests that the current HRM agenda comprises the following elements (Kluytmans, 1989, 1990; Fisscher et al., 1992; Sorge, 1992).

1. The human resources of a firm are an important source of competitive advantage. The claim is that by making full use of its human resources a firm can gain competitive advantage. The HRM function should therefore seek to harness the full potential of the workforce in the pursuit of organizational goals and objectives.
2. HRM issues should be an integral part of the strategic planning process in such a way that the strategic goals of the organization and the human resource policies are mutually reinforcing. In this sense the HRM function and HRM issues have an important role in determining the strategic direction of the company rather than responding to a situation over which they have had little, or no, influence.
3. To facilitate the above the responsibility for many HRM issues and policies has to be decentralized to lower levels in the organization. If HRM is one, or for some *the*, major source of competitive advantage, it follows that it is too important to be left to a centralized, specialist function but should be a concern for all managers.
4. The different aspects of HRM – such as recruitment and selection, employee development and performance appraisal – should be integrated. Furthermore, they should be flexible and adaptable enough to take account of different strategies being pursued.

These themes in the Dutch literature have a high degree of overlap with the Anglo-American literature on HRM. For example, Beaumont (1992) on the basis of a detailed review of the American HRM literature points out that one of the leading themes is the link between business planning and competitive strategy and HRM planning. Similarly, in the UK Sisson (1990, p. 5) has identified the focus on internal (the alignment of HRM policies with one another) and external (the close linkage of HRM strategies with corporate strategy) integration and the increasing role of line management in personnel matters as two of the central features of HRM. Furthermore, Brewster and Larsen argue (1992) that the two core elements in the Anglo-American literature on HRM are integration and devolvement. By integration they mean the degree to which HRM issues are considered as part of the strategy formulation process, and by devolvement they mean the degree to which the responsibility for HRM practice is located with line managers. Both of these are key elements in the Dutch HRM literature.

Since the four components of the Dutch approach to HRM detailed above are, to a large extent, derived from the Anglo-American literature, they may clash with a number of aspects of the Dutch context elaborated earlier in the chapter. In particular, the second and fourth principles, which are most strongly associated with the work of Fombrun et al. (1984), are problematic. These writers propose a *human resource cycle* in which selection, appraisal, rewards and development are all viewed as mechanisms which can be moulded by managers in order to determine the performance of the individual. According to Storey (1992) this is a 'hard' model of HRM in that human resources are treated and managed like any other organizational resource. As a consequence there is little room in this model for aspects such as working conditions and other care or welfare activities (that is, 'soft' HRM issues) that are so important in a feminine culture nation such as the Netherlands (Kluytmans and Paauwe, 1991). Furthermore, the emphasis on *individual* performance implies competition between employees in order to achieve the best performance. Again this is at odds with the Dutch management culture since it implies that individuals have to strive to be the best. They must outshine their work colleagues. Yet if they do this they will stand out. (As we suggested earlier, the Dutch have a tendency to modesty and are therefore not predisposed towards any activity which makes them stand out).

The human resource cycle also suggests that employees are like any other organizational resource and so should be used as effectively and profitably (and sparingly) as possible. Hence, the needs and feelings of employees are subordinated to the competitive requirements of the company. This approach contrasts with that adopted by the Dutch industrial-relations system. During collective bargaining sessions the government, employers' associations and employee representatives actively consider their societal responsibilities in terms of reducing unemployment or the impact of industrial conflict on economic performance.

This discussion suggests that the Anglo-American concept of HRM cannot be transplanted to the Dutch context without adaptation. As a consequence, the likely impact of the features of the Dutch national culture, business system and industrial-relations system on the components of HRM will be discussed below.

In the Netherlands employee turnover rates are fairly low. Wolfs (1992), for example, reports that 72 per cent of the Dutch work-force has been with their present company for more than ten years. This low level of inter-company labour mobility is due to a number of factors that are rooted in the Dutch business and industrial-relations systems (King, 1994).

- Dutch workers tend to be very loyal to the companies they work for. The companies themselves are deterred from recruiting their employees from rivals by the existence of powerful employers' associations which disapprove of such practices.
- Strong regional identities with their associated religious affiliations tend to discourage people from moving between regions.
- Pension rights, which are highly valued, are not easily trans-ferred from one company to another. Since employees appar-ently do not frequently move between employers, recruitment and selection via the external labour market is not strongly emphasized. Large companies prefer to fill vacancies from the internal pool of candidates (IVA, 1988).

Performance appraisals are frequently conducted, mostly as a joint effort of line management and personnel staff. The use of performance appraisals does not, however, automatically imply that rewards are linked to an individual's performance. Rather, as was pointed out earlier, since wage levels tend to be set col-lectively, wage competition is relatively unknown or at least rare. In recent years, a number of larger companies have been forced to downsize and therefore make drastic cuts to their workforces. As a result, employee exit – especially 'outplacement' – has become a prevalent HRM activity. Where this used to be an activ-ity that was contracted out to specialized agencies, it now takes up a significant amount of time of the personnel officer's job. This relates to the Dutch emphasis on care for personnel – 'Out is out but let's do it properly'.

Employee development, by means either of vocational educa-tion or company training programmes, is an important HRM activ-ity. Dutch companies spend a total of 3 billion guilders – 1.7 per cent of the companies' direct labour costs – on this HRM activity (CBS, 1990). The larger companies (those with more than 500 employees) account for the largest share of the expenditure (2.2 billion guilders). In 1990 every other employee in companies of this size participated in some kind of training and development activity. The transport and communication industries have the highest expenditures per employee. Again, the state's role appears prominent since its expenditure on training per civil servant amounted to 4.5 per cent of total direct labour costs. However, since companies in the Netherlands feel that the Dutch vocational education system is inadequately matched to the demand side of the labour market, they frequently design their own in-house programmes directed towards company-specific knowledge and skills. These in-house programmes account for 26 per cent of participants in vocational education and training activities. The regular education system covers 43 per cent of this market, while private educational institutions take the remaining 31 per cent with seminars and training that seek to meet company demands (Thijssen, 1988). The Dutch system of industrial relations, however, complicates matters. Since employee development is often part of the collective labour agreements and companies of different size differ substantially in their preferences for labour qualifications, a conflict emerges. The employers' associations representing the large and small companies remain divided on this point. Because of these differences, decentralization – yet again – is widely being required.

In accordance with other countries, the Dutch personnel management function has undergone significant changes in recent years due to a number of developments in the strategic context of Dutch organizations. The emphasis is now on cost effectiveness, employee flexibility, employee commitment and quality rather than on the employee interests which were the traditional focus of personnel departments. While a 'hard' version of HRM with an emphasis on people as an economic resource is still not prevalent in this country, a 'softer' version with investment in human resources in terms of development has become widespread. The result is a diverging pattern within personnel management. On the one hand, there are companies that have adapted their personnel function to the changing contextual demands by rigorously reorganizing their personnel departments. In these cases personnel management has become re-oriented towards internal consistency, intense involvement in strategic decision-making and a focus on long-term developments. The highest-ranked personnel officer is often also a member of the executive board. On the other hand, there are companies in which the evolution of personnel management to HRM has yet to begin. Here, the use of personnel management instruments as key levers of human capital accruement has only recently started. Companies operating in industries where few company-specific skills and knowledge are required tend to belong to this latter category. This divergence also explains why some firms decentralize their HRM function while others operate in the opposite direction, stressing a centralized, company perspective on the human factor. In both cases, however, the involvement of employees' interests is ensured by the consultative structure in large Dutch organizations.

An Empirical Study of HRM in two Dutch Industries

As a result of the economic demography in the Netherlands the majority of employees work in small and medium-sized companies. However, the development of Dutch research on HRM is closely linked with a few large companies that dominate much of Dutch business life, since these are pre-eminently influenced by international competition and thus have gained considerable freedom in determining their personnel policies. At Hoogovens Steel, Philips Electronics, DAF Trucks and other large companies a number of initiatives have been undertaken in order to investigate the functioning of employees in their work environment. These have covered topics such as optimal recruiting, job analysis and shift work. Thus, Dutch HRM research began with company-sponsored investigations of their own staff.

The interest of the Dutch government in HRM issues can be illustrated with reference to the initiatives taken and funds allocated to several research programmes. One example of a government-sponsored research project is a comprehensive review of all HRM research being conducted in the Netherlands (see Maenhout and van Hoof, 1993). This study reported that the two dominant topics of Dutch HRM research were: (1) the internal labour market (not surprising given the lack of labour mobility between companies indicated earlier); and (2) the role of the HRM function in the organization (including the relationship between the HRM function and corporate strategy, the position of the HRM function in the organizational structure and so on).

HRM has become a popular research topic within the academic community. There are many different ways, however, in which researchers have attempted to capture the shift from 'traditional' personnel management to HRM in organizations (Guest, 1990; Storey, 1992). To explore the type of changes occurring in the Netherlands the authors investigated the employee-management policies and practices of twelve of the largest Dutch companies. The purpose of this research was to reveal: (1) how these organizations labelled their personnel function (Guest, 1987, 1990); (2) where the personnel department was positioned within the structure of the organization (Brewster and Larsen, 1992); and (3) whether personnel issues were considered part of the strategic planning process (Schuler, 1992).

The data for the study were collected through interviews with personnel directors, inspection of annual reports, recruitment brochures and other relevant internal company documents. The organizations were either in the chemical or food and drink industries. The choice of these two industries was not arbitrary since in the Netherlands there is a concentration of chemical, fibre, food and drink and similar processing industries. Thus most large Dutch companies are located somewhere between large-batch production and continuous-process production in terms of the technology scale put forward by Woodward (1965). Accordingly, most of the products made by these companies are either composite (consisting of many separate parts) and made in large numbers, or 'integral' (homogeneous fluid, gaseous, viscous or solid substances – Sorge, 1992). The sample of companies in our study is therefore indicative of the type of companies which form the industrial base of the Netherlands.

The food and drink industry

In the food and drink industry, seven companies were examined of which four were divisions or business units of larger corporations. Three organizations were 'stand alone' companies. A potential shift from traditional personnel management to HRM was examined using the three issues outlined above.

In respect of the first issue – how the organizations label their personnel department – only one of the companies, which had a Harvard alumnus as CEO, had retitled its personnel department as a human resource management department. Furthermore, this company was the only organization to make an explicit reference to the importance of its employees in its mission statement.

Although this expression of an HRM philosophy may indicate how the company treats and values employees it does not of course automatically imply that HRM policies, programmes and practices are being implemented (Schuler, 1992). No additional information was available, however, on whether an HRM strategy was actually being implemented.

The other six food and drink companies all had a personnel and organization department for administering employee-relations matters. In these companies no retitling of this department had taken place. Although the term HRM was nowhere explicitly mentioned in three of these six companies features of HRM could be detected. This brings us to the second issue: the position of the personnel department in the structure of the organization. In these three companies personnel policy was decentralized to the unit where production and marketing decisions were by and large made autonomously. This also indicates a relatively high level of devolvement in the sense that the personnel department delegates responsibility for employee relations matters to line management. This is illustrated by a remark in one of the companies' annual reports that, with respect to training and development, personnel specialists should act as brokers between employee(s) and management. In addition, in these three companies some indication of a strategy-personnel link was detected – the third issue mentioned above. Management development, training and development, individualizing of working conditions, and selection based on a 'company culture-personality' fit were all stressed. Furthermore, in two of these companies the personnel manager was a formal member of the management team.

Thus, for the four companies discussed above one could conclude that some features of a HRM approach to employee management were indeed present either in terms of an actual HRM department or in terms of a decentralized, strategically integrated personnel function. In the remaining three companies features of a HRM approach were less evident in terms of the characteristics just mentioned. Two of these three companies, however, were interviewed less than a year after a merger took place, suggesting that these organizations were still in a state of flux. Here the personnel department was not (yet) very decentralized. Moreover, in one of these two companies, the personnel department was shared by two divisions. In the other company a personnel department was present in the division which could only operate within the context of a centrally established personnel policy. Investments in management development and training and development, were considered necessary in both companies, but were not yet implemented.

The third company in which HRM did not seem to be present, was a relatively small independent company employing 160 people. It is an example of the many small firms that flourish in the Netherlands in which personnel management is less professionalized and occurs in the more co-operative and corporatist context that is in line with Dutch values (Sorge, 1992). For example, one way in which employers and employees communicated according to the study, is through the works' council, where all matters concerning employees are discussed. Because of the relatively small size, interaction and co-operation between line management and the personnel function can prevail in conjunction with a rather centralized personnel function.

On the basis of the previous discussion it could be concluded that these seven companies in the food and drink industry differ markedly in their degree of strategic integration and decentralization. A higher degree of strategic integration at the business unit or division level appears to be related with decentralization in three cases (and vice versa: a low degree of strategic integration is associated with centralization). As for the existence of HRM in the seven companies, a partial shift from traditional personnel management to HRM could be observed in four companies – although only one introduced the HRM label. This is not the case in the other three firms. These results are summarized in table 6.4.

The chemical industry

In the chemical industry, five companies were examined of which four were divisions or business units within a larger group. In terms of the first indicator of HRM – how the companies labelled their personnel function – none these of five chemical companies had retitled the personnel function: the traditional 'personnel and organization' label still prevailed. However, one of these companies made reference to the importance of HRM as a vital strategic function in its recruitment brochures. It explicitly recognized that people were the key to success since they provide the strategic resources of information, knowledge and creativity. However, this was not directly reflected in the organization of the personnel function at the business unit level. Although job rotation programmes, career development, training and the creation of an internal labour market were considered to be important, all personnel decisions were made at a division level leaving little discretion for the business unit managers. Thus, although production and marketing decisions were decentralized this was not the case for HRM issues. The latter were determined at the divisional level and then imposed on the business unit. So in terms of the second issue – the position of the personnel function in the organization – it can be concluded that no decentralization had taken place. There was one other company in which the personnel function was highly centralized. Personnel policy in this case was based on information provided by the business unit but determined at headquarters. The personnel function in the business unit merely executed the centrally established policy. In the remaining three companies the personnel function was decentralized to the division, business unit or plant level.

In terms of the third indicator of HRM not one of the companies had a personnel manager who was a formal member of the main policy-making forum. In all of the companies the Personnel and Organization Department served as an administrative department focusing on staffing issues such as recruitment and selection, career planning, management development and job rotation programmes. These activities reflected the desire of the companies to create their own internal labour market for employees at the management level.

From the above, it can tentatively be concluded that, although the level of strategic integration appears to be fairly low, programmes fitting within an HRM philosophy are present in each company interviewed. The level of decentralization appears to be relatively high in all but two cases since most HRM-related programmes are initiated and implemented at the business unit level. So, although none of the chemical companies indicated the use of HRM explicitly, programmes fitting within the HRM philosophy were present or were being developed. These results are summarized in table 6.4.

Table 6.4 The level of strategic integration of personnel policy and its position in the organization

	High level of strategic integration	Low level of strategic integration
High level of decentralization	'True' HRM strategies 3 (4) food and drink companies	'Evolving' HRM strategies 3 chemical companies[a]
Low level of decentralization	'Imposed' HRM	'Traditional' personnel management 3 food and drink companies 2 chemical companies[a]

[a] In all of these organizations, however, evidence is found that programmes fitting with the HRM philosophy are implemented.

HRM or Traditional Personnel Management?

Does the previous discussion indicate a shift from personnel management to HRM in the Dutch companies studied? Table 6.4 seeks to answer this question in terms of the extent to which these companies have integrated HRM issues with business strategy (the horizontal axis) and decentralized the control and responsibility for HRM issues to lower levels in the organization (the vertical axis).

The top left-hand box represents an HRM approach to employee management. In four food and drink companies HRM is fully integrated with the business strategy and decentralized to lower levels in the organization. These companies can therefore be said to be pursuing 'true HRM strategies'.

At the opposite end of the spectrum, the bottom right-hand box represents a low level of integration between HRM issues and business strategy and little or no decentralization of HRM to lower levels in the organization. Three food and drink companies and two chemical companies are classified in this quadrant. This approach to employee management can be tentatively termed 'traditional' personnel management. However, programmes fitting within the HRM philosophy are still present in the majority of these companies since they were planning to introduce a number of HRM type policies, such as the creation of an internal labour market via the introduction of job rotation and career development programmes. A possible explanation for this finding could be that the involvement of employee representatives in the development of personnel policy is often ensured by the consensual approach of Dutch management.

Those companies in which personnel management shows little evidence of being integrated with business strategy but nevertheless have decentralized responsibility for HRM matters, can be considered to be pursuing 'evolving' HRM strategies (the top right-hand box). Three chemical companies are classified in this box. However, these companies face the risk that as a result of the low level of strategic integration the HRM programmes being implemented may not reflect, and indeed may diverge from, the strategic needs of the organization. In these circumstances 'the potential for incoherence, inconsistency and a strong employee reaction is obvious' (Brewster and Larsen, 1992, p. 415).

In the box in the bottom-left corner of table 6.4 high integration is coupled with low decentralization. No examples of this situation were found among the sample of companies. In this instance the personnel policy is developed in accordance with the strategy pursued, but at a higher level in the organization. So the personnel department at the division or business unit level simply executes this policy. We therefore term this position 'imposed' HRM. Although we found no examples of this type of HRM we would expect it to characterize highly centralized companies.

This discussion suggests that multiple HRM strategies are feasible in the Netherlands, partly due to the minimum requirements the Dutch business system imposes. This also implies that the boundary between HRM and traditional personnel management is diffuse.

Conclusion

This chapter reveals that national culture and the business system in the Netherlands together determine the degrees of freedom companies have in developing their personnel or HRM strategies. The Dutch business and industrial-relations systems, with their consensus orientation, appear to slow down the development of HRM in practice. HRM implies that policies and structures are contingent upon specific circumstances. In those instances where flexibility is required, however, the centralized employers' organizations and trades unions appear to take their time before deciding to whom they will give the discretion to decide on such highly charged issues. This is illustrated by our research findings of companies in the chemical and food and drink industries, where personnel policy was shown generally not to be highly integrated with the generic strategy pursued. It would be too easy, however, to conclude that the concept of HRM is therefore non-existent in the Netherlands. It merely appears to be a matter of definition. If strategic integration is the determining factor then it would appear that HRM is not extensively practised by Dutch companies. If however the emphasis is on employees as human resources and as a critical source of competitve advantage then HRM is indeed present in Dutch companies. This is indicated by, for example, a strong commitment to extensive training and development activities. Additionally, the results of our research reported in this chapter reveal that programmes fitting within the HRM philosophy are prominent within a number of large Dutch companies. It could therefore be concluded that a Dutch version of HRM is emerging. It comprises elements of the original American-based theory but moulded to the Dutch system of industrial relations and based on assumptions that are rooted in the Dutch national culture.

References

Albeda, W. and Dercksen, W. J. (1989), *Arbeidsverhoudingen in Nederland* (4th edn). Alphen ad Rijn: Samsom.

Beaumont, P. B. (1992), 'The US human resource management literature: a review'. In G. Salaman (ed.), *Human Resource Strategies*. London: Sage, pp. 20–37.

Brewster, C. and Larsen, H. H. (1992), 'Human resource management in Europe: evidence from ten countries', *International Journal of Human Resource Management, 3*, pp. 409–34.

CBS (1990), *Volwasseneneducatie. Bedrijfsopleidingen, 1990, deel 1: Particuliere Sector.* Heerlen: CBS.

CBS (1993), *Statistiek van het ondernemingsbestand 1993.* The Hague: CBS.

CBS (1994), *Statistical Yearbook of the Netherlands.* Heerlen: CBS.

Coopers and Lybrand/Berenschot (1994), *Ken- en Stuurgetallen voor Personeelsmanagement. Resultaten Nederland 1994.* Utrecht: Coopers and Lybrand and Berenschot.

CPB (1993), *Macro-economische Verkenning 1994*. The Hague: CPB.

Dijk, N. van and Punch, M. (1993), 'Open borders, closed circles: management and organization in the Netherlands'. In D. J. Hickson (ed.), *Management in Western Europe: Society, Culture and Organization in Twelve Nations*. Berlin: Walter de Gruyter, pp. 167–90.

Fisscher, O. A. M., Middel, H. and Vinke, R. H. W. (1992), 'Inleiding. HRM: een ontwikkeling maar ook een visie'. In O. A. M. Fisscher, H. Middel and R. H. W. Vinke (eds), *HRM. De Praktijk Gewogen*. Deventer: Kluwer Bedrijfswetenschappen.

Fombrun, C., Tichy, N. M. and Devanna, M. A. (1984), *Strategic Human Resource Management*. New York: Wiley.

Guest, D. (1987), 'Human resource management and industrial relations', *Journal of Management Studies*, **24**, pp. 503–21.

Guest, D. (1990), 'Human resource management and the American dream', *Journal of Management Studies*, **27**, pp. 377–97.

Hampden-Turner, C. and Trompenaars, F. (1993), *The Seven Cultures of Capitalism*. London: Piatkus.

Heijltjes, M. G., Sorge, A. and Witteloostuijn, A. van (1993), *International Organizational Observatory: Descriptive Report of the Netherlands – 1993*. Maastricht: University of Limburg.

Hertog, F.J. den (1991), *De Kwaliteit van Ontwerpgericht Onderzoek. De Kennisvraag*, Research Memorandum, University of Limburg, Maastricht Economic Research Institute in Innovation and Technology (MERIT).

Hofstede, G. (1980), *Culture's Consequences: International Differences in Work-Related Value*. Beverly Hills, CA: Sage.

Hofstede, G. (1991), *Cultures and Organizations: Software of the Mind*. London: McGraw-Hill.

Iterson, A. van and Olie, R. (1992), 'European business systems: the Dutch case'. In R. Whitley (ed.), *European Business Systems: Firms and Markets in their National Contexts*. London: Sage, pp. 98–136.

IVA (1988), *Werving en Selectie in de Praktijk*. The Hague: SER.

Janssen, A. M. C. (1992), 'Knelpunten op de arbeidsmarkt', *Gids voor Personeelsmanagement*, **1**, pp. 8–11.

Jong de, A. C. and Paauwe, J. (1993), 'Management buy-out en sociaal ondernemingsbeleid', *M and O*, **3**, pp. 172–86.

Kerckhoffs, C., Neubourg, C. de and Palm, F. (1994), 'The determinants of unemployment and job search duration in the Netherlands', *De Economist*, **142**, pp. 21–42.

King, P. (1994), 'The business culture in the Netherlands'. In C. Randlesome (ed.), *Business Cultures in Europe* (2nd edn). Oxford: Butterworth-Heinemann, pp. 322–64.

Kluytmans, F. (1989), 'Tussen verzakelijking and vernieuwing. De belofte van human resource management'. In F. Kluijtmans (ed.), *Human Resource Management. Verzakelijking of vernieuwing?* Deventer/Heerlen: Kluwer Bedrijfswetenchappen/Open University.

Kluytmans, F. (1990), 'Ontwikkelingen in het personeelsmanagement: een historische schets'. In F. Kluytmans and C. Hancké (eds), *Leerboek Personeelsmanagement*. Deventer/Heerlen: Kluwer Bedrijfswetenschappen/ Open University.

Kluytmans, F. and Paauwe, J. (1991), 'HRM denkbeelden. De balans opgemaakt', *M and O*, **4**, pp. 279–303.

Laurent, A. (1986), 'The cross-cultural prize of international human resource management', *Human Resource Management*, **25**, pp. 91–102.

Lawrence, P. (1986), *Management in the Netherlands*. Unpublished manuscript. Loughborough: University of Loughborough

Maenhout, J. M. M. and Hoof, J. J. van (1993), *Personeelsresearch in Kaart Hebracht. Een Overzicht van Personeelsonderzoek en Uitvoerende Organisaties in Nederland, SISWO-informatief, 1*. Amsterdam: Instituut voor Maatschappijwetenschappen.

McKinlay, A. and Starkey, K. (1992), 'Strategy and human resource management', *International Journal of Human Resource Management*, **3**, pp. 435–50.

Miles, R. and Snow, C. (1984), 'Designing strategic human resource systems', *Organizational Dynamics*, Summer, pp. 36–52.

OSA (1994), *Vraag naar Arbeid, Organisatie voor Strategisch Arbeidsmarktonderzoek*. Amsterdam: OSA.

Rowland, K. M. and Ferris, G. R. (1982), *Personnel Management*. Boston, Mass.: Allyn and Bacon.

Samson, R. and Brongers, E. B. (1993), 'De toekomst van de Europese arbeidsverhoudingen', *Economisch Statistische Berichten*, **78**, pp. 472–5.

Schuler, R. S. (1987a), 'Personnel and human resource management choices and organizational strategy', *Human Resource Planning*, **10**, pp. 1–17.

Schuler, R. S. (1987b), *Personnel and Human Resource Management*. St Paul, Minn.: West Publishing.

Schuler, R. S. (1992), 'Strategic human resource management: linking the people with the strategic needs of the business', *Organizational Dynamics*, Summer, pp. 18–32.

Sisson, K. (1990), 'Introducing the Human Resource Management Journal', *Human Resource Management Journal*, **1** (1), pp. 1–11.

Sorge, A. (1992), 'Human resource management in the Netherlands', *Employee Relations*, **14**, pp. 71–84.

Stokman, F. N., Wasseur, F. W. and Elsas, D. (1985), 'The Dutch network: types of interlocks and network structure'. In F. N. Stokman, R. Ziegler and J. Scott (eds), *Networks of Corporate Power*. Cambridge: Polity Press.

Storey, J. (1992), *Developments in the Management of Human Resources*. Oxford: Blackwell.

Thijssen, J. G. L. (1988), *Bedrijfsopleidingen als Werkterrein. Een Oriëntatie*. The Hague: Vuga Uitgeverij.

Visser, J, (1989), 'The coming divergence in Dutch industrial relations'. Paper presented at the Eighth World Congress of the International Industrial Relations Association, Brussels, September.

Visser, J, (1992), 'The Netherlands: the end of an era and the end of a system'. In A. Ferner and R. Hyman (eds), *Industrial Relations in the New Europe*. Oxford: Blackwell, pp. 323–56.

Whitley, R. (1992), 'The comparative analysis of business systems'. In R. Whitley (ed.), *European Business Systems: Firms and Markets in their National Contexts*. London: Sage, pp. 5–45.

Wolfs, G, (1992), *Firm Internal Labour Markets in the Netherlands: A Contract Theoretical Approach*. Maastricht: Universitaire Pers Maastricht.

Woodward, J. (1965), *Industrial Organization: Theory and Practice*. Oxford: Oxford University Press.

7 Denmark: Human Resource Management under Collective Bargaining: The Sociological Perspective*

STEEN SCHEUER

Introduction

Human Resource Management (HRM) has swept across the Western world (or at least the business school part of it) replacing older labels in the field such as 'personnel administration' and 'personnel management'. It has become a distinctive field of academic enquiry which challenges, and in some instances incorporates, elements which were previously the exclusive preserve of 'industrial relations' and 'personnel management'. But what is so special about *Human Resource* Management?[1] What marks it out as distinctively different? The replacement of the prefix 'personnel' by 'human resource' is supposed to represent a change in paradigm with regard to the planning and management of employees. Previously 'personnel' were considered an expense while the 'human resources' of an organization are now viewed as a critical source of competitive advantage and therefore something which requires considerable investment. In addition, HRM appears to be connected with certain practices in the employee relationship, which are probably not so novel in themselves, but which, via their association with the appellation HRM, have become essential parts of the 'modern' management toolbox and represent a break with the past. These HR policies include, among others, career planning for employees, management development, performance appraisals, performance-related pay and culture programmes.

At present much of the HRM literature has a strongly normative character, focusing on what HR practitioners and managers *should* do rather than on what they actually *do* do. This change in, or extension of, the *normative* approach can be traced to many places, such as business school courses, curricula and support- ing textbooks. However, whether there has been a concomitant change in the ideology of managers with regard to the employ- ment relationship which in turn has resulted in a change in the relationship between employers and employees is less clear (see Legge, 1989; Clark, 1993; Evans and Hudson 1993; Marginson et al., 1994).

Whether a HRM approach to the employment relationship is attractive to employees is questionable. For instance, is it better to be thought of, or referred to, as a 'human resource' or simply as a worker? This labelling of employees as human resources sug- gests that they should be considered like any other resource in a firm's possession: that is, physical or technical resources (build- ings or machines). This is almost a Marxist reduction of the worker, if not to a commodity then to a 'resource'. Such a con- ceptualization lies squarely within the rationalist management economic literature. Used in this sense the term may appeal more to managers than workers with the latter group probably interested in the term so long as it modifies and supports (and 'improves' as they see it) those management actions, policies and practices targeted at employees.

In essence, HRM is an approach to the management of the employment relationship which contrasts sharply with other approaches. Indeed, HRM is to some extent seen as a break with the past (that is, with personnel management). Therefore, the introduction of a HRM-inspired employee management style should be discernible to the average employee. If they do not feel that they are being treated differently or that there has been little change in the actions of managers directed towards them, then the personnel management/HRM distinction is meaningless.

The purpose of this chapter is to attempt to identify some of the changes which have occurred to the management of the employ- ment relationship – that is those that can be felt by employees, not only by managers. To achieve this the chapter begins by con- sidering a number of factors from the Danish institutional context, focusing in particular on the dual system of industrial relations, which impact upon the nature of HRM. A sociological theory of cultural change is then outlined in order to determine the different ways in which employee relations practices can be modified. Following this the policy goals associated with an HRM approach to employee relations are identified. The available empirical evidence is then considered to determine the extent to which HRM-type policies have been introduced into the Danish workplace.

Before proceeding it must be recognized there has not been any major academic debate in this country as to the nature of HRM, and in what respects it differs from previous approaches to managing the employment relationship such as personnel administration and personnel management. Any teaching or debates that have taken place within Danish business schools are largely based on the Anglo-American literature. A vigorous indigenous debate has yet to emerge. As we will discuss later, one consequence of this is the paucity of data when it comes to examining the extent to which HRM has entered into management reality. This chapter therefore represents a summary of a debate and topic which has only recently entered Danish academia.

The Danish Context – A Dual System

From a legal point of view the contractual relationship between the employer and employee in Denmark is relatively unencumbered by tight controls contained in numerous employment laws (Jacobsen, 1994; Nielsen, 1994). Unlike a number of other European countries (for example France and Italy) Denmark has neither a statutory minimum wage nor a legal maximum working week. However, the Law of Salaried Employees (*Funktionærloven*) gives this large group of employees a number of additional legal rights specifically relating to protection from dismissal. In contrast, manual workers have little legal protection from arbitrary dismissal. A number of laws regulate holiday pay, health and safety at work and sexual discrimination, and ban closed shops (cf. OECD, 1994: Chapter 4). With these qualifications the Danish labour market is relatively free from legal intervention into the employment contract and the employment relationship.

However, in practice the employment relationship in Denmark is more regulated than it first appears. This arises from the high level of unionization in Denmark. The level of unionization has increased significantly since the beginning of the 1960s. For example between 1960 and 1992 union density increased from

Table 7.1 Union densities of occupational groups in the private and public sectors in Denmark, 1991

Occupational status:	Private manufacturing (%)	Private sector services (%)	Public sector services (%)	All (%)
Higher salaried employees	76	80	94	85
Middle salaried employees	83	83	96	92
Lower salaried employees	87	79	90	87
Skilled manual workers	87	..	85	86
Unskilled manual workers	92	88	87	88
All employees	88	80	90	87

Source: Bunnage (1992), p. 311

60 per cent to 87 per cent (Scheuer, 1990, 1992). Table 7.1 shows that union density in Denmark is high for all classes of employees; it makes little difference whether one is a manual worker or senior manager. Furthermore, women are as unionized as men (Scheuer, 1992, p. 178). Thus, in Denmark the great majority of employees are members of a union.

The slightly lower level of union density in the private service sector shown in table 7.1 reflects the dominance of small and medium-sized enterprises in that sector. The great majority of Danish companies are small. Only eighty-one companies (1.1. per cent of all companies) have more that 500 employees (Fivelsdal and Schramm-Nielsen, 1993, p. 35).

A major reason for the high level of unionization in Denmark is the linkage between unemployment insurance and union membership. In Denmark there is no compulsory state unemployment insurance scheme. Rather there are a number of voluntary schemes known as unemployment insurance funds (UIFs). Many of these are organized by unions on behalf of their members. Indeed, from the very early days of Danish trades unionism UIFs were established alongside the union together with strike funds, sickness insurance funds and so on. These schemes are supported by members' dues and employer contributions (about one-third) and funds from the state (two-thirds). The dominance of state funding has meant that many of the UIFs have become financially and legally separated from the unions. In practice, however, a close link remains since virtually every member of the

Danish Federation of Trades Unions (Landsorganizationen i Danmark – LO) has its own UIF. Recent figures indicate that 76 per cent of the Danish workforce is a member of a UIF (Danmarks Statistik, 1993, p. 52).

The linkage between the UIFs and trades union membership has been further bolstered by the introduction of an early retirement scheme – the so-called 'post-employment wage' – by the social democratic and liberal coalition government in 1979. This programme was designed to release jobs for the younger members of the workforce by offering pensions at the age of 60 (the normal age of retirement in Denmark is 67) for those individuals who had been UIF members for five of the previous ten years (amended in 1980 to ten of the previous fifteen years). The scheme was a great success in that it encouraged a large number of those eligible to take early retirement. For the unions this meant that older members had to remain members of the union since to leave would disqualify them from the scheme. It was therefore, in effect, an early retirement scheme for union members (or more strictly UIF members only).

The high level of union density does not imply, as one might think, an equally high coverage by collective agreements. Collective bargaining agreements are an important issue with regard to HRM since such agreements may limit or in some instances prohibit the introduction of certain HRM policies or initiatives, such as performance-related pay, flexible working hours and so on. Survey evidence from 1985 suggests that almost 60 per cent of all employees in the private sector are covered by a collective agreement (Scheuer, 1990, p. 29). More manual workers are covered by these agreements than salaried employees. When the public sector is included 74 per cent of all employees are covered by collective agreements. The level of coverage is somewhat higher than in the UK. The British Workplace Industrial Relations Surveys found in 1984 that 62 per cent of all employees were covered by collective agreements. By 1990 this figure had dropped sharply to 48 per cent (Millward et al., 1992, p. 71). In other European countries the level of coverage is much higher with a few countries having coverage rates of over 90 per cent (Traxler, 1994, p. 172). While the coverage of collective agreements in Denmark may not be as high as in other European countries, in those companies where they apply many work-related conditions are determined by the collective bargaining process.

The previous discussion indicates that a dual system of industrial relations operates in Denmark. This has important implications for the development and character of HRM in Denmark. On the one hand there is the majority of companies whose employee-management system is subject to the provisions contained in collective bargaining agreements. These companies experience regulation beyond that which results from the relevant legislation. The levels of pay, overtime, bonuses, the role of shop stewards and so on are all the subject of collective bargaining agreements. Yet, on the other hand, those firms outside such agreements experience little regulatory control beyond that of the market itself (in the form of a high level of employee turnover resulting from dissatisfaction with working conditions). As a consequence, these firms have greater scope in their choice of HRM policies and practices. In Brewster and Larsen's terms (1992, pp. 414–15) these firms can range from a 'Wild West' approach to HRM where every manager is free to develop their own style of relationship with employees (the firm shows little consistency in its attitude to its employees), to that of the 'guarded strategist' where HR issues are integrated with the corporate strategy and responsibility for HR policies is located with the HR function rather than being devolved to line managers. In both of these cases the nature of the employment relationship will depend upon such factors as the management style of individual managers, the nature of the strategy being pursued by the organization and so forth. Employment conditions may therefore be better or worse than those in the more regulated sector.

Those firms covered by collective bargaining agreements will usually also be covered by the general collective bargaining rounds in Denmark. Collective bargaining in Denmark is highly co-ordinated and synchronized with agreements usually expiring in the spring of every second year (1991, 1993, 1995 and so on). Before the 1970s, collective bargaining in Denmark normally resulted in voluntary biennial agreements. Deadlock between the negotiating sides was rare, such as in 1956 and 1963. However, in the 1970s the 1975, 1977 and 1979 rounds all ended without agreement. So the norm of one in five 'going wrong' in the 1950s and 1960s was replaced by four out of five 'going wrong' in the 1970s. Nevertheless, the pre-1970 pattern was restored on the 1980s.

Until the mid-1980s collective bargaining was highly centralized, taking place between the two main national organizations representing employers and workers – the LO for the workers and salaried employees' unions and the DA (Dansk Arbejdsgiverforening) for the employers. Since then, bargaining has become decentralized, but only to the extent that today national unions bargain with sector-level employers' associations. Thus, in manufacturing, CO Industri (a cartel of unions including the General Workers' Union, the (skilled) Metal Workers' Union, the Electricians' Union, the Female Workers' Union, etc.) bargains with Dansk Industri (DI – the Danish Employers' Association for Industry) over pay and working conditions. In other sectors something similar takes place, always roughly co-ordinated in February to April by the state mediator who makes sure that compromises are reached (cf. Scheuer, 1993; Due et al. 1994). Agreements in recent years have increasingly moved away from stipulating industry-wide pay norms ('normal pay agreements') to agreements that leave scope for local flexibility so that pay can be adjusted to the firms' economic capabilities (their ability to pay) and to the efforts and qualifications of the workforce ('minimum pay agreements'). These changes can be seen as moves in a direction which accords with the principles of HRM, a theme that will be returned to later in the chapter.

Having identified the main contextual elements (that is, the industrial relations and collective bargaining systems) which are likely to impact on the character of Danish HRM, in the next section we turn to a discussion of the nature of organization culture, culture change and how HRM may impact on this.

The Theory of Agency and Change in the Workplace

Workplace cultures can be thought of as the attitudes, beliefs, meanings, norms and values that are shared and enacted in an organization or a place of work (Gowler and Legge, 1986; Schein, 1992; Hatch, 1993). The introduction of a new approach to managing the employment relationship, such as HRM, should have an identifiable impact upon this culture. This leads to the question of whether the introduction of an HRM approach to employee relations in the workplace has implied agency – whether it significantly influences the attitudes, beliefs, rules and basic assumptions which comprise the culture of the organization. In other words, is HRM an agent of change? Does its introduction lead to discernible changes in the workplace?[2]

In adopting an agency perspective, the culture of a group can be viewed as 'the set of rules held by members of that group' (Dietz and Burns, 1992, p. 188). This implies that culture is embodied in the individuals that carry it. Thus, a culture can be thought of as a population of rules, and for each rule there is a frequency of occurrence which is determined by the number of individuals in a population who hold to that rule. Cultural change, then, is a change in the frequency distribution of rules in a group or a population. These rules (or social norms – Elster, 1989, p. 97) guide the behaviour of individuals by indicating which actions are appropriate or legitimate.

Such an approach does not presume that a culture is necessarily (or becoming increasingly) integrated (see Archer, 1988). Rule systems are complex and sometimes inconsistent and contradictory. A culture may contain contradictory rules covering the same action thus resulting in choice and/or ambiguity for social actors. The members of a population may therefore have to choose between two (or more) different rule systems (cultures) in a particular situation. One of the sources of this variation and contradiction is the fact that different spheres of life can carry different norms systems: norms of reasonable and legitimate behaviour in one sphere may differ quite significantly from those applicable in other spheres.

How do cultures change? First, because the rule systems which comprise a culture cannot be exhaustive and all-encompassing there will always be room for interpretation within any system (we are not automata) with the consequence that specific interpretations may become more prevalent at certain times. These will then underpin the dominant value system of the group (Dietz and Burns, 1992, p. 189). Second, as mentioned above, members of a culture may have a number of different sets of rules or norms to refer to when making a choice between alternative actions. This permits interpretation and improvisation. Where this is tied to 'trial and error' learning – the individual invents a rule, tries it out, assesses the results and accepts, modifies, or rejects the rule on the basis of the results of one or more trials – the process of interpretation may be time-consuming and costly. As a consequence, most social actors tend to apply 'social learning', imitating the actions and rules of others. Whom we choose to imitate represents a further form of interpretation.

In summary, one must assume a substantial variability of cultures or rule systems in a society. The sources of this variability include, among other things, defects in the process by which individuals learn the rules (that is, during socialization), migration and shifts of location between societies or workplaces and finally agency, which may be interpreted as those domains where rules are not fully consistent and where, as a consequence, individuals are aware of more than one rule that could be enacted – in other words, there is room for improvisation and choice (Dietz and Burns, 1992, p. 189).

In order to attribute agency to a social actor (for example, to management introducing HRM), three criteria must be met:

1. **The actor must 'make a difference'** – i.e. possess some sort of power. As Dietz and Burns (1992) write, 'There can be no agency without power' (p. 191). In addition, there must be an element of free play for the agent. There must be other choices available in addition to the one which is chosen. Agency thus involves choices between alternative possibilities.
2. **Actions must be intentional.** Unintentional acts cannot be considered agency.
3. **There must be reflexivity**. The actor must have the resources to monitor effects of chosen actions and then possibly modify actions or rules where deemed necessary.

There are, however, a number of constraints on agency. Three main constraints can be identified: (1) the given technical repertoire of the society in question excludes certain types of action, even if they are desired by the actor; (2) the existing repertoire and structure of rules may make some types of action 'impossible' or 'unthinkable', while they make other types quite natural; (3) the agency of some actors affects the ability of other actors to exercise their own agency.

This last point is important, since – in the HRM context – the reactions of employees to changed HR practices is crucial to the successful implementation of new employment policies. Furthermore, these reactions may actually alter the outcomes of intended changes, sometimes in ways not anticipated by the first actor (in this case management).

To illustrate this last point one can model three different 'fates' that may characterize the introduction of new HRM policies. These are illustrated in table 7.2.

Table 7.2 From present policies to new policies: model of the theoretical outcomes of introducing new personnel or HRM policies

Policies (t)	Theories	New policies (t + 1)
PP_1	NP_1	NP_1
PP_2	NP_2	NP_2
PP_3	NP_3	NP_{3a}

If we think of three different areas of personnel policies and practices in a firm (using the suffixes 1, 2 and 3) the introduction of HRM may change the nature of these policies. Thus the present policies (PPs) should, according to the theory, be converted into new policies (NPs) in the different areas. At least three outcomes are possible. In the first row, i.e. in the case of PP_1, the new policy is accepted by the parties and NP_1 is enacted successfully. In the second row, the case of PP_2, the introduction of new policy NP_2 is thwarted – perhaps due to resistance by employees or by lack of commitment by management. Therefore, PP_2 remains in place. In the third row, one party is unable to accept that PP_3 is replaced by NP_3. However, they are willing to accept some but not all changes. The result is not NP_3, but NP_{3a} – that is, an alternative NP_3, adjusted and accommodated to take account of local conditions or interests. NP_{3a} in this case may be an unintended consequence (or at least: an unanticipated consequence) of trying to introduce NP_3 instead of PP_3.

This way of depicting a change from one set of policies to another may appear simplistic. Nevertheless, it is useful to understanding the discussion in the next sections of this chapter since the introduction of HRM practices do not always occur in the way originally planned since changes to employee-relations practices can be exploited by any of the parties – management or employee representatives – to further their particular interests.

The approach outlined above has a number of implications for any analysis of the introduction of HRM in Danish firms:

1. HRM can be viewed as one more rule system within the organization. It therefore makes certain types of action legitimate for both managers and their subordinates. These actions may not have been legitimate or acceptable previously within the organizational context. Such changes to the rule systems

within organizations should be identifiable in terms of their impact on the nature of employee management practices and policies.

2. Although much of the literature on HRM promotes it as an integrative device with regard to workplace culture (that is, the notion that HRM should integrate employees more closely with the aims and objectives of the organization thus reducing levels of collectivism and conflict), there is no *a priori* reason to assume that it either can be, or has been, successful in this respect. This may arise in part as a result of the contradictions and conflicts at the core of HRM (see Legge, 1989), but also because the very norms that are promoted and legitimized by HRM may be in conflict with the existing organizational culture. Therefore, HRM may in certain circumstances reduce friction between different employee groups but in others intensify those frictions, especially if one group of employees reacts negatively to HRM initiatives and they are large (or vociferous) enough not to be ignored.

3. Dietz and Burns (1992, p. 188) note that 'agents shape history in complex ways that do not lead to predictable or intended outcomes'. Since cultures are not necessarily integrated and homogeneous, alternative rule systems may operate in a single organizational context (see Hyman and Brough, 1975). As a consequence, the implementation of HRM policies may not be straightforward. Indeed, its introduction is likely to be subject to considerable modification with the consequence that the reality (the outcome) must be carefully examined and distinguished from the rhetoric. What is implemented may bear little resemblance to the initial intentions.

The previous discussion leads to the following three important questions in the Danish context: (1) Is there any evidence that new practices have been introduced in the workplace and if so have they superseded previous practices? (2) Has the introduction of HRM led to integration or to conflict? and (3) is what is implemented that which was intended or do HRM policies and intentions change during the implementation process? These three questions structure the remaining discussion in this chapter. To answer them a number of specific HRM policies will be considered in order to examine the empirical evidence available as to their introduction and fate. Before we can provide some tentative answers to these three questions, however, the term HRM must first be defined.

What is HRM?

There are many and varying definitions of HRM but perhaps one of the more general and all-encompassing is that proposed by Gospel (1992, p. 3). He suggests that HRM covers three main areas:

1. **work relations** – which refers to the way work is organized, the division of labour and its sequencing, and the deployment of workers around technologies and production processes;
2. **employment relations** – which includes recruitment and selection, training, job tenure and promotion, employee turnover and the remuneration system;
3. **Industrial relations** – these are the representational systems in the enterprise which include the role of shop stewards, union recognition, management–union relations and the process of collective bargaining.

In a Danish context this definition of HRM is too broad. Decisions in connection with work relations are generally taken by either senior management or line managers in a specific part of the organization depending on the importance of (in most cases the amount of investment involved in) the decision. While they may have major impacts on employees these decisions do not usually involve HR managers. Similarly, while, as we suggested above, the Danish industrial relations system is becoming more decentralized this implies a movement away from national to industry-level bargaining. Hence, the HR manager at the firm level has little impact on the content of these agreements, rather they are charged with implementing that which is agreed and contained in an industry-wide agreement. Thus in Denmark HRM is conceived mainly in terms of employment relations (number 2 in the above list).

Our concern then is with those policies and practices applied within the firm which constitute a break with the past and are designed to enhance employee commitment, flexibility, the internal labour market and the role of the individual over that of the unions. Since these policies are directed at employees they are assumed to have measurable consequences for the latter. Below we outline each of these policy goals prior to examining the extent to which these HRM type policies have been introduced, and therefore exist in Denmark.

Employee commitment

The introduction of HRM may result in greater permanence and stability in the employment relationship resulting from individual employees feeling committed to the organization. Similarly, the organization itself may show greater commitment to its employees. As a consequence, a significant proportion of the workforce should have 'tenure' in the sense that their (formal) employment contract guarantees them protection from dismissal due to seasonal and other short-term variations in demand. This in turn results in the development of an 'internal labour market' for the employees of larger firms. For these employees career progression occurs *within* rather *between* organizations. The key questions are these: Are changes of job by moving between firms becoming less frequent? Are more people gaining longer tenure? Are dismissal policies changing?

Flexibility

Building on the previous point, part of HRM thinking suggests that if organizations are to be successful they need to be adaptable in order to meet new challenges as they arise. One requirement for adaptability is what has been termed 'functional flexibility'. This suggests that firms should move away from numerical flexibility (hire and fire in accordance with the fluctuations of the market) and should assist employees to become functionally flexible by training them to develop flexible skills so that they may be able to undertake more than one work task. This is something which challenges the 'old-fashioned' notion of rigid demarcations between work tasks which can sometimes impede the rational allocation of employees. Since some of these demarcations are defences erected by employees and their representatives, moves toward functional flexibility can be perceived as an attack on collectivism.

To obtain functional flexibility, firms should invest increasingly in the training and development of employees. Under an HRM approach to employee relations such training should be 'internalized' – that is, provided by the firms themselves – not 'externalized'

– that is, based on (public or private) educational institutions, apprenticeship systems, or other such arrangements. The aim is to be able to move employees around in the firm, horizontally as well as vertically, although mostly the former.

This is connected with the shift towards 'individualization' mentioned in many HRM textbooks. The main focus switches from management–trades union relations to management–employee relations. One consequence of this is the upsurge of interest and use of the 'personal appraisal' or 'personal development' interview. This is both an investment by the manager in aiding the employee to develop and improve (by positive and negative feedback), but it is also a way (in some instances) to circumvent the influence of the shop steward and improve direct relations between the manager and the individual employee (in other words, to effect the switch from an emphasis on trades unions to individuals).

The previous discussion leads to the following key questions. Is on-the-job training becoming more prevalent? Is the dependence on external providers becoming less marked? Are personal development interviews becoming more extensively used? Does this diminish the influence of the shop steward?

Internal labour market

The 'logic of the internal labour market' (if such a logic exists) would appear to imply that the development and nurturing of internal candidates for management positions (resulting in less reliance on external supply) should become more widespread. As firms devote more resources to the training and development of their employees, what evidence is there that their 'home-grown talent' stay? Internal promotion has long been the rule in some types of large organizations, such as banks, real estate and insurance companies and in areas of the civil services (post, railways). Can it be shown that the proportion of internal candidates being appointed to management and other organizational positions has increased in recent years?

Individualization

One consequence of the move towards individualization associated with HRM is the introduction of remuneration policies based more on the individual employee's merits than on the norms of collective bargaining (wage relativities, linking pay to company profits, etc.). Furthermore, the increasing emphasis on tenure and training may imply that pay is being linked, to some extent, to the level of formal education reached, together with participation in company training and personal results. It is in this area that the introduction of HRM represents the most potent threat to the industrial relations systems described earlier in the chapter. If pay is increasingly negotiated and awarded on an individual basis then these new practices may undermine the existing arrangements based on collective bargaining and collective representation. However, a reduction in collectivism does not necessarily imply greater individualization, or a move towards HRM (Evans and Hudson, 1993). Conversely, it may also be that remuneration can be individualized *without* collective bargaining arrangements being dissolved. Some attention will be given to these issues in the discussion which follows.

Finally, given the Danish context outlined earlier, it is impossible to deal with the issue of the impact of HRM without considering the changing roles of the trades unions and shop stewards. Does HRM mean less influence of shop stewards? Does it mean a reduction in collective bargaining agreements? Have there been attempts to circumvent the trades unions for shop stewards and, if so, have they been successful? If HRM implies greater individualization in the employment relationship then it may be the case that the unions today play a more modest role and have less influence on working life than they had previously. Again this point will be dealt with in the discussion that follows.

Having outlined a whole series of issues related to the introduction of HRM in the Danish workplace we now turn to consider the evidence which may assist us to provide some tentative answers to the questions just posed.

The State of HRM in Denmark: Some Evidence

Two recent studies have examined the extent to which the employment-relations system has changed in Denmark in recent years. Jørgensen (1990) and his colleagues at Aalborg University conducted a large scale study of employment relations in Danish companies sponsored by the Ministry of Work. This is known as the 'ATA' project (hereafter referred to as ATA). This study focused on the 'personnel planning practices' of Danish private sector firms as well as their interaction with public sector institutions (such as labour exchanges, educational institutions, etc.) with regard to the recruitment and training of employees.

The second study is the Danish part of the Price Waterhouse Cranfield survey (referred to hereafter as PWC) a comparative study of HRM practices and policies in nineteen different countries. In Denmark Henrik Holt Larsen at the Copenhagen Business School is responsible for conducting the survey (Larsen 1991; Larsen and Svendsen, 1992; Brewster and Larsen, 1992). To date two PWC surveys have been conducted in Denmark (1991 and 1992).

At present, these two studies represent the main major empirical investigations of HRM practices in Denmark. They are, however, quite different in character, thoroughness and focus. The ATA project is analytical, detailed and critical. In contrast, the PWC project is more 'strategic' in its focus, concentrating on what HRM managers think about their own position and policies rather than on the employees' experiences of HRM. The findings from these two survey are elaborated and discussed below under the following headings: flexibility, training, role of the personnel department and collective bargaining. This structure is adopted since while these two studies represent the empirical base for discussion of the reality of HRM in Denmark they were not designed to answer all of the questions raised above.

Flexibility

As mentioned earlier, a fundamental goal of HRM is to reduce numerical flexibility and increase functional flexibility. Table 7.3 shows the extent to which the firms participating in the ATA study considered each form of flexibility to be important. Rows 1, 3 and 4 are examples of numerical flexibility while row 2 refers to functional flexibility. It is striking that a little under half of the firms (44 per cent) participating in the survey considered the hiring and dismissing of employees to be a very important method for regulating the size of the workforce, and that a further 41 per cent considered it to be of some importance. Table 7.3 also indicates that regulating 'working time' is an important form of numerical flexibility, whereas changes to 'work speed' seem to be less prevalent. These findings do not indicate that functional flexibility is

Table 7.3 Danish firms' methods for adapting personnel resources to production demands, 1990[a]

	Very important (%)	Important (%)	Not important (%)
1. By increasing or reducing the number of employees	44	41	14
2. By moving employees between types of work	34	46	20
3. By changing working time (overtime, flexitime, reduced time etc)	26	46	28
4. By changing work speed	12	28	60

[a]*N*: 1,523 firms
Source: Jørgensen (1990), p. 191

unimportant. Rather table 7.3 shows that about a third of the sample of firms considered it to be a very important form of flexibility, and a further 46 per cent rate it as being of some importance.

These results suggest that Danish firms do not favour one form of flexibility over another. Instead they use several forms of flexibility at the same time. As a consequence, these authors view the emergence of the 'flexible firm' in Denmark with some scepticism (Jørgensen 1990, p. 171). In contrast, a more recent study (DTI, 1994, Report 2, p. 13) indicates a decline in the use of numerical flexibility. This study emphasizes that Danish firms are increasingly considering the linkages between numerical and functional flexibility. This may be indicative of the emergence of the 'flexible firm' concept in Denmark (DTI 1994, Report 2, p. 14).

Table 7.4 shows the different planning horizons firms use when estimating their future human resource requirements. For salaried employees, the planning horizon for the vast majority of firms ranges from one month to over a year. In contrast, for manual workers the planning horizon is much shorter with 25 per cent of firms planning on a day-to-day basis, 36 per cent planning up to a month ahead and 32 per cent using a time horizon of between a month and a year.

Table 7.4 Planning horizon of firms' personnel recruitment by category of employee, 1990[a]

Planning horizon	Manual workers (%)	Salaried employees (%)
From day to day	25	2
One month ahead	36	9
One month to one year	32	58
More than one year	6	30
Total	99	99

[a]*N*: 1,523 firms
Source: Jørgensen (1990), p. 202.

Table 7.5 shows the planning horizons firms use when considering the training and development needs of their manual employees. A little over a third of firms plan these questions within less than a month, against almost two-thirds with regard to recruitment. Furthermore it is notable that 'day-to-day planning' declines with increasing company size, but it should be noted that the qualitative shift downwards comes only when companies move beyond the size of 200 employees. Since 60 per cent of all employees in Denmark are employed in firms with less than 200 employees, exposure to the effects of short-term planning with regard to recruitment and training is certainly a fact of life for many Danish employees, especially manual workers.

Table 7.5 Planning horizons of firms' training and education of manual workers, by company size, 1990

Planning horizon	Number of employees[a]				
	6–19 (%)	20–49 (%)	50–199 (%)	200+ (%)	All (%)
From day to day	16	13	10	5	14
One month ahead	23	26	23	15	24
One month–one year	49	47	56	65	50
More than one year	12	14	10	15	12
Total	100	100	99	100	100

[a]*N*: 1,523 firms
Source: Jørgensen (1990), p. 206

Training

As we established earlier, training is a central HRM issue. Training is essential if firms are to achieve functional flexibility through the possession of 'flexible' skills by the workforce.

First we identify the amount Danish firms spend on training. The DTI (1994) study estimated the direct and indirect costs to Danish firms of on-the-job training to be 7 billion kroner. This figure represents 1.6 per cent of the total pay bill in Denmark. This figure only includes the training expenses incurred by the firms themselves; it does not include state spending on training which is substantial (DTI, 1994, p. 12). According to the PWC surveys investment in training declined between 1991 and 1992. The DTI survey suggests an opposite trend. Employees spend about 3.3 per cent of their time on on-the-job training.

Recent studies show that the personal appraisal interview is increasingly important in identifying the training and development needs of individual employees (Larsen and Svendsen, 1992, p. 28; DTI, 1994, Report 2, p. 10). In the PWC survey almost half of the respondents indicated that they utilized such interviews to identify the training needs of their employees. Table 7.6 shows the various ways in which firms seek to enhance the skills of their employees. The table indicates that firms tend to emphasize on-the-job training in preference to other forms of training provision. Formal training courses, whether in-house or external, are not extensively used.

The DTI (1994) survey investigated the existence of formalized educational plans for employees (these are not the same as personal development plans – but close). There seems to have been a slight increase in their use since about a third of firms participating in this study used them when determining the training needs of their employees.

Next we consider whether training is available for all groups of employees, or whether it is reserved for a narrow and select range of employees (see Sisson, 1993, p. 209). Although previous evidence indicates that the amount spent on training by Danish companies is considerable, to which groups of employees are these resources being targeted? The PWC and the DTI surveys seem to point to the existence of what might be labelled a 'Matthew effect'[3] (see Elster, 1989, p. 57). This suggests that the least qualified receive the least training and that the most

Table 7.6 Methods used by Danish firms to enhance the skills of employees, 1990[a]

	Very important (%)	Important (%)	Not important (%)
1. Training by participating in normal work	68	13	1
2. Special tailor-made courses in working hours	26	40	35
3. Public educational institutions	21	38	41
4. Course offered by suppliers (of machinery etc)	14	39	47
5. Introductory courses before employment	8	21	72
6. Special tailor-made courses outside working hours	6	30	64

[a]*N*: 1,532 firms
Source: Jørgensen (1980), p. 214.

qualified receive the most training. Thus, manual workers receive less training than their salaried counterparts. Unskilled workers receive the very least training. Among salaried employees, participation in training generally increases with seniority. So while the amounts invested in on-the-job training appear impressive, they are heavily concentrated on the training of salaried employees. To paraphrase George Orwell: 'All human resources are equal but some are more equal than others'! (1945, p. 114). This picture is confirmed by a survey conducted by Anker and Andersen (1991). The relevant results are summarized in table 7.7. This shows the extent to which different groups of employees have participated in training.

One of the most striking features of table 7.7 is the substantial difference in participation rates between manual workers and salaried employees, especially higher salaried employees. The table shows that over two-thirds of all salaried employees participated in on-the-job training in the previous sixteen months. In contrast, about a quarter of all manual workers had participated in on-the-

Table 7.7 Extent to which different groups of employees participate in training activities

Occupational status	Have ever participated (%)	Participated within the last 16 months (%)
Higher salaried employees	86	63
Middle salaried employees	82	57
Lower salaried employees	67	42
Skilled manual workers	57	27
Unskilled manual workers	49	21
All employees	66	40

Source: Anker and Andersen (1991), pp. 250–1

job training in the previous sixteen months. One interpretation of these findings could be that HRM thinking has not yet 'devolved' to manual workers but may be on its way. A more critical interpretation (as in the DTI analysis) is simply that the more senior an individual is within the organizational hierarchy the greater are the training opportunities.

Role of personnel department

The existence of a personnel (or human resource) department and a written personnel plan are often considered central aspects of HRM (Larsen 1991; Larsen and Svendsen, 1992; Brewster and Larsen, 1992). Table 7.8 shows their frequency in different sized firms in Denmark.

Table 7.8 Extent to which personnel departments and written personnel plans exist in different sized Danish firms[a]

Number of employees	With personnel dept (%)	With written plans (%)
6–19	5	11
20–49	14	34
50–199	25	45
200+	54	53
All firms	12	22

[a]*N*: 1,523 firms
Source: Jørgensen (1990), p. 20

It is perhaps not surprising that their frequency increases as the size of firms increases. Thus they are less frequent in small firms and more frequent in large firms. Overall it is interesting to note that written personnel plans are more prevalent than personnel departments. This may indicate that while at the workplace level a little over one-tenth of the ATA respondents had established a personnel department, collective bargaining agreements and the collective bargaining process may encourage those firms that are affected to plan and monitor their personnel policies.

Collective bargaining

Finally, we consider whether there is any evidence that collective bargaining and collective representation (trades unions) have diminished with the advent of HRM in Denmark? Has the increasing awareness of HRM among Danish managers meant that unions have become circumscribed and collective agreements less prevalent? Findings from the two PWC surveys suggest that this might be the case. In the more recent (1992) survey about a third of respondents indicated that the influence of the trades unions had diminished. However, these results may have a certain in-built bias in that the respondents were personnel managers. These findings may therefore be indicative of their wishful thinking. Furthermore, does HRM undermine collective representation, or is collective representation something that mediates, partly changes and partly assists in the implementation of central aspects of HRM? These questions will be considered in the discussion which follows.

There is general agreement that the process of pay setting in Denmark has become: (1) more decentralized; and, (2) more related to the qualifications and productivity of the individual employee. Before we can claim that this represents a 'rolling back' of the 'traditional' Danish collectivist infrastructure two points need emphasizing. First, the decentralization of pay setting reflects the type of pay agreements being set. Collective bargaining arrangements are increasingly concerned with setting 'minimum' pay levels rather than 'actual' pay levels – in other words, they are increasingly becoming agreements which presuppose some local bargaining and flexibility over pay levels. This implies that decentralization is taking place with the tacit approval of the trades unions.

Recent survey evidence seems to indicate an erosion of the extension of collective bargaining (though not nearly as sharply as in the UK). Survey evidence of collective bargaining coverage from 1994 seems to indicate a fall from 57 per cent to 52 per cent among private sector employees between 1985 and 1994 (see table 7.9). The table also shows that manual workers and salaried employees have not experienced a similar drop. Rather among these employees the percentage covered by collective agreements has remained virtually unchanged thus indicating that the aggregate decline reflects that manual workers make up a diminishing share of the workforce (a trend present in virtually all the advanced economies).

The decreasing level of coverage of collective bargaining agreements between 1985 and 1990 may be seen either as an expression of general macro-economic tendencies, unrelated to HRM policies, or as an expression of attempts by firms to individualize the employment relationship by increasing the share of the workforce enjoying protection under the law of salaried employees and in this way attempting to take them out of the collective bargaining framework. That some firms have such a policy is known, but whether it makes this kind of a macro-impact is uncertain, although possible.

An elaborate system of merit pay ('the payment system of the 1990s') has been designed by the Dansk Industri employers' association and the CO Industri union cartel. Although this system envisages greater individualization, it is based on union acceptance. An essential precondition of this agreement has been that the criteria for individualization have been made explicit

Table 7.9 The percentage of private sector employees covered by collective bargaining agreements in 1985 and 1994

	1985 (%)	1994 (%)
Salaried employees	40	39
Manual workers	71	72
Men	56	50
Women	59	56
All employees	57	52

Source: Scheuer (1996)

and objective – that is that an individual's pay should not the result of the whims of any one employer. Recent surveys have confirmed that these new payment systems are always introduced with the agreement of the workers' representatives (Ibsen, 1994, p. 161; Ibsen and Stamhus, 1993).

Since, at the same time, there are no indications of a drop in union density there is no reason to believe that the increasing use of HRM terminology has undermined the position of the unions. In fact, it would appear that the unions have successfully exploited those parts of HRM which appear most attractive from their point of view and blocked those aspects which appear less appealing. For example, in the 1993 general bargaining round one part of the agreement guaranteed any employee in manufacturing industry two weeks of on-the-job training per year. Not everyone exploits this, of course, but it does create new opportunities for firms and for employees. The same agreement laid down rules for better sickness pay and a longer period of notice in case of 'lay-offs'. All these are aspects of HRM: caring more for employees; reducing numerical flexibility; and emphasizing functional flexibility, while trying to obtain it through training and job rotation.

As a result several features of HRM have been realized not by the autonomous actions of individual employers, and not in the face of opposition from employees' collective representatives (unions and shop stewards), but by the means of collective bargaining and collective agreements between employers' associations and trades unions.

Summary

The previous discussion gives a rather sombre picture of the nature of HRM in Denmark in the late 1980s and early 1990s. Training involvements of firms do not appear to be very dominant, planning horizons – especially when it comes to manual workers – appear shockingly short, and the level of professionalization of the HR/personnel functions does not appear advanced. The latter point is related to the fact that Denmark has many small and medium-sized enterprises. In a country where legal regulation of the employment relationship is very limited, especially with regard to manual workers, and where the coverage of collective bargaining (despite the very high union density levels) is not all-encompassing, these are perhaps disquieting facts. They do not seem to imply a very advanced approach to the management of the employment relationship and if the innovatory capabilities of firms are thought to be contingent upon training and functional flexibility, this cannot be said to be too prevalent in Denmark.

A comparative analysis of the PWC data in ten European nations by Brewster and Larsen (1992) would appear to support these conclusions. They sought to locate each country on a two-by-two matrix with the horizontal axis as the extent to which responsibility for HR matters is devolved to line managers (low to high) and the vertical axis as the extent to which HR issues are considered as part of the strategy formulation process. They locate Denmark in the quadrant of high devolution of HR responsibilities to line managers and low integration of HR issues with the corporate strategy. They term this position in matrix as 'the Wild West'. This suggests that 'every manager is free to develop his or her own style of relationship with employees and, in extreme cases, would have the power to 'hire and fire', to reward and invest in employees as they wished. The potential for incoherence, inconsistency and a strong employee reaction is obvious' (pp. 414–15). However, the collective bargaining process provides a strong countervailing force encouraging greater similarity and uniformity between employers.

Conclusion

This chapter has sought to examine the nature of HRM in Denmark. It has argued that this has to be viewed within the context of the industrial relations and collective bargaining systems. The impact of this context on Danish companies suggests that the anti-union message contained in many (particularly American) HRM textbooks needs to be modified in view of the employee-management system operating in Denmark. Much of this literature has either downplayed or ignored the importance of unions in those companies where HRM is believed to prevail. Indeed, there is a tendency to believe that the introduction of HRM and strong union representation are incompatible; HRM is a feature of non-union and 'greenfield' (or start-up) operations. Yet, the role of the unions remains significant in Denmark and cannot be ignored. Furthermore, it is clear from the previous discussion that the unions remain strong in Denmark despite any apparent growth of

HRM thinking in Danish companies. HRM-type policies, if they have been introduced in Denmark, have been done so in the context of strong trades unionism, not in the face of diminishing levels of unionization. Sisson's (1993) discussion of the most recent Workplace Industrial Relations Survey (WIRS3) in the UK stresses this point. Whereas in the USA HRM is thought of as an *alternative* to collective representation and bargaining, in the UK evidence from WIRS3 clearly shows that where fragments of HRM policies appear they are much more prevalent in union than in non-union workplaces. Therefore, the assertion that HRM is strongest in non-union organizations is not borne out. In Denmark the idea that 'traditional collectivist' forms of industrial relations are being, and have been, challenged and replaced by an approach to employment relationship which emphasizes the 'individual' over collectivist concerns is too simplistic. Rather the evidence suggests that where new employee relations practices are introduced they occur *with* the agreement and consent of the unions (Sisson, 1993, p. 208).

How much these developments and moves towards HRM will result in fundamental change for the ordinary employee remains to be seen since these moves are still very new. However, there is no doubt that without the collective effort of unions HRM in Denmark could easily have become an investment in managers and other senior employees to the exclusion of those lower down in the hierarchy.

The empirical evidence presented in this chapter suggests that there has been little measurable change in the recruitment, retention and dismissal practices of Danish firms. A move away from 'hire and fire' practices by many employers is not (yet) observable and a greater emphasis on internal candidates for promotion cannot be discerned. The amount spent on training is large and Danish firms appear to be stressing on-the-job training. Training is increasingly being targeted towards the attainment of externally validated qualifications. Since these are not firm-specific they provide employees with qualifications that are generally recognized and valued, in the external, as well as internal, labour market. Thus there appears to be a move by firms towards increasingly developing and nurturing the talent of their employees but not in a way which restricts their employment opportunities to the firm which funded the training. This flies in the face of some HRM notions since it does not appear to support the development of a strong internal labour market.

Whether payment systems and the employment relationship are becoming more individualized is more difficult to determine. In Denmark these trends are inextricably linked to the future development of the trades union movement and collective bargaining system. There is evidence that some organizations and industries have introduced individualized payment systems for particular kinds of employees. But these have been introduced with the explicit agreement of the unions since they have formed part of a collective arrangement. The respondents to the PWC studies indicate that the future role and influence of the unions is likely to diminish. However, these findings may simply reflect the hopes of the personnel managers who responded. The movement towards individualized pay systems may reflect a small shift towards HRM, but as we stated earlier this has occurred with the consent of the unions. This particular aspect of an HRM approach to employee relations has not sought to alienate and minimize the role of the unions. Rather it has if anything strengthened their traditional role.

This discussion also has implications for the nature of 'agency'. An HRM approach to employee relations places considerable stress on certain personnel policies (especially those related to employment security and training). These appear more important and more legitimate to management. As a consequence, some of the policies that fall within the general rubric of HRM (such as individualization of pay) and which have traditionally been opposed by the unions have begun to be more common in Danish organizations. What appears to have happened is that the way in which they have been introduced has emphasized and legitimized the existing industrial relations system. Since employers have continued to use and stress 'normal channels' the unions have been less critical and more conciliatory than might be expected.

Earlier in the chapter three questions were asked: (1) Have any new policies been introduced in the workplace and if so have they replaced previous policies? (2) Has the introduction of HRM led to integration or to conflict? and (3) Is what is implemented that which was intended or do HRM policies and intentions change during the implementation process?

There is some evidence that new policies have been introduced and have replaced previous policies – but this is not widespread. Where HRM policies (or policies that can be said to fall under the general rubric of HRM) have been introduced, they seem not to have been the cause of new conflict, but rather to have had an integrating effect on the workforce. This follows from the fact that Danish firms have generally introduced changes to their personnel policies in accordance with the collective bargaining process and have therefore sought to consult widely with employee representatives prior to their introduction. Union acceptance of these changes to personnel policies legitimizes management's actions, which results in a higher level of acceptance by the workforce. On the other hand management may be forced to concede part of its prerogative to the unions by accepting workers' demands for fairness in wage relativities and fairness in rationalizing wage differentials. However, these arguments and agreements occur within a general framework which is being established by management. The unions are therefore negotiating within and to an agenda established by management. Hence, agency and 'counter-agency' results in the implementation of new policies but not in the way envisaged by many HRM textbooks (NP3a in table 7.2 perhaps).

This argument suggests that changes in ideologies (here the ideologies of managers and would-be managers) can and do change organizational employee-relations practices and cultures. However, these are highly contingent upon existing subcultures and institutional arrangements. Thus, the importance of the values and attitudes of the other, non-management, groups in shaping and changing the outcome of these changes cannot be ignored.

Notes

* An earlier version of this text was presented to the Research Committee 44 (Labour Movements) at the XIII World Congress of Sociology in Bielefeld, Germany, July 1994. Comments from participants in session 12, and also from Richard Hyman, University of Warwick and Henrik Holt Larsen, Copenhagen Business School, are gratefully acknowledged.
1 In Danish, HRM is termed *ledelse af de menneskelige ressourcer*, which is the direct translation; it has a slightly strange ring in Danish ears. Most HR managers are still called personnel managers or directors, although a few firms have started using the new acronym HRM in their job titles.
2 Does Danish *national* culture play any role in setting the context for HRM implementation? The study of cultural differences in management styles by Hofstede (1984) and recent contributions on the nature of Danish or Scandinavian management imply a linkage between national culture and behaviour in organizations (Lindkvist, 1992; Fivelsdal and Schramm-Nielsen, 1993).
3 'Unto every one that hath shall be given, and he shall have abundance: but from him that hath not shall be taken away even that which he hath' (Matthew 25: 29).

References

Anker, N. and Andersen, D. (1991), *Efteruddannelse*. Copenhagen: Danish National Institute of Social Research.

Archer, M. (1988), *Culture and Agency*. Cambridge: Cambridge University Press.

Brewster, C. and Larsen, H. H. (1992), 'Human resource management in Europe: evidence from ten countries', *International Journal of Human Resource Management*, **3** (3), pp. 409–35.

Bunnage, D. (1992), *Living Conditions in Denmark*. Copenhagen: Danish Statistics Office.

Clark, J. (ed.), (1993), *Human Resource Management and Technical Change*. London: Sage.

Dietz, T. and Burns, T. R. (1992), 'Human agency and the evolutionary dynamics of culture', *Acta Sociologica*, **35** (3), pp. 187–201.

Danmarks Statistik (1993), *Statistisk tiårsoversigt*. Copenhagen.

Det Økonomiske Råd (1994), *Dansk økonomi 1994*. Copenhagen.

DTI (1994), Ploughmann, P., *Privat efteruddannelse*. Copenhagen: Danish Technological Institute.

Due, J., Madsen, J. S. and Jensen, C. S. and Petersen, L. K. (1994), *The Survival of the Danish Model*. Copenhagen: DJØF Publishing.

EIRR (1993), 'The reduction and restructuring of working hours in Denmark: compromise and implementation', *European Industrial Relations Review*, **231**, pp. 25–8.

Elster, J. (1989), *The Cement of Society*. Cambridge: Cambridge University Press.

Evans, S. and Hudson, M. (1993), 'Standardized packages individually wrapped? A study of the introduction and operation of personal contracts in the port transport and electricity supply industries', *Warwick Papers in Industrial Relations*, No. 44, University of Warwick, Coventry.

Fivelsdal, E. and Schramm-Nielsen, J. (1993), 'Egalitarianism at work: management in Denmark'. In D. Hickson (ed.), *Management in Western Europe*. Berlin: Walter de Gruyter, pp. 27–45.

Gospel, H. (1992), *Markets, Firms and Management in Modern Britain*. Cambridge: Cambridge University Press

Hatch, M. J. (1993), 'The dynamics of organizational culture', *Academy of Management Review*, **18** (4), pp. 657–93.

Hofstede, G. (1984), *Culture's Consequences* (abridged version), London: Sage.

Hyman, R. and Brough, I. (1975), *Social Values and Industrial Relations*. Oxford: Blackwell.

Ibsen, F. (1994), 'Effekterne af den decentrale løndannelse'. In *Arbejdsmarkedspolitisk Årbog*. Copenhagen: The Danish Ministry of Labour.

Ibsen, F. and Stamhus, J. (1993), *Decentral lønfastsættelse. En virksomhedsundersøgelse*. Copenhagen: DJØF Publishing.

Jørgensen, H., Lind, J. and Nielsen, P. (1990), *Personaleplanlægning og politik*. Ålborg: ATA Publishers.

Jacobsen, P. (1994), *Kollektiv arbejdsret.* Copenhagen: DJØF Publishing.

Larsen, H. H. (ed.) (1991), *HRM 91. Human Resource Management i danske virksomheder. En rapport om strategisk personaleledelse i private og offentlige virksomheder.* Copenhagen: Dansk Institut for Personalerådgivning.

Larsen, H. H. and Svendsen, L. K. (eds), (1992), *HRM 92. Human Resource Management i danske virksomheder. En rapport om strategisk personaleledelse i private og offentlige virksomheder.* Copenhagen: Dansk Institut for Personalerådgivning.

Legge, K. (1989), 'Human resource management: a critical analysis'. In J. Storey (ed.), *New Pespectives on Human Resource Management.* London: Routledge, pp. 19–40.

Lindkvist, L. (1992), *Management in the Nordic Countries: Differences and Similarities* (mimeo). Copenhagen: Copenhagen Business School, Institute of Organization and Industrial Sociology.

Marginson, P., Olsen, R. and Tailby, S. (1994), 'The eclecticism of managerial policy towards labour regulation: three case studies', *Warwick Papers in Industrial Relations,* No. 47, University of Warwick, Coventry.

Millward, N., Stevens, M., Smart D. and Hawes, W.R. (1992), *Workplace Industrial Relations in Transition.* London: Dartmouth Press.

Nielsen, R. (1994), *Lærebog i arbejdsret* (5th revised edn). Copenhagen: DJØF Publishing.

OECD (1994), *Employment Outlook.* Paris: OECD.

Orwell, G. (1966 [1945]), *Animal Farm: A Fairy Story.* Harmondsworth: Penguin.

Schein, E. (1992), *Organization Culture and Leadership.* San Fransisco: Jossey-Bass.

Scheuer, S. (1990), 'Struktur og forhandling. Aspekter af fagbevægelsens strukturudvikling i efterkrigstiden: Ekstern struktur, medlemstal samt strukturen i de kollektive overenskomstforhandlinger'. In *Årbog for Arbejderbevægelsens Historie* (Vol. 20). Copenhagen: Selskabet til Forskning i Arbejderbevægelsens Historie.

Scheuer, S. (1992), 'Denmark: return to decentralization'. In A. Ferner and R. Hyman (eds), *Industrial Relations in the New Europe.* Oxford: Blackwell, pp. 168–97.

Scheuer, S. (1993), 'Leaders and laggards: who goes first in bargaining rounds?'. In T. Boje and S. Olsson (eds), *Scandinavia in the New Europe.* Oslo: Scandinavian University Press.

Scheuer, S. (1996), *Faelles aftale eller egen kontrakt i arbejdslivet: Udbredelsen af kollektive overenskomster, faglig organisering og skriftlige ansaettelsesbeviser blandt privatansatte.* Copenhagen: New Social Science Monographs.

Sisson, K. (1993), 'In search of HRM', *British Journal of Industrial Relations,* **31** (2), pp. 201–10.

Traxler, F. (1994), 'Collective bargaining: levels and coverage'. In OECD (1994), Chapter 5, pp. 167–94.

8 Sweden: the Fate of Human Resource Management in a 'Folkish' Society

JOHAN BERGLUND AND JAN LÖWSTEDT

Introduction

The term 'human resources' is not new. It was introduced by Raymond Miles in 1965 when he made a distinction between three models of management: 'traditional', 'human relations' and 'human resources'. In human resources there is a concern with peoples values and abilities:

> which focus attention on all organization members as reservoirs of untapped resources. These resources include not only physical skills and energy, but also creative ability and capacity for responsible, self-directed, self-controlled behaviour. Given these assumptions about people, the manager's job cannot be viewed as one of giving direction and obtaining co-operation. Instead, his primary task becomes that of creating an environment in which the total resources of his department can be utilized.
>
> Miles, 1965, p. 150

However, according to Pieper (1990, p. 2) this definition became an umbrella definition for a variety of related approaches rather than a single theory. One common and unifying theme of these approaches is that people are viewed as having the potential to grow and develop. As the above quotation suggests people constitute a dynamic resource pool which managers need to nurture and develop. Hence, the work of organizational humanists such as Argyris and McGregor can be seen as an important precursor to modern writing on human resource management (HRM). Both these writers saw a conflict between the interests and needs of the organization and that of the employees in that the represent-atives of the former (the managers) frequently apply tight controls to ensure that individuals act in accordance with the overall goals of the organization thereby stifling their individuality and potential. Both these authors, in their own way, argue that such an approach to the management of people is too restrictive and nar-row. Accordingly they stress that people want to take responsib-ility for their development, are willing to learn and want to grow as human beings. As a consequence, they view work not as a painful and soul-destroying experience which is necessary for survival but as an important part in the development of self-identity and an opportunity for self-actualization.

Similarly, Swedes are strongly committed to the development of the individual and consequently tend to view work as an opportun-ity for self-development. Indeed, the value of work and people's right to be employed are central dimensions of the 'Swedish model'. There is a strong feeling that people need to express themselves economically. Therefore everyone should have the opportunity to work. As a consequence, some commentators have suggested that Sweden could be more adequately char-acterized as a 'workfare' state, rather than a welfare state (see Hampden-Turner and Trompenaars, 1993). Such an approach to work stresses 'the fullest use of human resources'. This is reflected in the Swedish view that unemployment is a failure of society to include everyone, and that work should be adapted to people, rather than people to work (Hampden-Turner and Trompe-naars, 1993). One explanation for the strong emphasis on the high value of work in Sweden is that it is seen as one of the most important activities in creating meaning and a social identity. According to Daun (1989) Swedes generally have a more positive attitude towards work than people in other European countries (see also Zetterberg, 1983). The Swedish orientation towards work with its positive connotations raises the following question: is this relatively committed and motivated workforce a conse-quence of a widespread application of an HRM approach to employee management, or is it better explained by other factors such as the societal context, which would suggest that an extens-ive application of HRM was not needed in the first place?

To answer this question we will examine how HRM is perceived and discussed in the cultural setting of Sweden. Different arenas are considered to be important for transmitting and modifying HRM, or HRM-related, ideas – industry, business schools and popular management books. All of these are examined below; but, before we proceed any further it is first necessary to define HRM for the purpose of this chapter. We use the term in its generic sense to refer to those policies and practices which represent a break with previous approaches to the management of the employment relationship in that they are concerned with: (1) the decentralization of the employment relationship; and (2) the individualization of the employment relationship. HRM therefore includes subject areas which have traditionally been the concern of industrial relations, management, occupational psychology and sociology. As the chapter unfolds we will gradually reveal more specifically what is meant by this concept in Sweden as well as how it is perceived by Swedish writers.

We begin by detailing the key features of the 'Swedish model' and then examining the nature of Swedish culture. We argue that the paradoxical combination of strong collectivism and independence in Swedish society has created the conditions upon which succeeding governments have sought to create a *Gesellschaft* within the framework of a *Gemeinschaft*. This argument is then applied to the development of HRM. In order to determine the current state of HRM in Sweden we examine the emergence of the personnel function in SCANIA, the output of the seven business schools and departments of administration in Sweden as well as the key themes contained in prize-winning management books. This leads us to argue in the final sections of the chapter that an HRM approach to the employment relationship has failed to emerge because Swedish society lacks an elaborated idea of the unit to which the policies are targeted – the individual. We conclude by arguing that the future of HRM in Sweden is inextricably linked to the future of the Swedish model.

Institutional Factors – One People, One Model

The characteristics which are often used to describe (working) life in Sweden include consensus, participation, industrial democracy, corporatism and a highly developed public sector. These characteristics can be seen as central elements in what is often

referred to as the 'Swedish model'. In 1938 the 'historical compromise' was reached in the Saltsjöbaden agreement after a long
and bitter fight between employers and employees. This is often
considered to be the starting point for a period of central negotiations and joint agreements between these two parties (Trägårdh,
1990).

In the beginning, the 'Swedish model' was considered by many
as a good example of a capitalist welfare state – a utopia in the
north. According to Gould (1993), 'it seemed to some that Sweden had achieved an impressive balance between the needs of
the business community to respond to the changing conditions of
private markets, thereby generating profits and the demands for
employees for security and a good standard of living' (p. 163).
Even the prototypical liberals in America seemed to take an interest in this 'Middle Way' model . This is shown most notably in
Marquis W. Childs' best-seller *Sweden: the Middle Way*
(1936/1974) which described the Swedish model in glowing
terms emphasizing that this approach was actually working at a
time when so many other approaches adopted in other market
economies were failing. The 'Middle Way' model mediates
between capitalism and socialism and is based on a thorough
specialization between these two opposites (SOU, 1990, pp. 44,
119). While private ownership is the dominating form in industry,
the social welfare system and decisions concerning resource allocation are governed by the public sector.

What does the Sweden model look like in more detail? Before
answering this question it should be noted that to talk of a single
Swedish model obscures its dynamic nature and the inherent contradictions and tensions within it. Thus, the Swedish model
should not be seen as a precise, static and unambiguous concept. In spite of these caveats there are a number central features of the model which are commonly identified by
commentators. The final report of the five-year interdisciplinary
research programme titled Power and Democracy in Sweden
(SOU, 1990, p. 44) identified some of the core dimensions of the
'Swedish model'. Among other things the Swedish model has
been referred to as a certain way of handling conflicts in the
labour market. A central notion in the history of Swedish politics
from 1938 to the present day has been the non-interventionist
stance of the state. Kjellberg (1992) has argued that the Swedish
industrial relations system is one of 'centralized self regulation'.
He writes that 'the relatively passive stance of the Swedish state

reflects historical factors such as the relatively non-repressive character of the state in the early years of 'the union movement; the deep disunity of the bourgeois parties, vitiating several attempts at legislation; and the prominent role of the employer and union confederations, paving the way for self-regulation as an alternative to state regulation' (Kjellberg, 1992, p. 94). Issues relating to salaries and working conditions are therefore handled by the parties in the labour market without any interference from the state.

The distribution of power in the negotiations relating to salaries and working conditions is another important aspect of the Swedish model. The fact that centralized negotiations were held between a small number of central and homogeneous organizations representing the main parties in the labour market facilitated the development and implementation of a 'solidaristic wage policy'. The general ideal of centralization has long been a key characteristic of the Swedish model. Centralization and advantages of scale were thought of as important for growth and efficiency in general. The state was supportive of structural rationalizations both in the public and the private sectors of the economy.

The concept of the Swedish model has also been used to refer to a certain kind of political climate or culture in Sweden. The historical compromise between labour and capital, embodied by the Saltsjöbaden agreement in 1938, helped in the creation of a Swedish political culture based on a *culture of consensus*. Collective decisions, negotiations and agreements are seen as important aspects of this political culture.

Another common characteristic is the idea of the *strong society.* This idea is manifested in one of the largest and most extensive public sectors in the Western world. As Gould (1993) writes 'the range of services and personnel, the scope and generosity of benefits, the all-embracing pervasiveness of the programmes testify to a formidable structure' (p. 200). Certain services – for example health care, child care, education – are supplied by public organizations in order to guarantee the welfare and equal treatment of all citizens. In Sweden the public service system was founded on the idea of high quality standard solutions, or as Gustav Möller (Minister of Social Affairs 1924–6 and 1932–51), and one of the major architects of the model, put it: 'only the best is good enough for the people' (Rothstein, 1992, pp. 25–6). The central idea underpinning the development of the public service system was to offer the same high quality service to everyone, thereby ensuring broad support and equal treatment of all citizens.

Cultural Factors

Although a society is a collection of unique individuals some experiences and values are collectively shared. These collectively shared experiences and values are important aspects of the web of significance that binds people together in what is commonly described as a national culture. The similarities in thinking, reasoning and acting among people are seen as manifestations of a shared national culture. The Swedish national culture is considered comparatively homogeneous (Daun, 1989). Consequently, when contrasted with other cultures the 'Swedishness' of the people of Sweden is often clearly discernible. It is important to note that when comparing national cultures different values between cultures imply that something which is viewed as a negative trait by foreign observers may be looked upon as something natural or positive in another nation and vice versa. While there may be a number of similarities between national cultures (such as language and religion), for the purposes of this discussion we focus on the differences. This raises the question: when asking foreigners about their observations of Sweden and Swedes, and asking Swedes about their own self-images, what are the typical elements of Swedish culture that are emphasized?

Sweden is often depicted as a culture of consensus, where rational discussions and agreements pave the way for collective action. Reaching consensus is important. This image is understandable in the light of some central cultural characteristics often ascribed to Sweden.

1. One important characteristic is that Sweden is a low-context culture (Daun, 1989, p. 127), that is, relatively homogeneous and integrated, consisting of people who more or less share the same moral values, language, religion and so on. Sweden was, until recently, a country of low immigration. This means that the differences between Swedes are small thus facilitating communication between different groups and opening up the possibility of consensual agreement and collective action.

2. Following from the previous point, conflict avoidance is an important dimension of the Swedish culture. Face-to-face conflict tends to be avoided. According to Daun (1989), in a conversation Swedes typically avoid emotional subjects and subjects where opinions are divided and conflict and differences are likely emerge. In conversations one is not supposed to raise one's voice, or lose one's temper. Calm and friendly discussions are preferred. Consequently, there is a generally negative attitude towards aggressiveness and aggressiveness in the public arena in particular. The exception is during sporting activities where aggressiveness is often seen as a positive trait.

3. As a consequence of this tendency to avoid conflict Swedes are often seen as 'shy', 'reserved' and 'indifferent'. To speak in public in general, and to strangers in particular, is something to be avoided if at all possible. Although communication-anxiety is something that is shared with other nations, such as USA, people in the latter nation attempt to overcome this anxiety and therefore show greater willingness and competence to communicate with others. One of the reasons for this is that shyness is perceived more negatively in USA than in Sweden. Cultural norms differ between these countries: shyness in USA is thought of as a sign of a lack of competence and intelligence, whereas shyness in Sweden is seen as a positive trait, as a sign of sensitivity, thoughtfulness and consideration of others.

4. A fourth characteristic of Swedish culture is its rationalistic bias. Traditionally, different groups of experts have participated in the design and implementation of the Swedish model. The belief in experts, and their ability to plan and design 'the good society', has traditionally been strong. Hence, rational social engineering has been seen as something that is both desirable and possible (Hirdman, 1989). According to Zetterberg (1984, cited in Daun, 1989) there exists a Swedish version of rationality in which the technical or practical usefulness of knowledge is emphasized over abstract theoretical reasoning. As Czarniawksa-Joerges (1993) notes 'in Sweden, academics teaching practitioners rarely have a substantial advantage over the practitioners' awareness of current issues, whereas teaching programmes in e.g. Great Britain seem to have remained about 10–20 years behind current research concerns' (p. 238). Hence, in Sweden academic research

tends to be more practical, aimed at solving particular problems. This may be because to solve a problem in a rational manner in Sweden is to seek a *lagom* (reasonable) solution, not necessarily the one best solution. This idea of *lagom* – not too much, not too little, somewhere in between – is central in the Swedish culture, and it manifests itself in several different areas of society. As observed by Michael Maccoby:

> The Swedes have a term for fairness, *lagom*, which means 'just right'. . . . Swedish children learn that putting either too much or too little on the plate is not *lagom*, and Swedish unions demand that wages be *lagom* enough to create solidarity. The value of *lagom* permeates Swedish culture and is a way of minimizing the envy and sibling rivalry that could destroy the solidarity of the Swedish national family.
>
> Maccoby, 1991, p. 6.

In everyday life, according to Daun (1989, p. 260), Swedes have a 'strong preference for rational arguments, facts and concreteness, as opposed to emotional and speculative imagination'. As a consequence, 'professional talk' as opposed to 'small talk' is something that most Swedes are familiar with, and feel more comfortable discussing. Symptomatically, at more or less formal occasions, where conversation or 'small talk' with strangers is expected (and often unavoidable), one common opening phrase seems to be: 'What do you do for a living?' One summary of Swedish mentality might be: about facts one may speak, otherwise one should be silent (or only discuss other subjects with friends within one's private sphere).

This culture of consensus – in which reason prevails and joint agreements are reached between parties that are supposed to be in conflict (for example, representatives of labour and capital) – is sometimes characterized as a collectivistic culture. Gould (1993), for example, argues that Sweden is a collectivistic country. Partly basing his discussion on the work of Heclo and Marsden (1986), he suggests that Swedes are dominated by organizations, both in their working and social life. Furthermore, they seem to be very conformist in their participation in different types of organizations where their individual interests are subordinated to those of the organization or the group. According to Gould (1993, p. 177) 'as a result of excessive paternalism and authoritarianism, Swedes have become self-policing'. In contrast, Swedes view their private life as very private and therefore seek to protect it from invasion. According to Heclo and Marsden (1986, quoted in Gould, 1993, p. 177) 'just as American individualism creates a land of the gregarious, so Swedish communitarianism creates a land of the truly solitary'. Thus, in the public arena while the typical Swede is described as friendly and polite they find it difficult to engage in small talk. Their inner thoughts and feelings are reserved for a chosen few (their close friends). In short, Swedes do not seem to think it is appropriate to mix their public and private lives. Their home is their castle in an almost literal sense. This apparently deep paradoxical combination of strong collectivism and independence in Swedish society has been termed by Hampden-Turner and Trompenaars (1993) the 'ethic of socially oriented individualism' (pp. 243–7). They state that 'Swedes begin with the individual, his or her integrity, uniqueness, freedom, needs and values, yet insist that the fulfilment and destiny of the individual lies in developing and sustaining others by the gift of his or her work and energy' (p. 243).

A *Gesellschaft* within the Frames of a *Gemeinschaft*

Institutional factors cannot be separated from cultural factors. Institutional factors (whether one defines them as rules, conventions, laws, formal organizations, government agencies and so forth) are embedded in a social and cultural context (see Chapter 1). This section is an attempt to show how some of the underlying ideas of the Swedish 'Middle Way' model manifest themselves.

Our main argument is that Sweden could be seen as a country which attempted, and some would argue succeeded, to create a modern industrialized society within an all-embracing community. To put this another way, it could be argued that Sweden tried to create a *Gesellschaft* within the framework of a *Gemeinschaft*. Let us first take a closer look at these two concepts developed by Ferdinand Tönnies – *Gemeinschaft* and *Gesellschaft* – which are central to the analysis which follows. Accordingly to Tönnies (1963) life a *Gemeinschaft* society is characterized by among other things unity, harmony and intimacy. A *Gemeinschaft* society is comprised of brothers and sisters. It should be understood as a living organism, as something natural, not a construction of people. In a *Gemeinschaft* society thought and action are one, they comprise a unity. In contrast, a *Gesellschaft* society is comprised of strangers; people act in isolation by themselves and for themselves. No individual action takes 'place on behalf of those united with him' (Tönnies, p. 65). Thus, in a *Gesellschaft* society *homo oeconomicus* rules. Furthermore, thought and action are separated with the former preceding the latter. The organizing principle in a *Gesellschaft* society is conflict, but of a narrow, economical kind – that is, competition. People compete with each other trying to maximize their own utility.

We wish to suggest that the Swedish model is intimately connected with a folkish ideology which attracted large groups of people (not individuals)[1] uniting them in an organic community 'forged by common blood and deep roots in the native soil' (Trägårdh, 1990, p. 30). The themes of the folkish ideology were elaborated by the Social Democratic party with Per Albin Hansson as the figurehead, although the famous term *Folkhem* (the peoples' home) was apparently borrowed from the conservatives (Trägårdh, 1990, p. 42). Gradually the different political parties joined in supporting this folkish discourse, except for the Communists who clung onto their more narrow and less inclusive concept of the worker. Soon the bourgeoisie, the workers and the farmers spoke a similar language, living comfortably in their people's homes. Thus the Swedish model can be seen as an attempt to realize a *Gesellschaft* within the framework of a *Gemeinschaft* – it was an attempt to create the best of two worlds – the romantic and the enlightened one. After a while, the *Gesellschaft* elements became dominant. The central agreement between the employers and the employees reached in 1938 'signalled the end to worker-employer hostilities and paved the way for the economic basis of the welfare state' (Trägårdh, 1990, p. 48). The wheels of the *Gesellschaft* started to spin faster and faster. Without suggesting any evolutionary necessity Sweden witnessed a shift in emphasis from the ideal of a *Folkhem* – the *Folkmovements* and the spirit of Saltsjöbaden – to the corporate machine – Sweden Inc. However, we would suggest that some of the *Gemeinschaft* ideals have remain strongly entrenched in the Swedish culture and have consequences for the way in which the employment relationship is managed – or is supposed to be managed.

HRM in Practice – the Case of Scania Trucks

As a reaction to the negative consequences of the industrial revolution, social movements were formed in both Europe and the USA. In Sweden this movement was institutionalized in 1922, when the SAIA (Social Workers for Industry and Working Life) was formed. Women mainly worked in the SAIA and the focus of their concern and efforts was the workplace. Gradually, companies began to establish offices with the purpose of improving the working conditions of their employees. The task of these offices was to reduce work hazards, improve sanitary conditions, training and primary education for young workers and so forth. These offices are a part of the history of the modern personnel department.

According to Hampden-Turner and Trompenaars (1993, p. 246) the development of these early, and hardly recognizable, personnel departments may stem from Swedish organizations' dedication to the development of the individual. In their study Swedish respondents indicated that they believed that Swedish organizations should go to the trouble of redesigning jobs to fit the individual. This is also complemented by their belief in making the 'fullest use of human resources' (Hampden-Turner and Trompenaars, 1993, pp. 247–50). As we suggested earlier this is supported by the belief that in order to assist *everyone* to work, work should be adapted to people, rather than people to work.

The development of the personnel department at SCANIA, the Swedish truck manufacturer, is perhaps typical of Swedish companies. The story of this company indicates that modern personnel departments have their origin in the administration of wages on the one hand and the social responsibility for workers on the other hand. An informal personnel department (for example a working group) was established in 1946. The main purpose of this department was to deal with social issues such as contacts with social authorities (for instance education and employment). One example is contacts with the church to help arrange funerals in the case of a death in the family of the worker.[2] Another main activity was employees' accommodation. The growth of the company resulted in an increasing need to hire people from more distant parts of the country – and later on immigrants as well. All these people needed help with temporary accommodation, and then as their families joined them permanent housing. Until 1949 the senior accountant of the company was responsible for personnel-related issues concerning white-collar workers. In this year these concerns were integrated with recruitment which had previously been the responsibility of line managers. At this time there were eleven people working in the personnel department at SCANIA looking after a workforce of 2,000 employees.

The personnel department grew at a faster rate than the company in the following period. During the 1950s and 1960s the proportion of employees working in the personnel department tripled. The major part of this growth consisted of people working in the area of recruitment. One consequence of this was that the administrative tasks outnumbered social tasks during the period. Thus, the focus of the work of the personnel department shifted from the needs of the individual to the needs of the organization, in line with the major trend in Swedish industry during this time (Damm, 1993). The social responsibilities of the company increased during the 1960s when safety and work conditions for employees became increasingly important. At the same time the company began to become involved in organizing the leisure time of its employees. Examples of this include the establishment of holiday homes at the seaside for employees and their families, and the construction of sports facilities.

During the 1970s, the expansion of the personnel function came to a halt. There was a growing awareness that the management of employees had become too specialized and too separated from line management. As a consequence, the company decided to redefine the mission of the personnel department. The responsibility for managing personnel, it was argued, should be taken by managers at all levels. Therefore, the role of the personnel specialists became one of providing services and expertise to line managers in order to support them in their task of managing those employed in their departments.

During the 1970s, the relationship between the employers' federation and the unions became strained. In line with the general trend in society, the collaborative spirit which had existed between the parties was broken. The strongly Social Democratic government aimed at a democratization of working life which resulted in laws and regulations instead of agreements between the parties in the labour market. This led to a shift in the content of the tasks carried out in the personnel department. Negotiations with the unions in accordance with the procedures set out in the Co-determination Act, and the training of managers to act in accordance with the provisions of the law, became priorities. During the initial period after the implementation of the Co-determination Act in 1977 there was a considerable number of disputes with the union about decisions taken by the company and on procedural matters. During the 1980s the Co-determination Act became an integral part of the industrial-relations system in the company. Furthermore, as it emerged that the Act had not altered the balance of power between the company and workers' representatives to any great extent its impact on the nature of the work performed by the personnel department diminished.

Managers in the personnel department at SCANIA currently describe themselves and their work in a very pragmatic way: 'Of course we keep up with new ideas in the field but we always ask ourselves if these new ideas are sensible before we try them. Maybe we are unnecessarily disobliging . . . Qualified behavioural methods carry more costs than benefits. They are not only expensive approaches to use, they also raise expectations that are difficult to meet'.

Is this description of the development of the personnel function in SCANIA similar to that in other organizations in Sweden? According to Damm (1993), four phases in the development of the role of personnel/HR departments can be identified.

1. The initial phase (1910–49) was characterized by a focus on social issues, where special concern was given to the poor and uneducated working-class families.
2. The next phase (1950–69) was characterized by a shift from social work to personnel administration.
3. The third phase, the democratization of Swedish working life (1970–79), resulted in new laws, regulations and agreements to be handled by the personnel department.
4. During the present phase (1980 onwards) personnel issues have grown more important. They have become more and more a managerial concern, and sometimes even an issue of strategic importance. It is during this period that the Anglo-American term HRM has become increasingly used to describe the nature of and the activities of the personnel function.

The descriptions of the development of the personnel department in SCANIA and the more general development in Swedish industry described by Damm (1993) show a shift in the work of the personnel department from an administrative to a managerial focus. In

Swedish industry, both the use of the term HRM, and a managerial perspective on personnel issues, is a recent development. If this is the case in industry is the topic of HRM considered important in academia as well?

HRM in Academia

During a series of lectures held in the end of the 1950s on the theme 'Social Psychology in the Service of Work-life' Professor Gunnar Westerlund argued that the organization can be considered as a social system of co-operating groups. As a consequence, the design of work should acknowledge the social needs of employees. Westerlund was Professor of Social Psychology and Personnel Administration at the Stockholm School of Economics. He was the first professor in this field in Sweden. He was also a leading proponent of human relations ideas and, according to Damm (1993), in his work he attempted to synthesize ideas from the classical administrative school with those of industrial psychology, in other words, he attempted the synthesis of rational interests with human needs. Although not a professor of personnel management or HRM his work was very much in this area. Recently attempts have been made to create a chair in Human Resource Management in Sweden. However, these attempts have failed as a result of the government arguing that this area was already well represented in other traditional academic disciplines (Damm, 1993). Indeed, when Westerlund retired in 1978 rather than creating a chair in personnel management his chair was incorporated into the general discipline of business administration. This unwillingness to consider personnel management, or HRM, as a distinctive discipline and field of study has two important implications:

1. Its constituent parts are spread out in a number discipline areas with the consequence that the research being conducted in this area is similarly dispersed.
2. Since HRM is not at present a distinctive and separate field of study in Sweden, identifying that research which is being undertaken within the general area of HRM is not an easy task. Indeed, in many cases such research may not even be considered as HRM research but as research in management or occupational psychology and so on.

In order to determine whether HRM has infiltrated the academic agenda in Sweden we examined all publications emanating from the seven business schools and departments of administration in Sweden between 1983 and 1994.[3] If HRM had entered the academic arena we would expect a number of these 1,339 publications to reflect this in their titles and content. The results of this survey show that only *five* publications included some version of the term 'human resource management' in their titles:

- Larsson (1991; and Larsson et al., 1993) – two papers on 'strategic human resource management';
- Katarina Östergren at the University of Umeå – a report entitled *Människan en kritisk resurs. En studie av mönster i kunskaps-människans beteende* (1989) (The Human Being a Critical Resource: A Study of Patterns in the Behaviour of the Knowledgeable Human Being);
- Jörgen Sandberg's book entitled *Human Competence at Work* (1993)
- Norbäck-Targama's book entitled *Människan i organizationen* (1988) (The Human Being in the Organization).

However, HRM is a broad subject encompassing a number of distinctive academic fields such as industrial relations, organizational behaviour, occupational psychology, sociology and general management. Hence, simply looking for publications with HRM, or some variant, in their title may not reflect the total picture. Thus, when the search was widened to include publications about employee management and work organizations in general (in other words, with more of an industrial-relations perspective) the number of hits increased to fifty-seven. This indicates that 4 per cent of the 1,339 Swedish academic business-related publications during the period 1983–94 dealt with HRM related issues. Furthermore, according to table 8.1 only two of the fifty-seven HRM-related publications explicitly used the term HRM.

If one examines these publications in more detail, it becomes apparent that more than 60 per cent of them seem to cover topics more related to industrial relations (that is, they focus on the institutions – the state, employers and the unions – concerned with central collective bargaining procedures) than to HRM (focusing on the management of the relationship between the organization and the individual). Consequently, when it comes to issues about employees and their development in a broad sense of the term the perspective applied is from the employee's viewpoint

Table 8.1 The incidence of HRM-related topics in Swedish academic research publications between 1983 and 1994

HRM-related topics	Number of reports	% of total reports
Co-determination	10	18
Competence and knowledge in organizations	10	18
Union activity	9	16
Transformation of work	7	12
Work-related values and attitudes	5	9
Work environment	4	7
HRM	2	3
Others	10	18
Total	57	101

rather than the managerial elite's. It should be noted though that most of the titles concerning co-determination, work environment and union activity are from the early part of the 1980s. This focus on industrial-relations-related issues rather than HRM is understandable in the light of research and development programs initiated during the period. These issues have been of central concern to government agencies and the parties in the labour market thus attracting research funds.

In summary, the previous discussion would appear to indicate that HRM is not a significant topic of discussion within the academic discipline of business administration in Sweden. Considering that the concept of HRM is used by some of the professionals working within personnel management in industry one might expect to find this topic discussed in publications directed in the main at this audience. Consequently, we now turn to examine some of the management books published in Sweden.

Management Books – the HRM Discourse in Sweden?

Every year the *Swedish Association for Human Resource Management* (SPF)[4] awards a prize to the book which it considers to have dealt best with issues concerning personnel and personnel management in the past year. Most of the winning books are written primarily for a practitioner audience. In the discussion which follows we examine the awarded books during the period 1983–94. We wish to determine whether any patterns emerge from this literature on how managers currently manage, or ought to manage, the employment relationship.

One of the key themes in the literature was the emphasis, and possibly increasing emphasis, on the individual. The growing importance of the individual was highlighted in these texts in a number of different ways. One common argument was that changes in the values in Swedish society have lead to a greater emphasis on the individual rather than the collective. This may reflect a weakening in the Swedish 'ethic of socially orientated individualism' referred to earlier. Another related argument has been the increasing importance of knowledge workers and knowledge-intensive organizations (KIOs). In these circumstances an organization's employees are its main asset and a key source of competitive advantage. As a consequence, employees are considered as a strategic resource, and HRM is therefore viewed as an important activity within these companies for creating and sustaining the competitive edge by harnessing the full potential of employees. An important tool or instrument for achieving this is the creation and maintenance of a corporate culture. We now turn to examine some of these themes in more detail.

Lindstedt (1985) argues, in one of the winning books, that during the last decade something has happened in Sweden: to show initiative is not only acceptable nowadays, it is considered desirable and necessary. Gone is the economical and technocratic mentality of the 1970s, to be replaced by a more individualistic perspective. Similarly, Jöever (1984) argues:

> Look at this book as a source of inspiration. Look at it also as a product of a decade with growing awareness of the individual's responsibility and importance, regardless of whether the person is a manager or an employee. It has emerged in a climate of greater openness and a climate in which achieving results is both important and demanded.
>
> Jöever, 1985, p. 7

One of the arguments propounded by Sveiby and Risling (1986) is that Swedish society is becoming more dependent upon the acquisition and development of sophisticated knowledge. Mass production is becoming less important as the focus changes from quantity to quality. They describe this as a significant shift from the 'paradigm of maximization' to the 'paradigm of quality'. The implication is not that those organizations which focus on mass production will disappear, but that these organizations will have to face the implications of the Knowledge Society – changes which are manifested by the increasingly pivotal position being adopted by knowledge producing companies (KIOs) in the Swedish economy.

Another important consequence of this new era seems to be the emergence of a new type of individual with a new mentality. But what does these new human beings look like? They are well-educated, confident, sure of themselves and young (Sveiby, 1991). Furthermore, they consider self-realization to be more important than material rewards. While this post-materialist person is not a modest consumer, he or she will tend to focus consumption on experiences rather than tangible goods. These knowledgeable individuals will tend to want to do things their own way, as far as is possible. They are loyal to no one but themselves. These individuals represent a new management challenge according to Sveiby (1991). How do you control well-educated individuals with little, or no, loyalty to the organization? One solution is to develop a strong organizational culture. He writes: 'The decisive advantage of using corporate culture as a management tool is that it could be created as a frame, as "the ten commandments" . . . A well defined and strong culture makes it possible for the managers to let the entrepreneurs loose, knowing that they will work within the pre-set frames' (Sveiby, 1986, p. 109).

Although borrowed from anthropology it is evident that the concept of organizational culture is usually interpreted in the pragmatic, or instrumental, manner so familiar to management discourses. This is clearly the case with all the awarded books discussing this topic. Corporate culture is viewed as yet another variable added to the manager's arsenal of tools for motivation and control, rather than as a metaphor (Smircich, 1983). Companies are seen as having (manageable) cultures, rather than being cultures, or cultural manifestations, beyond the clear-cut control of man.

In summary, when examining the central themes of these awarded books the notion that 'a company's employees are the firm's most valuable asset' appears to be an outdated one. Given the themes contained in these books this notion is fast being replaced by the idea that 'a company's *individuals* are its most valuable asset'. One of the major changes that the authors frequently propose is that Sweden is currently going through what one may termed a shift toward an individualistic orientation. The historically valued centralistic and collectivistic tendencies in Swedish society are changing. The new trends point towards decentralization and local initiatives. The individual is becoming more important, more strategic, more skilful and knowledgeable. As a result of this change in orientation from collectivism to individualism, earlier positive Swedish traits are now depicted more negatively. For example, striving towards consensus solutions is now seen as conflict avoidance, and arguing for equality is now depicted as a pressure towards uniformity (Czarniawska-Joerges, 1993).

In a discussion of different definitions of HRM in British and American literature, Legge identifies some common themes.

> In the majority of these definitions several common themes stand out: that human resources policies should be integrated with strategic business planning and used to reinforce an appropriate (or change an inappropriate) organizational culture, that human resources are valuable and a source of competitive advantage.
>
> Legge, 1989, p. 25

When comparing the common themes identified by Legge with the themes identified in Swedish management books, the similarities appear self-evident. Hence, the management books in Sweden seem to be an important arena for the Swedish HRM discourse.

The Swedes and their Institutionalized Model

Before we try to answer the question posed at the beginning of this chapter – whether or not the relatively committed and motivated workforce in Sweden is a consequence of a widespread application of HRM, or whether it is better explained by other factors such as national culture – let us summarize the previous arguments.

The discussion of the development of the personnel department SCANIA suggests that personnel management was traditionally built on paternalistic values with an emphasis on looking after the well-being of the workforce. The result of growth in the Swedish economy on the back of export success led to more time being spent on administrative tasks such as wages and recruitment. Owing to the more legalistic strategies of the unions during the 1970s, the task of the personnel departments became more focused on the negotiation and interpretation of the new emerging laws and regulations. During this period several research programmes were initiated by government agencies, employers and trades unions. As suggested above (and to be argued below in more detail) the researchers from a variety of academic disciplines which have shown interest in the employment relationship have been more concerned with industrial relations – where issues concerning work environment, co-determination, industrial democracy were studied and implemented[5] – rather than with management techniques such as HRM. When it comes to HRM business research, on the other hand, is silent. As discussed earlier, the researchers within business and administration departments in Swedish universities have shown little interest in studying HRM.

In contrast, when studying more popular books on management, the rhetoric related to HRM could be heard more frequently. Judging by the awards given by SPF, there is an ongoing HRM discussion in Sweden which has much in common with the international discussion on the subject. Furthermore, it seems as though this discussion is a fairly recent phenomenon. In short, the rhetoric of HRM is not found in the research produced either in the field of sociology of organization or business and administration. To find similar rhetoric one has to turn to more popular management books.

Historically the Swedish model since the 1930s has been characterized by a highly centralized system, in which union and employer federations, in the name of progress and the collective good, negotiated such overall issues as wages, working conditions and technology agreements. The underlying model guiding much of the public discourse, research and practice in Sweden during this period has been an industrial relations model (IR – Söderström and Lindström, 1994). In such a model three parties are seen as the main actors – the state, the unions and the employers – all of whom are represented as having conflicting interests. In contrast, in Sweden, the relations between these parties have been charaterized by harmony and mutual understanding since the 'historical compromise' was signed at Saltsjöbaden. The ideological model which underpinned these values emphasized the importance of national and collective interests and central negotiations as a way of fulfilling welfare goals and improving the economic position of the nation. This ideological model contrasts sharply with the HRM model which places a greater emphasis on the individual and on company-level negotiations. According to Söderström and Lindström (1994) proponents of this latter model have only appeared recently in Sweden with the consequence that the negotiations between the parties in the labour market in Sweden are characterized by a clash between these two perspectives.

The answer to the question with which we began this chapter has to be that the relatively committed workforce in Sweden is not an example of an extensive application of an HRM approach to employee management. One explanation for the low influence of HRM in Sweden could be that the underlying Industrial Relations model, with its high degree of central regulation and negotiation, coupled with strong unions, hinders the diffusion of an HRM approach. According to Pieper (1990), these factors have, in different degrees, obstructed the development of an HRM approach to employee management in many Western European countries. This is very much the case in Sweden. The scope of choice for Swedish companies in designing work organizations and managing employees is relatively narrow and is restricted. According to this explanation there has been no room for HRM approaches.

The explanation just offered is an institutional one that uses a narrow definition of institution (as the rules, laws, regulations and agreements that govern the function of the labour market). As mentioned earlier, in our view institutional arrangements are always embedded in a cultural context because institutions are cultural manifestations. Using this wider definition of an institution as 'a set of cultural rules that give generalized meaning to social activity and regulate it in a patterned way' (Meyer et al., 1987, p. 36), we wish to suggest an alternative, although related, explanation. We argue that historically there has been *no perceived need* for HRM approaches due to the limited role of the individual in this Folkish society. In a society where collective interests are considered more important than individual interests in the public arena and where this is considered to be the most natural way of seeing things, HRM approaches appear strange and unnecessary. Thus, when certain values and ideals become institutionalized they eliminate alternative interpretations (Meyer et al., 1987). To substantiate our argument we will discuss in more detail why the individual only plays a small part in the public arena in Sweden.

A collective or corporatist society (*Gemeinschaft*) is often contrasted with a individualistic or liberal society (*Gesellschaft*). Often these two opposites are treated dualistically, where the one extreme is considered incompatible with the other. In other words *either* a society has a collectivistic nature or it has an individualistic one. Each of these types of society is organized differently with different approaches to the question of control so central in the sociological literature. We wish to suggest that both these extremes are two sides of the same coin and that they therefore cannot be considered separately. To understand how society is (re-)constructed one must understand how the individual is (re-)constructed and *vice versa*. There is a dialectical relationship between these two (re-)constructions (Asplund, 1983). Nowhere is this dialectical relationship between the individual and society clearer than in a liberal society where the emphasis is on the individual and any form of supra-individual agency (in other words, society) is weak.

> For instance, the elaboration of theories of self-esteem lead to personal projects and rights to self-actualization and fulfilment resulting in both organizational programs and commodities that promise these outcomes. Conversely, commodities from the automobile, television and personalized personal computers to a shampoo that meets the 'ever changing needs' of one's hair . . . all greatly expand the legitimate domain of the self and highly articulate subtle nuances of fulfilled selfhood.
>
> Meyer et al., 1987, p. 23

This quotation, which describes American society, suggests that 'no person is an island'. For individuals to act and in so doing to express their individuality, they need institutions in various forms to legitimate and give meaning to their actions. Their actions are influenced by, and defined as such, by the institutional setting in the society. At the same time, their actions legitimate, or (re-)produce, the institutions. It is a reciprocal process. In this view then, the more elaborated the individual in a society the more elaborated is the institutional setting which enables, as well as hinders, him or her to express individuality.

In Sweden the individual and his or her relationship to society is (re-)constructed differently. Rather than adhering to a liberal or an American celebration of the individual, the Swedish view of individualism is influenced by German ideas and ideals. In Sweden the German romantic idea of individuality (*individualität*) – the notion of the human being as original and unique – 'became transformed into an organic and nationalistic theory of community' (Lukes, 1973, p. 20). Society was considered a spiritual whole, and individuality was ascribed not only to persons, but to the state and nation as well. This view stands in stark contrast to the liberal view of individuality in which society was conceived of as a rational construction, as a series of contractual arrangements between sterile and abstract individuals. This different view of the individual, we suggest, has consequences for the way in which a HRM approach to the employment relationship is received in Sweden.

We wish to suggest that the key explanation for the lack of an HRM approach to the employment relationship could be that Sweden as a society lacks an elaborated idea of the central unit to be organized – the individual. This does not mean that we are suggesting that there are no individuals in Sweden. Rather, we are arguing that they are perceived differently than in more liberal societies and as a consequence they seem to be most clearly discernible in the private sphere – within the walls of their home. Our argument is that in the public or societal arena 'the loaded gun of legitimated actor hood and legitimated interests' (Jepperson and Meyer, 1991, p. 220) is not given to individuals but to groups or organizations which perform legitimated social functions.

In contrast to a liberal/individualist society such as the American one, in which individuals are given a high degree of authorization as public actors, a corporatist society such as Sweden confers this authorization on groups. According to Guillet de Monthoux (1991) decisions in Sweden are results of a group process and individuals are only taken seriously 'when they speak 'on behalf' of a group' (p. 29). As we have seen this emphasis on the collective rather than the individual is clearly a central dimension in the 'Swedish model'. In addition, this emphasis on the collective is reflected in the terms of employment. In Sweden, the

details and terms of employment contracts are the result of negotiations between the unions and employer federations. In contrast, in USA the terms of the contract are invariably determined
between the individual and the employer (Brulin and Nilsson,
1991). Furthermore, an underlying ideal of these central agreements in Sweden is the solidaristic wage policy – equal pay for
equal work.

HRM approaches to employee management with their clear
bias towards an American notion of individuals with interests of
their own and authority to follow them in the public arena do not
fit comfortably with the ideals of a corporatist society. For a HRM
approach to employee management to become established in a
society, a highly elaborated individual in the public arena or organization is required in addition to highly elaborated and active individual demands. The myth or ideology works both ways.

In the next section we consider the implications of changes in
the Swedish model for the long-term future of HRM approaches to
employee management in Sweden.

The Demise of the Swedish Model

Several authors argue that the Swedish model has been changing
for the last decade or two. The president of the Swedish Employers' Federation (SAF), Ulf Laurin, even pronounced the death of
the model in 1990. According to Czarniawska-Joerges (1993) the
study of *Power and Democracy in Sweden*, a five-year interdisciplinary research programme, 'could be seen as performing the
task of peacefully burying the "Swedish model" ' (1993, p. 234).
As mentioned earlier, the central joint agreements between the
parties in the labour market were dependent upon the existence
of a few centralized organizations which shared, more or less, a
similar view of the overall welfare goals of the society and how
these should be reached. According to several authors this is no
longer a valid description of how the Swedish model works,
because today 'organizations are neither few, centralized, or
homogenous' (SOU, 1990: 44, p. 390).

Other authors describe the changes in the Swedish model as a
transformation from a more centralized form to a more decentralized one (Brulin and Victorin, 1992; Brulin and Nilsson, 1991;

Gould, 1993). It could be seen as a transformation from a societal to a managerial corporatism, in which the 'disintegration at the
central level' (Brulin and Nilsson, 1991, p. 328) is partly the
result of the emergence of new forms of work organization
(market-oriented and flexible organizations) to meet the competitive challenge in international markets on which the Swedish
economy is so dependent. One of the characteristics of managerial corporatism in contrast to societal corporatism is that the
former, by regulating the employment relationship at the firm
level, establishes collective and class identity at the enterprise
level rather than at the societal level. This makes it harder for the
unions to create solidarity among employees across the borders
of enterprises. 'Work organization issues are specifically local
matters, and, unlike wage issues, cannot easily be handled by the
main parties at the central level, a fact which became apparent in
Sweden during the 1970s and onwards' (Brulin and Nilsson,
1991, p. 328). Furthermore, the continuation of a solidaristic
wage policy, which could be proposed as an argument for central
negotiations at least when it comes to wages, is also being questioned. An example of this is the rapid development of alternative
remuneration schemes (company level schemes for bonuses,
profit sharing, convertibles and so forth) (Brulin and Nilsson,
1991; Gould, 1993).

The general trend towards decentralization is reflected in the
research and development programmes initiated during the
period as well. At the beginning of the 1970s, several socio-
technical research and development projects were initiated with
the employers and employees jointly participating (Brulin and Nilsson, 1991). These projects 'were created in the spirit of societal
corporatism in order to get away from Taylorism' (Brulin and Nilsson, 1991, p. 336). But what started as a broad national strategy
of joint participation for organizational change broke down in the
late 1970s owing to conflicts between the parties. Instead, the
parties went separate ways initiating so-called one-party research
and development projects. This precipitated a general trend
towards decentralization in Swedish society. As Brulin and Nilsson (1991) write 'paradoxically, these centrally initiated programmes facilitate the path away from societal corporatism. One
characteristic feature of both programmes was the aim to support
local initiatives to create change in work organization' (p. 338).
According to these authors writing at the beginning of the 1990s

it seems that the initiative in work organization issues was held by the local parties to the employment relationship.

Alongside these changes has been a shift in a number of societal values. Nowadays more liberal and individualistic values are seen as important. These changes are most obvious among the younger generations. Somewhat paradoxically Rothstein (1992) argues that the 'success' of the model in itself partly explains the questioning of its relevance today. The author argues that the strengthening and the liberation of the citizen's capacities, as an employee, as a consumer and as a tenant, has created strong citizens with demands for more individual choice.

Conclusion

In this chapter we have argued that HRM approaches at the firm level presuppose an elaborated ideal of the individual. Due to the centralistic and collectivistic focus of the Swedish model the individuals at the firm level have not been that discernible and, hence, not amenable to an HRM approach to employee management. However, HRM-related issues have been integrated at a more central level because groups rather than individuals have been given interests. Thus demand for an HRM approach, in the sense of applicable models and recipes for managing employees, has been low in a folkish society like Sweden. But, as has been suggested by several authors, the Swedish model is presently being questioned and transformed. Hand in hand with the move towards the decentralization of what is left of the Swedish model and towards more individualistic ideals, the individual may become more and more prominent as a public actor. If this is the case and a more elaborated and stronger self emerges in the public arena, raising legitimate claims, the fate of HRM approaches in Sweden may be more promising in the future. In the next few years, then, one might expect to find more researchers, more specialists, helping managers to assist individual employees in their project of self-realization. A project, one might add, realized within the frame of the common good (as defined by management?).

Notes

1 The German word *Volk* or the Swedish equivalent *folk* is, according to Trägårdh (1990), difficult to translate directly into English. In its German or

Swedish use the term focuses on the collective unit, people as a group or a nation rather than people as individuals or citizens. From this perspective the liberal society consists of individual citizens artificially bound together in a *Gesellschaft*. In contrast, the folk is united in the organic and natural *Gemeinschaft* 'by common blood and deep roots in the native soil' (Trägårdh, 1990, p. 30). In a *Gemeinschaft* sisters and brothers dwell together in harmony, whereas a *Gesellschaft* is comprised of strangers. This Germanic ideology of the *Volk* is incompatible with Marxism. The holistic quality of the Volkish ideology does not mix well with the Marxist focus upon a specific segment of society (the less inclusive concept of the working class) and the idea that class struggle is the motor of history. Needless to say, although the ideology of the Swedish Social Democratic party is rooted in similar ideas and ideals as the German ideology of *das Volk*, the ideas in Sweden were elaborated within a democratic context, and stand in sharp contrast to their development in Germany.

2 From the earliest times of industrialization in Sweden companies paid the salaries of the local priest and schoolmaster. Thus Swedish companies became committed to developing a strong social role. This is supported by Macoby's (1991) article, which suggests that Swedish managers believe that success in the marketplace follows from building a better society. The two are intertwined.

3 The seven business and administration departments are: Stockholm School of Economics, the University of Stockholm, the University of Uppsala, the University of Linköping, Gothenburg School of Economics, Umeå Business School and Lund University. At Lund University data on dissertations was collected from 1983 and data on publications from 1988.

4 It should be noted that a more 'direct' translation of SPF (Sveriges Personaladministrativa Förening) would be 'The Swedish Association for the Administration of Personnel'. The organization changed its English translation in 1986 from The Swedish Association for Personnel Management.

5 Frequently action-research projects were attempted within these research and development programmes. Hence, the researchers often took a more active part in trying to change the conditions (for employees) in the organization.

References

Ahrnell, B.-M. and Nicou, M. (1989), *Kunskapsföretagets Marknadsföring*. Malmö: Liber Hermods.

Alvesson, M (1990), 'On the popularity of organizational culture', *Acta Sociologica, 33*, pp. 31–49.

Asplund, J. (1983), *Tid, Rum, Individ och Kollektiv*. Stockholm: Liber.

Brewster, C. and Tyson, S. (eds) (1991), *International Comparisons in Human Resource Management*. London: Pitman.

Brulin, G. and Sandberg, A. (1987), 'Sociology of organization in Sweden'. In U. Himmelstand (ed.), *The Multiparadigmatic Trend in Sociology*. Stockholm: Almqvist and Wiksell.

Brulin, G. and Nilsson, T. (1991), 'From societal to managerial corporatism: new forms of work organization as a transformation vehicle', *Economic and Industrial Democracy,* **12**, pp. 327–46.

Brulin, G. and Victorin, A. (1992), 'Improving the quality of working life: the Swedish Model'. In OECD (ed.), *New Directions in Work Organization: The Industrial Relations Response.* Paris: OECD.

Childs, M. W. (1936/1974), *Sweden: The Middle Way.* New Haven: Yale University Press.

Czarniawska, Joerges, B. (1993), 'Sweden: a modern project, a postmodern implementation'. In D. J. Hickson (ed.), *Management in Western Europe.* Berlin: Walter de Gruyter, pp. 229–47.

Damm, M. (1993), *Personalarbete. Yrke Eller Passion.* Götenborg: BAS.

Daun, Å. (1989), *Svensk Mentalitet.* Stockholm: Rabén and Sjögren.

Guillet de Monthoux, P. (1991), 'Modernism and the dominating firm: on the mentality of the Swedish Model', *Scandinavian Journal of Management,* **7**, pp. 27–40.

Gould, A. (1993), *Capitalist Welfare Systems: A Comparison of Japan, Britain and Sweden.* London: Longman.

Hampden-Turner, C. and Trompenaars, A. (1993), *The Seven Cultures of Capitalism.* London: Piatkus.

Hansson, J. (1988), *Skapande Personalarbete. Kompetens som Strategi.* Stockholm: Prisma.

Heclo, H. and Marsden, M. (1986), *Policy and Politics in Sweden.* Philadelphia, Penn.: Temple University Press.

Hirdman, Y. (1989), *Att Lägga Livet Tillrätta. Studier i Svensk Folkhemspolitik.* Stockholm: Carlsson, Maktutredningens Publikationer.

IDE (1981) Industrial Democracy in Europe – International Research Group, *European Industrial Relations.* Oxford: Clarendon Press.

Jacobsson, B. (1989), *Konsten att Reagren.* Stockholm: Carlssons.

Jepperson, R. L. and Meyer, J. W. (1991), 'The public order and formal institutions'. In W. W. Powell and P. J. DiMaggio (eds), *The New Institutionalism in Organizational Analysis.* Chicago: The University of Chicago Press.

Jöever, M. (1985), 'Kulturen speglar helhetskommunikationen'. In M. Jöever (ed.), *Informationens Mojligheter.* Malmö: Almqvist and Wiksell.

Kjellberg, A. (1992), 'Sweden: can the model survive?' In A. Ferner and R. Hyman (eds), *Industrial Relations in the New Europe.* Oxford: Blackwell, pp. 88–142.

Larsson, R. (1991), *Barriers to Acculturation in Mergers and Acquisitions: Strategic Human Resource Implications.* Lund University: Working Paper Series, 1991/20.

Larsson, R., Svensson, K. and Ulvenblad, P.-O. (1993), *Strategic Human Resource Management of Services: Matching Customers, Employees and Job Design in Banks.* Lund University: Working Paper Series, 1993/21.

Legge, K. (1989), 'Human resource management: a critical analysis'. In J. Storey (ed.), *New Perspectives on Human Resource Management.* London: Routledge, pp. 19–40.

Lindstedt, M. (1985), *Initiativets Makt. Om Chefer och Förändringsarbete.* Stockholm: Prisma.

Lukes, S. (1973), *Individualism.* Oxford: Basil Blackwell.

Mabon, H. (ed.) (1983), *Personaladministration.* Stockholm: P. A. Norstedts and Söners Förlag.

Maccoby, M. (1991), 'Introduction: why American management should be interested in Sweden'. In M. Maccoby (ed.), *Sweden at the Edge.* Philadelphia, Penn.: University of Pennsylvania Press.

Meyer, J.W. (1987), 'Self and life course'. In G. M. Thomas, J. W. Meyer, F. O. Ramirez and J. Boli (eds), *Institutional Structure: Constituting State, Society, and the Individual.* Newbury Park: Sage.

Meyer, J. W., Boli, J. and Thomas, G. M. (1987), 'Ontology and rationalization in the Western cultural account'. In G. M. Thomas, J. W. Meyer, F. O. Ramirez and J. Boli (eds), *Institutional Structure: Constituting State, Society and the Individual.* Newbury Park: Sage.

Norbäck-Targama (1988), *Människan i Organizationen.* Göteborg: BAS.

Nordhaug, O. (1990), *Strategisk Personal Ledelse. Menneskelige Resurser i Omstilling.* Tano.

Östergren, K. (1989), *Människan en Kritisk Resurs. En Studie av Mönster i Kunskapsmänniskans Beteende.* Working Paper No. 112, University of Umeå.

Pieper, R. (1990), 'Introduction'. In R. Pieper (ed.), *Human Resource Management: An International Comparison.* Berlin: Walter de Gruyter, pp. 1–26.

Rothstein, B. (1992), *The Crisis of the Swedish Social Democrats and the Future of the Universal Welfare State.* Paper presented at the VIII International Conference of Europeanists, Chicago, 27–9 March.

Sandberg, J. (1993), *Human Competence at Work.* Göteborg: BAS.

Scheuer, S. (1996) *Faelles aftaler eller egen kontrakt i arbejdslivet. Udbredelsen af kollektive overenskomster, faglig organisering og skriftlige ansaettelsesbeviser blandt privatansatte* Copenhagen: New Social Science Monographs.

Smircich, L. (1983), 'Concepts of culture and organizational analysis', *Administrative Science Quarterly,* **28**, pp. 339–58.

Södergren, B. (1992), *Decentralisering. Förändring i företag och arbetsliv.* Stockholm: EFI (Diss.).

Söderström, M. and Lindström, K. (1994), *Från IR till HRM. Två Synsätt på Personalarbete.* Uppsala: IPF Report 28 June 1994.

Sveiby, K. E. (1991), *Kunskapsledning.* Stockholm: Affärsvärldens Förlag.

Sveiby, K. E. and Risling, A. (1986), *Kunskapsföretaget. Seklets Viktigaste Ledarutmaning?* Malmö: Liber.

Trägårdh, L. (1990), 'Varieties of *Volkish* ideologies: Sweden and Germany 1848–1933'. In B. Stråth (ed.), *Language and the Construction of Class Identity.* Report from the DISCO II Conference, Götenborg University.

Tönnies, F. (1963), *Community and Society: Gemeinschaft und Gesellschaft.* New York: Harper Torchbook.

Zetterberg, H.L. (1983), *Det Osynliga Kontraktet.* Vällingby: Sifo Förlag.

9 HRM: a Unified Understanding or a Multiplicity of Meanings?

TIMOTHY CLARK

Introduction

The previous chapters of this book have sought to describe and examine what is meant by HRM in seven European countries: United Kingdom, France, Spain, Germany, the Netherlands, and Sweden. In addition, the majority of chapters have considered the cultural and institutional context within which HRM notions and practices are situated. This book has *not* sought to examine the extent to which the features of a particular model of HRM are or are not present within a particular nations. It has been argued that this is an inherently ethnocentric approach to cross-national comparison. In essence, ethnocentric comparison proceeds from the assertion that one nation's models and understandings are superior to those of other nations. Indigenous models and understandings are ignored, or suppressed, in favour of those present and dominant in the country from which the comparisons are being made. The ethnocentric approach to cross-national comparison therefore seeks to answer the question: to what extent are one nation's models or notions of HRM present in other nations?

By contrast, this book has sought to encourage a more polycentric approach to cross-national comparison. In keeping with this aim the task of each contributor has been to compose a vignette which succinctly conveys what is meant by HRM in their respective countries. This approach differs from that described above in that it seeks to understand a phenomenon, in this case HRM, from the perspective of each nation. As Adler (1986) writes, 'polycentric studies are individual domestic studies conducted in various countries around the world' (p. 41). In an extreme sense, polycentric studies view phenomena as only being understandable in terms of the interpretative schema adopted by each nation. The Germans understand HRM one way, the French another, the Dutch another, and so on. If we are not German, French or Dutch we cannot possibly understand what they mean by HRM. If we adopt such a view cross-national comparison becomes an impossible and therefore redundant exercise since we cannot compare that which cannot be compared (that which is uniquely understood). This has been labelled the 'Malinowskian dilemma' by Goldschmidt (1966) after the anthropologist Bronislav Malinowski. According to Goldschmidt 'Malinowski was most insistent that every culture be understood in its own terms; that every institution be seen as a product of the culture within which it developed. It follows from this that a cross-cultural comparison of institutions is essentially a false enterprise, for we are comparing incomparables' (1966, p. 8). While few scholars take the extreme view of Malinowski some still deny universality. For example, Neghandi (1974, 1986) describes cultural uniqueness as equifinality: 'There is no one way of doing things. Managers may achieve given objectives by various methods' (1974, p. 62). This suggests that there are many equally effective ways to manage organizations. The most effective will depend, in part, on the character of the national culture involved. Different national cultures will support different recipes for managerial effectiveness and success.

Whilst we accept that there are many nationally distinct ways to reach a particular management goal (in this case to manage the employment relationship) we do not take such an extreme view as that detailed above (that is, deny universality). Rather the focus of this book has been on whether there are 'special understandings' of HRM in different countries. It has been about ascertaining and describing the 'many ways' rather than the 'one way'. By examining whether HRM is uniquely understood and practised in each nation, it can be determined whether these differences are centred around a number of core elements which are common across nations, or whether there are divergent understandings of HRM which cannot be integrated into a single truly 'European' model. This book has therefore heeded Hofstede's (1983) advice that 'what we need is more cultural sensitivity in management theories . . . It is unlikely to be the product of one single country's intellectual effort' (p. 89).

This chapter has two related purposes: (1) to identify the main elements of the notions of HRM in each of the seven European countries investigated in this book; and (2) to consider the extent to which notions of HRM have converged in these countries. With these aims in mind the chapter is structured as follows. It begins by examining the problems encountered by the authors in achieving their task. The main forces underpinning the shift towards an HRM approach to employee relations are then identified. Following this the central elements of HRM highlighted in the previous seven country chapters are determined. It is noted that there are a number of common elements to these notions of HRM. The final section discusses whether these overlaps between notions of HRM in different nations represent a trend towards convergence or whether there are a number of powerful countervailing forces which support, in some respects, continuing divergence.

Problems Associated with Identifying HRM

Before we can consider how HRM was conceived in each of the seven countries it is appropriate that we first examine the problems encountered by the authors when seeking to convey the meaning of HRM in their respective countries. This is important since these problems may have influenced the type of features which were highlighted as constituting HRM and consequently will impact on the discussion occurring later in this chapter. An examination of the country chapters suggests that the authors were confronted with three kinds of problems.

1. In some countries an indigenous debate and concept has yet to emerge. This is most clearly demonstrated by the Spanish chapter (Chapter 4) in which the author acknowledges that there has been little indigenous debate over the nature of HRM in Spain. To overcome this deficiency Josep Baruel turns

to an external conception of HRM in order to examine whether HRM exists in large Spanish companies. In adopting such an approach he imports a notion and model of HRM which is patently not indigenous. In this sense he is possibly guilty of reverse ethnocentrism. Rather than seeking to ascertain whether a domestic theory is applicable in other countries he takes a foreign notion of HRM with the intention of determining whether it applies to Spain. It is perhaps therefore not surprising that few large Spanish companies have a Director of HRM on the Board of Directors, or that the HR function has a low level of status and is excluded from a wide range of corporate decisions. However, this chapter is an admirable attempt to kick-start a debate where none previously existed. What better way to start an indigenous debate than by saying: if these foreign notions of HRM do not apply to Spain then what is special about HRM in Spain?

2. A number of contributors, but particularly those from Denmark, the Netherlands and Sweden, make the point that HRM is a multi-disciplinary area encompassing such social science discipline areas as economics, organizational behaviour, organizational psychology, industrial relations, and the sociology of work and organizations. In these countries HRM has yet to emerge as a distinctive academic subject area. The paraphernalia associated most notably with the development of HRM in the USA and UK has yet to materialize, particularly in the academic arena. At present there are no journals specifically devoted to the topic of HRM, no university departments of HRM and no academic appointments in the area of HRM. Indeed, Berglund and Löwstedt in the chapter on Sweden note that recent attempts to create a professorship of HRM in Sweden have failed since the government has argued that this area was already well represented in a number of existing discipline areas.

In these countries there is no, or at least very little, demarcation between HRM and other related academic subject areas. This makes it difficult if not impossible to isolate HRM from those parts of a number of different discipline areas which examine the employment relationship. Any person attempting to convey the nature of HRM in these circumstances can adopt one of two approaches. In the first they may conduct a broad survey of all of the relevant literature drawing together the relevant themes. This was the approach of the Swedish chapter. This has the advantage of breaking down some of the boundaries between different discipline areas with the consequence that the reader is forced to recognize the diversity of approaches to the study of the employment relationship. But there is also the danger that the review is too broad thus failing to capture the nuances of the different approaches. In the second approach the changes to the employment relationship are examined from the stance of one discipline area. The Danish chapter for example adopted a 'sociological perspective'. This has the danger that it fails to recognize the diversity of approaches, and therefore the distinctive contribution of a number of discipline areas to the development of the HRM debate.

3. Finally, in a number of countries (particularly UK and Germany) HRM has developed into a distinctive and fully-fledged academic area with all the accompanying paraphernalia (academic posts, books, journals, and so on). In these circumstances the meaning of HRM is contested. Different academics propose different definitions with the consequence that they look for different evidence to support their understanding of HRM. The empirical literature therefore gives a confused and muddied picture of the nature of recent developments. These chapters are consequently masterpieces of brevity and synthesis. However, because of the volume of material they seek to compress into their pages there is the danger that they give an incomplete picture – one that gives greater prominence to certain material while downplaying or ignoring the importance of other strands in the literature which, in a fuller context, may be of some importance.

These problems demonstrate the hurdles which the authors had to overcome in order to achieve their task. In writing these chapters some authors have achieved masterpieces of succinct synthesis and selection, while others have achieved masterpieces of creativity and originality. The aim has been to introduce the reader to the nature of HRM in each country in sufficient detail to meet their immediate needs while at the same time providing a strong foundation for those wishing to go further. A single chapter on such a topic cannot be, and none pretend to be, all-encompassing.

Forces Underpinning the Shift to HRM

The previous chapters confirm that the term 'human resource management' is increasingly being used by academics and practitioners in a number of different countries. In some countries there has been a marked change in terminology as HRM has largely challenged and replaced previous popular terms such as 'personnel administration', 'personnel management' and 'industrial relations', or indigenous variants of these. In other countries HRM's apparently inevitable rise to hegemony is only just beginning; although, even at these early stages its eventual ascendancy seems assured. The sudden and rapid emergence of this new term inevitably leads scholars to examine the reasons underpinning its initial and continued development? What are the factors which have triggered this inexorable move in the direction of HRM? In Chapter 1 it was suggested that the concept and practice of HRM initially emerged in the USA in the early 1980s primarily as a result of a number of critical changes in the product market environment. In addition, the influence of Japanese management methods, the decline in the level of unionization, the increasing level of interest attached to human resource issues by senior managers and the limited power and status of the personnel management function were all important factors underpinning the move towards HRM. However, these factors relate to the emergence of HRM in the USA in the 1980s. Since this book has focused on Europe it is pertinent to ask what were the equivalent factors which precipitated the change in terminology and practice in Europe? Are they the same as those in the USA? The previous contributions suggest that three factors have been of particular importance in the countries examined, although their relative strength will vary from country to country: turbulence of the product market environment, changes to the structure of employee representation and the increasing concentration of power in the hands of managers. Each of these points is considered in greater detail below.

Turbulence of the product-market environment

The 1980s and early 1990s was a recessionary period for much of Europe. In some countries the depth and length of the recession was unprecedented, with levels of unemployment rising to historically high levels. At the same time the European market, which is the main export market for the great majority of EU member countries, was deregulated and opened up to greater competition with the creation of the Single European Market on 1 January 1993. Thus many companies in the nations featured in this book were simultaneously facing two main pressures – declining demand and greater competition in domestic and international markets.

Changes in the structure of employee representation

The increasing decentralization of industrial-relations institutions and practices has reconstructed the role of employers and unions in the collective bargaining process thus resulting in a change in power relations. The firm is increasingly becoming the main arena for employee relations matters. In Denmark, The Netherlands, Sweden (and France and Germany to a lesser extent) the centralized models which have dominated the collective bargaining process for the past forty years (in Sweden even longer) have begun to break down. The importance of collective agreements determined centrally between the employers' organizations and employee representatives is lessening. Furthermore, these agreements are covering fewer employers and employees and their content is becoming narrower permitting greater interpretation and flexibility at the firm level. The shift towards decentralization and the growth of single-employer bargaining (and within that the increasing move to the subsidiary operating company or establishment level) has been most marked in UK. In addition, levels of unionization have fallen significantly in UK and union power has been severely curtailed by legislation.

The increasing concentration of power in the hands of managers

Following on from the previous point, managers have achieved greater autonomy over employee-relations matters and as a result have begun to operate in a less restricted environment, albeit within a framework often determined jointly with employees' representatives (the works' council). In this situation managers have sought to utilize a language which conceptualizes and legitimizes a 'new reality' in which they are once again supreme. Purcell

(1993, p. 515) has remarked that this represents a rediscovery of the management prerogative. Managers have sought to make use of a new language which reinforces their agenda by reclothing the traditional concerns of management (the achievement of productivity and profitability via command and control) by reconceptualizing management, organization, and employee, thus making the changes to the management of the employment relationship more acceptable. These developments are perhaps associated with a revival of the 'manager's right to manage'.

What is Meant by HRM?

If the three factors elaborated above are those which have lead to a shift towards a new approach to employee relations, namely HRM, what then are its main features. The central tenets of HRM identified in the previous seven chapters are summarized in table 9.1. This table shows that these various notions of HRM share a number of common elements. These elements therefore transcend national boundaries. In particular the following three elements are most frequently cited as being central to the notion of HRM in a number of different countries:

1. the importance of human resources as a source of competitive advantage;
2. the decentralization of responsibility for HR issues to the firm level and/or line management;
3. the integration of HR strategies with corporate strategies in the sense that they are mutually reinforcing.

The centrality of these three elements to notions of HRM in these different countries should come as no surprise given the earlier discussion which identified the key factors underpinning the shift towards an HRM approach to employee management in Europe. These three elements are, to a large extent, direct outcomes of those forces which have underpinned the move towards HRM. First, the rediscovery of the importance, or centrality, of human resources to the overall performance and continued success of the organization reflects the way in which firms have

Table 9.1 The central elements of HRM in seven European countries

United Kingdom

1. A belief that the human resources of an organization are an important source of competitive advantage
2. A recognition of the importance of establishing a close two-way relationship between the HR strategy and the corporate strategy

France

1. A belief that the human resources of an organization are an important source of competitive advantage
2. A belief in the decentralization of responsibility for certain HR issues to the firm level
3. A recognition of the importance of:
   (a) the integration of the HR strategy with the corporate so that they are mutually consistent and supportive
   (b) the integration of various elements of the HR strategies themselves

Spain

1. A belief that the human resources of an organization are an important source of competitive advantage
2. HR skills and expertise within organizations are accorded to a high status
3. HRM should be a high-status function with representation on the board of directors
4. The HR function participates in the strategic planning process (i.e. 'external' integration)

Germany

1. A belief that the human resources of an organization are an important source of competitive advantage
2. A recognition of the importance of establishing a close two-way relationship between the HR strategy and the corporate strategy

The Netherlands

1. A belief that the human resources of a firm are an important source of competitive advantage.
2. A recognition of the importance of the integration of the HR strategy with the corporate strategy
3. The decentralization of responsibility for HR issues to the firm and within this line management
4. A recognition of the importance of integrating the various elements of HR strategy

Denmark

1. A belief that the human resources of an organization are an important source of competitive advantage
2. A belief in the decentralization of responsibility for certain HR issues to the firm level
3. A number of policy goals designed to:
   (a) enhance employee commitment
   (b) foster functional flexibility
   (c) develop an internal labour market

Sweden

1. A belief that the human resources of an organization are an important source of competitive advantage
2. *Generally* it is a multi-disciplinary topic and therefore encompasses those aspects of industrial relations, occupational psychology, management and sociology which have traditionally focused on the employment relationship.
3. *Specifically* it refers to:
   (a) the decentralization of the employment relationship to the firm level
   (b) the individualization of the employment relationship

responded to increased competitive pressure. The previous contributions suggest that in general firms have responded to
increased competition in their product-market environments by
creating smaller, cheaper, better trained, and more flexible workforces. Fundamental to these efforts is the belief that employees
are a precious asset and that organizational success comes from
identifying, channelling and then harnessing this human potential
rather than stifling and constraining it. The deployment and
encouragement of this human potential is achieved by pursuing a
whole series of policies and practices which, according to Purcell
(1993, p. 515):

> constitute a break with the past and which are often associated
> with words like: commitment, individualism, competences,
> empowerment, motivation, satisfaction, flexibility, culture, perform-
> ance, assessment, appraisal, reward, teamwork, involvement, co-
> operation, harmonization, quality, learning, loyalty.

Second, the decentralization of employee relations matters to the
organization, and within that the devolvement of responsibility for
HR issues to line management, reflects two forces at play. At the
national level European states have increasingly recognized that
in order for firms to compete effectively and successfully they
must have greater freedom to determine HR policies which are
relevant to the competitive conditions of the product market environments within which they operate. Firms should therefore be
unencumbered by centrally determined agreements which apply
to a diverse range of industries regardless of their competitive
characteristics. Rather HR policies should be determined at the
firm level and should support the strategic objectives of the
organization. At the organizational level it is increasingly being
recognized that HR issues are too important to be left to a centralized and specialist function and should therefore become the
concern of all managers. This process transforms a belief in the
importance of human resources to organization success from
being a strictly senior management concern to a general management priority.

Finally, the notion that HR strategies should integrate with corporate strategies is linked to two forces already mentioned: (1)
the gradual withdrawal of the state from centralized collective bargaining procedures and the movement to single employer bargaining thus permitting organizations greater autonomy in determining

employee relations matters; and (2) related to the previous point the view that organizations can compete more effectively if they are free to implement employee relations policies which are appropriate to the competitive circumstances in which they find themselves.

This discussion suggests that in these seven European nations there are perhaps a number of core elements to notions of HRM which transcend national boundaries. These might loosely be considered as the foundation stones of any model of 'European' HRM. We say loosely because this book has only focused on seven European nations. Further research is required to determine whether these elements are also to be found in other European nations' notions of HRM. Given that there are a number of common elements to notions of HRM in some European nations does this suggest that the shift towards HRM represents a trend towards the convergence of employee management practices between different European nations? Is it that national differences in employee management practices are becoming less and less important with the consequences that European nations are headed in same direction? The answer to this question is considered in the next section.

Convergence or Divergence?

The convergence debate was inaugurated by Clark Kerr and his colleagues at Harvard University (Kerr et al., 1960). They argued that industrialism is a world-wide phenomenon. It is based on science and technology, which speak a universal language. Science is supranational, independent of the form of government or the culture of the people. Technology spreads out so that the world is apparently divided into nations which are industrialized and those in the process of becoming so. In Kerr's view, this is a major transition and all countries will participate in the inevitable process of industrialization. This logic is in all societies irrespective of their culture or their economic or political system. Few countries, the argument goes, will want to forgo the material benefits associated with increased industrialization. Although there are considerable costs, such as increased urbanization and environmental pollution, these have yet to dissuade many countries from seeking to industrialize. The world-wide diffusion of advanced technology creates a 'logic of industrialism' since it sets up a range of tasks and problems. The pressures towards efficient production will ensure that the most effective ways of tackling these common tasks will inevitably be adopted world wide. As this process continues, organizations tackling the same tasks, such as managing people, in whichever nation, will become more and more alike.

Subsequently, Hickson et al. (1974) developed the 'culture free' theory of organizational structure. Using the measures developed by the Aston Research Programme (see Pugh and Hickson, 1976) they studied whether relationships between structure (specialization, formalization, and centralization) and context (size of the organization, operating technology, and dependence on other organizations) were consistent in fourteen countries. They found that while there were variations in the levels of the scores between countries, the relationships were similar. This led to the argument that structure-context relationships were stable across nations. In other words, 'whether the culture is Asian or European or North American, a large organization with many employees improves efficiency by specializing their activities but also by increasing controlling and co-ordinating specialities' (Hickson et al., 1974). Thus, whatever the nation and culture, bigger organizations are more specialized and formalized in structure. In addition, organizations which are more dependent on others in their environment take decisions centrally. The strength and consistency of the relationships between organization structure and context suggest that it is more important to know the size of an organization and its dependence on other organizations than the nation in which it is located. Pugh (1992) has written 'the general tendencies are clear: increasing size and scale is everywhere monotonically related to increasing bureaucratic structuring of activities' (p. 17).

However, it is too simplistic to argue that all aspects of the design and management of organizations are becoming similar across nations. A more accurate interpretation of current trends is that certain features of organizations are becoming similar across nations while others remain nationally distinct (i.e. divergent across nations). According to Child (1981) it is the macro aspects of organizations, structure–context relationships for example, which are converging while it is the micro aspects, such as the behaviour of individuals, which tend to vary between nations. This suggests that 'organizations are becoming more similar in terms of structure and technology, whereas people's behaviour within those organizations continues to manifest culturally based dissimilarities' (Adler et al., 1986, p. 302).

The arguments and evidence presented in this book also support the view that convergence is occurring at one level while divergence is happening at another. The earlier discussion in this chapter has indicated that there are a number of powerful forces which are pushing organizations to change the ways in which they manage the employment relationship. In response to these various pressures organizations are increasingly adopting a new approach to employee relations, namely HRM, which appears to be centred around a number of common elements: (1) the belief in the importance of human resources; (2) the devolution of responsibility of HR issues to the firm and within this line management; and (3) the linking of corporate and HR strategies so that they are mutually reinforcing. This convergence is occurring at the macro-level in that these various elements combine to create a general, perhaps European, notion of HRM. But the divergence is occurring at the level of interpretation and application of the three elements in each country. Consider the following examples drawn from the previous chapters.

With reference to the first common element of HRM identified earlier in the chapter, the Swedish chapter suggests that while employees may be considered an important source of competitive advantage Sweden lacks an elaborated idea of the individual. It is groups rather than individuals which are the central unit to be organized in Swedish society. Sweden is a nation comprised of very private, 'shy', individuals whose individual interests are subordinated to those of the group. Individuals tend not to speak for themselves but seek representation through group membership. Therefore, the type of HR policies which can be targeted at employees in order to enhance their commitment, improve the quality of their output, and reward the achievement of organizational objectives differs from those pursued in less collectivist cultures such as the UK. Sweden is not a supportive environment for the development of a more individualistic orientation to the employment relationship. In contrast to Britain, merit and performance-related pay, appraisals, and different forms of individual participation and involvement such as quality circles or share ownership are currently less common in Sweden. The authors point out that the introduction of a more individualistic approach to the employment relationship depends upon the fate of the Swedish model. If this continues to disintegrate then a HRM (or individualistic) approach to the management of the employment relationship may become more wide-spread.

With regard to second common element of HRM – the decentralization of HR issues to the firm and within this line man-agement – the earlier chapters of this book indicate that certain features of the institutional context can act as a powerful break on the trend towards convergence. In all the countries featured there has been a move in the direction of the decentralization of collective-bargaining institutions and procedures. With the poss-ible exception of the UK these changes have occurred within a context of strong trades unionism. The Anglo-American literature of HRM which has dominated the debate surrounding its nature and incidence has tended to suggest that HRM is most applicable in non-union organizations or may be difficult to introduce (as a result of union opposition) in highly unionized firms (see Beau-mont, 1992). Purcell (1993) notes that, according to some, 'HRM is the visual embodiment of the unitarist frame of reference' (p. 517). As suggested above, the introduction of HRM is asso-ciated with the rise in the belief that managers have the right to manage unencumbered by trades unions or the need for joint regulation (in other words, the rediscovery of managerial prerog-ative). Yet, as the chapters on France, the Netherlands, Germany, Denmark, and Sweden show, trades unions continue to exert a powerful influence on the employment relationship. Indeed, the increasing decentralization of industrial-relations institutions and procedures in a number of these countries has modified rather than eradicated the power base of trades unions by shifting the locus of responsibility from national-level representation to the firm-level work's councils. The views of employee representatives cannot be ignored; in many European nations institutional arrangement ensure that employee representatives must be con-sulted by management on a whole range of issues. For example, in Germany works' councils have three sets of rights: the co-deter-mination right, the right to be consulted, and the information right. Furthermore, in Germany and the Netherlands employees repre-sentatives are able to delay certain managerial decisions by recourse to the courts. Thus, in a number of European countries management has sought to modify their approach to employee relations via negotiation with employee representatives. These negotiations have not only tempered the original objectives of management but may also have resulted in greater union acceptance of the changes. Thus, whereas in the UK and the USA decentralization tends to be associated with the resurgence of managerial authority at the expense of employee participation and representation, in a number of European nations it has reinforced the importance of existing consultative structures between employers and employees.

With reference to the third common element of notions of HRM identified above, the Dutch chapter suggests that the while the integration of HR strategies with corporate strategies is important, the Dutch cultural and institutional context tends to restrict this linkage to 'soft' HR strategies. Building on the work of Storey (1992), the authors distinguish between 'hard' and 'soft' HRM. The former refers to the view that employees, like other organizational resources, are utilized and disposed of according to the exclusive needs of the organization. In contrast, 'soft' HRM refers to a view in which employees are viewed as an organization's most precious asset, and therefore must be cherished, rewarded and developed in order to maximize their contribution to organizational effectiveness. The authors suggest that the 'hard' notion of HRM – the focus on strategies for rewarding individual performance and the subordination of the needs and feelings of employees to the competitive requirements of the organization are all alien in the Dutch context. Such concepts do not sit comfortably with Dutch employees who expect their managers to be caring and considerate of group relations (consonant with the 'feminine' aspects of Dutch culture), and that decision-making will be guided by consensus (downplaying rather than elevating individual contribution) and a long tradition of negotiation and consultation between employees, top management, and shareholders or owners (reinforced and institutionalized by a number of laws). The Dutch chapter suggests that the types of HR strategy organizations can pursue, and therefore the types of corporate strategy these can support, is in part determined by the cultural and institutional context of a nation. In some nations, for example the Netherlands, corporate strategies requiring 'hard' HR strategies may be difficult, if not impossible, to implement. In these nations the extent to which the corporate strategy and the HR strategy integrate and are mutually reinforcing will depend

upon the character of the corporate strategy being implemented.

Conclusion

The whole purpose of the previous chapters has been to describe
the nature of HRM in seven European countries. This chapter has
sought to examine some of the evidence presented in these chapters to consider to what extent notions of HRM are converging or
diverging. The strength of the trend towards convergence
depends upon the power and impact of a number of macro forces:
(1) turbulence in the product market, (2) changes in the structure
of employee representation and (3) the increasing concentration
of power in the hands of managers. These factors appear to be
pushing organizations in different nations towards adopting a new
approach to management of the employment relationship –
namely HRM. This centres around a number of common elements, namely, the belief in the importance of human resources,
the devolution of responsibility of HR issues to the firm and within
this line management, and the linking of corporate and HR strategies so that they are mutually reinforcing. However, although
there is evidence of some convergence between notions of HRM
at the macro level, the cultural and institutional context of different nations leads people to interpret these common elements
differently in different nations. Examples of this taken from this
book include: (1) Sweden's strong collectivism countering the
development of a more individualistic orientation to the employment relationship; (2) the role of the unions and the consultative
structures between employers and employees attenuating the
rise of the management prerogative; and (3) the antipathy of
Dutch employees to 'hard' HRM. Differences in cultural and institutional contexts therefore continue to have a major impact on the
nature of the employment relationship. Whether this will continue
in the future or whether there will be moves towards greater convergence will depend upon the relative strength of the pressures
towards convergence and the factors which maintain culture-
specific approaches to the employment relationship. So long as
the cultural and institutional contexts of different nations continue to be different and integrated they will remain powerful

countervailing forces which will at least attenuate and may even halt the march to convergence.

References

Adler, N. J. (1984), 'Understanding the ways of understanding: cross-cultural management methodology reviewed'. In R. N. Farmer (ed.), *Advances in International Comparative Management* (Vol. 1). Greenwich, CT: JAI Press, pp. 31–67.

Adler, N. J., Doktor, R. and Redding, G. S. (1986), 'From the Atlantic to the Pacific century: cross-cultural management reviewed', *Journal of Management* (Yearly Review), **12**, pp. 295–318.

Beaumont, P. B. (1992), 'The US human resource management literature: a review'. In Salaman, G. (ed.), *Human Resource Strategies*. London: Sage, pp. 20–37.

Child, J. (1981), 'Culture, contingencies and capitalism in the cross-national study of organizations'. In C. C. Cummings and B. M. Staw (eds), *Research in Organizations' Behaviour* (Vol. 3). Greenwich, CT: JAI Press, pp. 303–56.

Goldschmidt, W. R. (1966), *Comparative Functionalism: An essay in Anthropological Theory*. Berkeley, CA: University of California.

Hickson, D. J., Hinings, C. R., McMillan, C. J. and Schwitter, J. P. (1974), 'The culture-free context of organization structure: a tri-national comparison', *Sociology,* **8**, pp. 59–80.

Hofstede, G. (1980), *Culture's Consequences: International Differences in Work Related Values*. Beverly Hills: Sage.

Hofstede, G. (1983), 'The cultural relativity of organizational practices and theories', *Journal of International Business Studies,* **13** (3), pp. 75–89.

Hofstede, G. (1991), *Cultures and Organizations: Software of the Mind*. London: McGraw-Hill.

Hofstede, G. (1993), 'Cultural constraints in management theories', *Academy of Management Executive,* **7** (1), pp. 81–94.

Kerr, C., Dunlop, J. T., Harbison, F. H. and Myers, C. A. (1960). *Industrialism and Industrial Man*. Boston, Mass.: Harvard University Press.

Neghandi, A. R. (1974), 'Cross-cultural management studies: too many conclusions, not enough conceptualization', *Management International Review,* **14**, pp. 59–72.

Neghandi, A. R. (1986), 'Three decades of cross-cultural management research: Alice in Wonderland'. In S. R. Clegg, D. C. Dunphy and S. G. Redding (eds), *The Enterprise and Management in East Asia*. Hong Kong: University of Hong Kong, pp. 35–66.

Pugh, D. S. (1992), *The Convergence of International Organizational Behaviour*, Open University Business School Working Paper Milton Keynes.

Pugh, D. S. and Hickson, D. J. (1976), *Organization Structure in its Context: The Aston Programme 1*. Aldershot: Saxon House.

Purcell, J. (1993), 'The challenge of human resource management for industrial relations research and practice', *International Journal of Human Resource Management,* **4** (3), pp. 511–27.

Storey, J. (1992), *Developments in the Management of Human Resources.* Oxford: Blackwell.

Index